Combining Facts and Values in Environmental Impact Assessment

Social Impact Assessment Series

Combining Facts and Values in Environmental Impact Assessment

Theories and Techniques

Eric L. Hyman
and Bruce Stiftel
with David H. Moreau
Robert C. Nichols

Westview Press / Boulder & London

Social Impact Assessment Series

Published in 1988 in the United States of America by Westview Press, Inc., 5500 Central Avenue, Boulder, Colorado 80301, and in the United Kingdom by Westview Press, 13 Brunswick Centre, London WC1N 1AF, England

Library of Congress Cataloging in Publication Data
Hyman, Eric.
    Combining facts and values in environmental impact
assessment.
    (Social impact assessment ; 16)
    1. Economic development--Environmental aspects--Cost
effectiveness. 2. Natural resources--Cost effectiveness.
3. Environmental impact analysis--Cost effectiveness.
I. Stiftel, Bruce. II. Title. III. Series: Social
impact assessment series ; no. 16)
HD75.6.H95 1988   333.7'1   85-26630
ISBN 0-8133-7162-7

Printed and bound in the United States of America

10   9   8   7   6   5   4

Contents

Tables

Figures

Acronyms

```
AEA      --- Adaptive environmental assessment and
             management process
CEQ      --- U.S. Council on Environmental Quality
EES      --- Environmental evaluation system
EIS      --- Environmental Impact Statement
EQA      --- Environmental quality assessment method
HEP      --- Habitat evaluation procedures
KSIM     --- Kane simulation method
METLAND  --- Metropolitan landscape planning model
NEPA     --- National Environmental Policy Act
PAG      --- Policy Advisory Group
PEQIs    --- Perceived environmental quality indicators
PVNB     --- Present value of net benefits
SAGE     --- Social Judgement Capturing--Adaptive--Goals--
             Achievement--Environmental assessment
SWT      --- Surrogate-worth tradeoff approach
TJCOG    --- Triangle J Council of Governments
             (North Carolina)
WES      --- Wetland evaluation system
WPTF     --- Watershed planning task force
WRAM     --- Water resources assessment method
WTA      --- Willingness-to-accept compensation measure
WTP      --- Willingness-to-pay measure
```

Acknowledgments

This book has grown from a research workshop that began at the University of North Carolina under the direction of Maynard Hufschmidt. Professor Hufschmidt's long-held interest in the incorporation of environmental and other social values into benefit-cost analysis led to a research project entitled, "The Role of Environmental Indicators in Water Resource Planning and Policy Development," funded by the U.S. Department of the Interior (DOI project number 14-34-001-8408). That project brought together the authors of this volume for a two-year period during which the groundwork for this book was laid.

Several people provided essential assistance in the completion of the original Department of the Interior study. At the University of North Carolina, Asta Cooper and Mary Pettis managed project, administrative affairs and myriad day-to-day matters. Theodore Roefs was technical officer for the project at Interior.

After completion of the Interior project research continued with support from the Department of City and Regional Planning at the University of North Carolina, the Department of Urban and Regional Planning at Florida State University, and the Environmental Policy Institute at the East-West Center in Honolulu.

The book itself is a joint product of the two principal and two contributing authors. Eric L. Hyman assumed primary responsibility for chapters one, two, four, five, and six, and collaborated on chapters three, seven and eight. Bruce Stiftel assumed primary responsibility for chapters three and eight, and collaborated on chapters one, two and five. David H. Moreau collaborated on chapter eight. Robert C. Nichols collaborated on chapters six and seven.

Various scholars have commented in detail on portions of the manuscript for the book. They include: C.P. Wolf of the Social Impact Assessment Center, Ronald Bisset of the University of Aberdeen, Richard Carpenter of the East-

West Center, Duncan MacRae of the University of North
Carolina, Elizabeth Wilman of the University of Calgary,
Allan Kneese of Resources for the Future, and Richard
Smardon of the State University of New York at Syracuse.
Maynard Hufschmidt, now with the East-West Center, has
continued to exercise important direction of our work.

The book has benefited from the technical editing of
Ruth B. Haas of Washington, D.C. Graphics were prepared by
Stan Berns of Washington and Karen Zedeck of Tallahassee,
Florida. The typescript results from the work of Joan
Nakamura of the East-West Center, Catalino de la Paz of the
Philippine Ministry of Natural Resources, Beth Hendrix of
Tallahassee, and Kathy Mullis of Florida State University.
Final copy editing is the work of Kent Wimmer at Florida
State University.

At Westview Press, Dean Birkenkamp has been the
editor. He has worked with the assistance of acquisition
editors Krista Muller, Barbara Ellington, Amos Zubrow, and
Ellen Williams.

Eric L. Hyman

Bruce Stiftel

Introduction

Before 1970, development plans largely were carried out within a limited framework of objectives, primarily economic efficiency. The National Environmental Policy Act of 1969 required the preparation of environmental impact statements for major federal actions in the United States with a potential for significant impacts on the human environment. Many of the states in this country and a large number of other countries have adopted similar requirements.

These legislative mandates have encouraged much activity in the development of methods for assessing the environmental impacts of projects. Unfortunately, only a handful of these efforts have resulted in generally applicable methods; most have been *ad hoc* attempts to deal with specific cases. Often, environmental impact statements have been perceived to be a procedural burden rather than an opportunity to improve decision making. The principal reason for this disappointing experience is the failure to integrate facts and values in a framework that can assist in making tradeoffs among multiple objectives. A considerable amount of information is available on determining the physical, chemical and biological effects of human actions. Yet, most major public policy issues are transcientific; they cannot be resolved simply by weighing objective evidence without considering subjective values. The weakness in existing environmental assessment methods is in the valuation of impacts.

The usefulness of environmental assessment could be improved if greater emphasis were placed on the role and sources of values. Many conceptual and practical lessons can be learned by incorporating knowledge from the various social sciences with an understanding of the natural sciences. The purpose of this book is to stimulate the development of environmental assessment methods that integrate objective and subjective analysis in a way that is useful for decision makers.

This book is divided into two parts. The first part (chapters 1 to 6) focuses on theories and techniques from a variety of disciplines that have a bearing on environmental assessment. The second part (chapters 7 and 8) describes and evaluates specific impact assessment methods, including a new method developed by the authors.

Chapter 1 discusses the evolution of the main categories of environmental assessment methods: land-use planning tools; benefit-cost analysis, multiple-objective analysis, checklists, matrices, and networks; and modeling and simulation approaches. Chapter 2 discusses some common pitfalls in environmental assessment: the merging of facts and values; problems with the validity, reliability, and bias of information; the lack of a systems approach; an unsystematic treatment of risk and uncertainty; and the failure to present and communicate results in a way that facilitates decision making.

Most existing environmental assessment methods rely heavily on the value judgments of experts. Chapter 3 delves into political theory to justify a participatory approach for bringing a broader set of values into an environmental assessment. Public participation is important to allow consideration of a broad base of representative values, increase the accountability of government, and enlist the consensus needed for successful implementation of decisions. This chapter then discusses the pros and cons of various methods of obtaining public participation and integrating it into decision making.

Economic arguments often are persuasive in environmental planning and policy analysis. Chapter 4 examines the value judgments implicit in an economic analysis and addresses the particular problems of placing monetary values on various aspects of environmental quality that are not exchanged in markets. Although many advances have occurred in quantifying the benefits and costs of environmental services through hypothetical values and revealed preference techniques, most of these techniques underestimate environmental values. Nevertheless, in many instances, lower bound values are all that is needed to prove that a resource is more valuable preserved than developed.

Chapter 5 draws on theories from psychology which yield insights into how people experience and understand natural environments and how they form and express their value judgments. It also discusses perceived environmental quality indicators -- techniques for the direct analysis of the observations, opinions, and preferences of individuals with respect to their environments. There are three types of perceived environmental quality indicators: (1) descriptive assessments, (2) preferential judgments, and (3) evaluative appraisals. These indicators are more relevant in the areas of aesthetics, environmental amenities, and recreation than in the valuation of impacts on ecosystem functioning or human health.

Some ecologists and physical scientists have advocated the use of energy analysis as a substitute or supplement for economic analysis in an environmental assessment. Chapter 6 describes the types of energy analysis and critiques the conceptual and practical problems in applying them.

Chapter 7 describes fourteen of the most well-known attempts at developing broadly applicable methods for environmental assessment. Some of the methods are packages that rely on a variety of techniques from different disciplines of the natural and social sciences. This chapter also evaluates each of these methods in terms of the following criteria derived from conclusions reached in earlier chapters. These criteria are the treatment of the probabilistic nature of environmental quality; incorporation of indirect and feedback effects and the dynamic characteristics of natural systems; recognition of multiple societal objectives; a clear separation of facts and values; facilitation of a participatory approach to environmental assessment; and efficiency in resource and time requirements. In general, most existing environmental assessment methods either ignore the roles of values in decision making or are based on the values of experts or a small group of administrators. Few of the methods are concerned with valid ways of representing the values of a broad array of groups involved in the political process.

In response to the shortcomings of existing environmental assessment methods, chapter 8 presents a new method called SAGE. SAGE stands for Social Judgment Capturing-Adaptive-Goals Achievement-Environmental Assessment. This method focuses on eliciting and incorporating value weights in multiple-objective decision making. The value weights are inferred from the tradeoffs that people make in choices about alternatives. These weights are applied to scaled scores for accounts based on measurable attributes of each objective. To indicate the political ramifications of decisions and facilitate sensitivity analysis, the values held by various groups are presented in matrix form arrayed by group affiliation or by judgment types -- groups of people that share common values. This final chapter also presents the results of a trial application of SAGE to a land-use management problem in a growing urban watershed.

The intended audience for this book includes planners and professionals working on environmental assessments for government agencies, consulting firms, and private corporations. In particular, it would help natural scientists broaden their understanding of the relationships between their work and the political, social, and economic systems. This book can serve as a text for in-service training or for graduate students or advanced undergraduates in a number of fields: environmental management, planning, public adminstration, economics, and environmental sciences. This book also would be of interest to administrators or managers whose

responsibilities make them need to learn of the
possibilities of various techniques and methods even though
they themselves might not be involved in the efforts of an
environmental assessment.

1
The Evolution of Environmental Assessment

1.1 CHARACTERIZATION OF ENVIRONMENTAL ASSESSMENT

Environmental assessment consists of the prediction of future changes in environmental quality and the valuation of these changes. The purpose of environmental assessment is to provide decision makers with guidance for making informed tradeoffs among conflicting aspects of environmental quality and between environmental quality and other societal objectives. Our definition of environmental quality encompasses the functional and aesthetic attributes of natural systems that sustain and enrich human life.

The environmental assessment process has an objective component and a subjective component (figure 1-1). The objective component deals with facts and falls within the domain of the natural and physical sciences. It produces predictions of the resulting biological and ecological effects of these changes on plants, animals, and people. The expected effects are actually probabilities because of the variability and uncertainty that are inherent in natural systems. Often, the effects of alternative actions or projects are compared under different scenarios for the selected technologies, planning and regulatory strategies, and induced market activities.

There are established principles to follow in assessing objective effects on ecosystems (Walker and Norton 1982). Baseline data and predictions of changes in natural systems that would otherwise occur in the absence of the human action are needed so that effects can be attributed to the action. Yet, sometimes too much effort has been devoted to collecting baseline data at the expense of the predictions of impacts (Beanlands and Duinker 1983).

The subjective component deals with values and falls within the planning and institutional framework. It involves comparing diverse effects to develop measures of the overall impact on environmental quality and weighing the environmental impact against impacts on other societal objectives. Other societal objectives that may be

5

6

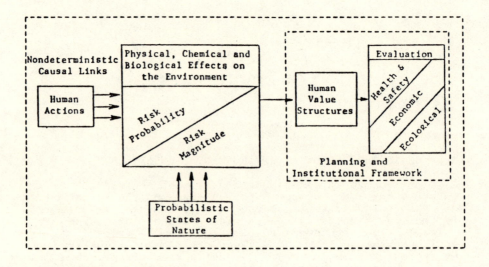

Triple arrows indicate that the causal links are
nondeterministic or subject to uncertainty.

Figure 1-1 The process of environmental assessment
(Adapted from Hyman, Moreau, and Stiftel 1984,
p. 211). Reprinted by permission.

considered in government decision making are national economic efficiency; regional economic development; equity within and across generations; and various effects on the sociocultural, psychological, and political well-being of people.

The following example shows both components. Suppose that anticipated growth in an area's population and economic activity will increase discharge of organic matter into a nearby river. These discharges can be predicted as a function of the technology of waste generation and treatment. Models of transport and transformation processes or statistical analyses can be used to estimate how concentrations of the organics are likely to vary by location in the river. These concentrations could then be compared with baseline levels and water quality standards and criteria to predict the number and types of fish and other organisms harmed as well as the number of people exposed to contaminated drinking water supplies. After that, an analyst can identify the diverse values placed on these losses and the costs of preventing or cleaning up the pollution. The final judgment on how much should be spent on prevention or mitigation of impacts and who should bear the costs and benefits of these activities is up to the decision makers.

This view of the environmental assessment process is based on a rational model of planning and decision making. The rational model assumes that societal decisions are made in a systematic way that maximizes individual or social well-being, given limited resources and costly information (Banfield 1955; Janis and Mann 1977). In its most basic form, the rational model consists of a five-step process: (1) identifying a problem or opportunity, (2) setting objectives, (3) developing planning guides and criteria, (4) formulating alternatives, and (5) evaluating and selecting the preferred alternative. More sophisticated forms of the rational model allow for feedback because they recognize that the above steps are interdependent (Quade 1975).

The rational model approximates reality best when alternatives can be well defined and decisions made by a single administrative agency (Hufschmidt 1974). In reality, decision makers aim to produce satisfactory rather than optimal decisions (Simon 1975) and often proceed in disjointed, incremental steps (Lindblom 1959). The rational model has a serious conceptual difficulty in that it provides no guidance on how decision makers can choose which of the diverse values held by individuals and groups should be adopted. Also, changes in conditions may alter the rankings of objectives as well as the means of achieving them (Frohock 1979).

1.2   THE CURRENT STATUS OF ENVIRONMENTAL ASSESSMENT

The National Environmental Policy Act of 1969 (NEPA) was a reaction by the U.S. Congress to the prevailing

public opinion that the conventional planning processes of
the executive branch did not adequately account for
environmental factors. NEPA requires U.S. federal agencies
to prepare an environmental impact statement (EIS) for
major federal actions that may significantly affect the
quality of the human environment. Such actions include
projects, investments, regulations, and legislative
proposals. An EIS must report on

1. Any adverse environmental effects which cannot be
   avoided should the proposal be implemented
2. Alternatives to the proposed action
3. The relationship between local short-term uses of
   man's environment and enhancement of long-term
   productivity
4. Any irreversible and irretrievable commitments of
   resources which would be involved in the proposed
   action (Section 192(2) (C)).

NEPA does not force federal agencies to select the
alternative that is preferable on environmental grounds or
even to use benefit-cost analysis to weigh tradeoffs
between environmental quality and other societal
objectives.

The first set of NEPA-implementation guidelines,
issued by the U.S. Council on Environmental Quality (CEQ)
in 1973, had the status of recommendations rather than
legally binding regulations. They provided little specific
guidance on how to prepare an EIS. Instead, federal
agencies were required to write their own regulations, and
thus, over seventy different sets of regulations of varying
quality were produced. As a result, the courts took over
the task of sharpening the substantive requirements with
the force of law to establish uniform standards for
preparing environmental impact statements. These
regulations outline a process rather than offering an
approach, but they do attempt to focus the analysis on
significant issues and avoid duplication of effort through
a "scoping" step.

By late 1985, federal agencies in the United States
had issued almost 23,500 environmental impact statements
(M. Henderson 1985). Many states have also enacted "little
NEPA" laws. Yet, the impact of this tremendous amount of
costly activity is unclear. Most impact statements have
been voluminous compendiums of largely irrelevant and
under-analyzed data. The major reasons for this
disappointing experience are the procedural rather than
substantive focus of the law and the inadequacy of existing
methods for environmental assessment with respect to the
treatment of facts and values. The EIS process has had two
positive contributions in the United States. It has
encouraged agencies to screen out some projects with large,
adverse, environmental impacts and has broadened
opportunities for public scrutiny and participation in
government decision making.

Since the U.N. Conference on the Human Environment at
Stockholm in 1972, international interest in maintaining
environmental quality has grown substantially. By 1980,
over 50 developed and developing countries had instituted
requirements for environmental impact statements, and 102
less developed countries now have government protection
(EIA Worldletter 1983). One example of a major EIS in a
less developed country is the one done for the Mahaweli
River Development Program in Sri Lanka (Tippetts-Abbett-
McCarthy-Stratton 1980). The major multilateral
development banks, U.N. project-implementing agencies, and
some bilateral aid donors have also adopted environmental
review procedures (Horberry 1983). Guidelines for
environmental assessment have been prepared by the
Organization of American States (1978) and the Mekong
Secretariat (1982), among others.

The experience in less developed countries shows that
environmental assessment procedures have promise, but have
been of limited effectiveness to date (Hyman 1984; Lim
1984; Hufschmidt 1985). In addition to the problems
encountered in the United States, less developed countries
often face stringent constraints on budgets, available
expertise, baseline data, and political feasibility.

1.3   THE DEVELOPMENT OF ENVIRONMENTAL ASSESSMENT METHODS

Environmental assessment methods have evolved from
work in five areas: (1) land-use planning tools; (2)
benefit-cost analysis; (3) multiple-objective analysis; (4)
checklists, matrices, and networks; and (5) modeling and
simulation approaches. During the 1970s, the evolution of
these methods accelerated resulting in generally greater
sophistication. Representative examples of the methods
mentioned below are discussed in detail in chapter 7.

1.3.1   Land-Use Planning Tools

Geologists, ecologists, landscape architects, and
urban planners have developed various tools for land-use
planning. Some of these tools focus solely on biophysical
features while others include economic and social aspects
as constraints on the selection of a site. Many factors
affect the biophysical suitability of a site for particular
land uses, including

1.   Climate--precipitation, temperature, wind,
     droughts, floods, storms, fire risk, and air
     pollution potential
2.   Geomorphology and geology--slopes, stability,
     location and uses of surface water and
     groundwater, mass movements of earth, depth to
     bedrock, and unique features
3.   Soils--nutrients, structure, depth, and
     erodability

4. Flora and fauna--biological diversity, ecosystem fragility, valuable species, pests and diseases

There are two main types of land-use planning tools: land classification and land-suitability analysis.

Land classification approaches identify the best land uses for each type of site in terms of its biophysical features. These classifications may be made at various levels for different purposes. A macro-level classification is a broadbrush scanning of large land areas to establish national or regional priorities. A micro-level classification is a task for public or private sector land managers who have such mandates as economic production, watershed management, wildlife conservation, or security.

Table 1-1 lists a variety of land classification techniques. Remote sensing may be extremely useful in applying these techniques. These techniques have some limitations. Most are oriented toward a particular land use such as agriculture or forestry. They are less suited for determining appropriate management practices for existing land uses or for predicting the consequences of proposed changes in land use policies (Mueller-Dombois 1981). None of the techniques measure land productivity directly or identify the impacts of land use conversions. Moreover, these techniques may neglect gradual changes in biophysical factors that result in varying limitations on land uses (Lee 1981). Often, they are more useful in ecological studies than in helping decision makers answer land management questions (Cameron 1981).

Methods of land-suitability analysis focus on the constraints that could inhibit a particular land use. They are used for screening out sites that have unacceptable physical or spatial characteristics for that type of development. There are three types of land-suitability analysis: gestalt, mathematical combination, and logical combination methods (Hopkins 1977). Gestalt methods ask a team of experts to determine appropriate future land uses by viewing "the lay of the land." The experts look at such variables as slopes, vegetation, soils, and existing land uses (Hills 1961; Lewis 1963). Mathematical combination methods apply numerical measures to represent the site's degree of suitability for development. The results may be displayed on maps or map overlays (McHarg 1969) or numerical scores (International Planning Associates 1978).

Logical combination methods define site suitability through a hierarchy of factors or constraints. Some of these methods have been computerized, (Fabos, Green, and Joyner 1978) and different areas of a site can be represented through grid cells, polygons, or image processing (Steiner 1983).

Land-use planning tools for a biophysical assessment are important, but financial and economic analyses are needed to maximize the values obtained from the use of land

TABLE 1-1
Common land classification methods

1. Australian Land System
    The Australian Land System (Christian and Stewart
    1968) uses aerial photos to survey large areas for
    agricultural, forestry, and recreational potential. A
    "site" is defined as a uniform land form with common
    soil types and vegetation. A "land unit" is a
    collection of related sites with a particular land
    form. A "land system" is a group of associated land
    units, usually bounded by a geological or topographic
    feature.

2. Ecological Series Classification
    The Ecological Series Classification (Mueller-Dombois
    and Ellenberg 1974) describes forest habitat types in
    bioclimatic terms: a plant community's soil, water
    and nutrient regimes; soil surface characteristics;
    and undergrowth plant distribution. The technique
    produces site indices for each habitat type that vary
    with the productive capacity of the trees, natural
    regeneration capability, the appropriate species for
    tree-planting, fertility requirements, and engineering
    properties.

3. Holdridge Life Zones System
    Holdridge Life Zones (Holdridge 1967) are broad
    bioclimatic units defined by mean annual
    precipitation, mean annual biotemperature (air
    temperatures adjusted to eliminate negative values),
    and potential evapotranspiration. These broad units
    can be subclassified by soil, seasonal rainfall
    distribution, drainage, and mature vegetation
    associations.

4. Canadian Biophysical System
    The Canadian Biophysical System (Lacate 1981) is a
    hierarchial classification. The basic unit used is the
    "land type," which is characterized by a homogeneous
    soil series and sequence of vegetation. Land types
    are subdivided into "land phases" according to their
    stage of vegetative succession. "Land systems" are
    groups of land types with a recurring pattern of land
    forms, soils and a sequence of vegetation. The next
    broader unit, the "land district" has a distinct
    pattern of relief, geology, topography, and a sequence
    of vegetation. Finally, there are "land regions,"
    distinct climatic zones associated with a particular
    climax vegetation.

(Continued)

TABLE 1-1 <u>Continued</u>.

5. <u>Webb's Structural Classification of Humid Forests</u>
This is a classification system for humid forests
based on vegetation structure and physiognomy
including such factors as forest structure,
composition, canopy closure, type of emergents,
species growth forms, and leaf size (Webb *et al.*).
The system correlates vegetation structure and
physiognomy with rain, altitude, cloudiness,
temperatures, soils, drainage, and wildlife habitat.

6. <u>Krajina's Biogeoclimatic Zonation System</u>
Krajina's Biogeoclimatic Zonation System (1973) is
based on forest habitat types. Each zone is
characterized by a climatic climax vegetation, climate
and soil type. However, a "climatic climax" might be
deflected into an "edaphic climax" due to poorly or
excessively drained soils or a "topographic climax" on
steep slopes or alluvial flats.

7. <u>USDA Soil Conservation Land Capability System</u>
The USDA Soil Conservation Land Capability System
(Klingbiel and Montgomery 1961) uses soil according
to the units grouped into eight classes according to
the capability to sustain cultivation, grazing,
forestry, wildlife, and recreation without erosion.
The classification system indicates the degrees of
limitation to intensive uses.

8. <u>California Soil Vegetation Survey</u>
The California Forest and Range Experiment Station
(1958) developed a classification system predicated on
the assumption that soil types are correlated with
differences in vegetation on undeveloped lands.
Aerial photos are used to observe the type, age,
density, and structure of the vegetation.

Source: Hyman 1984 (adapted from Hamilton 1982).
Reprinted by permission.

while conserving natural resources for the future. The
financial and economic impacts of land conversion depend on
the previous uses of the land, quantity and quality of
labor and capital required, energy-intensiveness of the
technologies, existence of infrastructure such as roads and
dams, location of markets, and size of the site. There may
be conflicts between the financial decisions made by
individuals and the decisions that would be preferred from
a societal perspective. Some proposed developments may be
infeasible because the necessary human resources are

unavailable or cultural values and legal or political
obstacles inhibit effective implementation.

1.3.2 Benefit-Cost Analysis

     Methods for applying benefit-cost analysis to
environmental planning were first developed in the area of
water resources planning. The Flood Control Act of 1936
established a legal mandate for benefit-cost analysis in
the formulation and evaluation of water resource projects.
Originally, benefit-cost analysis was confined to the
single objective of economic efficiency (mainly, the
development and protection of infrastructure). In 1950,
the Federal Interagency River Basin Committee suggested
having a benefit-cost analysis include "intangible"
benefits such as the displacement of people, modification
of wildlife habitat or scenic or historic sites, and
depletion of land and mineral resources. The state of the
art progressed substantially in the 1960s and 1970s so that
these techniques could be applied in assessing timber,
range, recreation, and other land uses. The U.S. General
Accounting Office (1984) and the World Industry Conference
on Environmental Management (1984) both concluded that
benefit-cost analysis can be useful in government decision
making on environmental regulations, despite its
limitations.
     Executive Order 12291 (President of the United States
1981) expanded the role of benefit-cost analysis in the
executive branch. It requires U.S. federal agencies to
conduct a benefit-cost analysis of any new regulations,
changes in existing regulations, or legislative proposals
that are expected to result in any of the following:

  1.   An annual effect on the economy of $100 million
       or more
  2.   A major increase in costs or prices for
       consumers; individual industries; federal, state,
       or local government agencies; or geographic
       regions
  3.   Significant adverse effects on competition,
       employment, investment, productivity, innovation,
       or the ability of U.S.-based enterprises in
       domestic or export markets [Section 1(b)]

This executive order requires identification of the level
and incidence of the monetary and nonmonetary benefits and
costs of the proposal and its alternatives. It also states
that the regulations must be devised to "maximize the net
benefits to society or if that cannot be determined, to
minimize the net loss to society taking into account the
condition of the particular industries affected, ...
condition of the national economy, and other regulatory
actions contemplated for the future." The

Office of Management and Budget is responsible for supervising implementation of this order.

1.3.3 Multiple-Objective Analysis

Once information is available on the likely biophysical, economic, and sociocultural impacts of a proposed action, decision makers need some way to judge the relative importance of the impacts. Techniques for multiple-objective analysis may be used to evaluate alternatives when there are diverse impacts on several planning objectives. Some of these techniques group impacts into separate accounts without trying to aggregate the different accounts. Other techniques attempt to derive a score representing the overall impact on all accounts. Interest in multiple-objective analysis grew in the mid-1960s and 1970s as a result of increased dissatisfaction with the inherent incompleteness of economic growth as a measure of social well-being (Mishan 1967; Cohon 1978).

Much of the early conceptual work on multiple-objective analysis also began in water resources planning. The Harvard Water Program (Maass *et al.* 1962) pioneered the use of computerized, multiple-objective optimization techniques in the design of water resource projects. The U.S. Water Resources Council (1973) institutionalized a multiple-objective planning process for the water and related-land resource activities of five federal agencies. These guidelines were later revised (U.S. Water Resource Council 1983) to emphasize national economic development as the principal planning objective although the importance of considering effects on regional economic development, environmental quality, and other aspects of social well-being was reiterated.

Multiple objectives have also been addressed in urban and regional planning through the "planning balance sheet" (Lichfield 1960) and the "goals-achievement matrix" (Hill 1968). However, neither of these approaches suggested valid ways of determining the value weights on objectives that are needed to carry out the approaches. Later examples of multiple-objective methods have derived the value weights through decision analysis (Haimes, Hall, and Freedman 1975; Keeney and Raiffa 1976).

Multiple-objective methods can improve the planning process in at least three ways. First, they can facilitate participation to increase the range of value judgments considered. Second, the inclusion of the full range of objectives can make the analyst's perception of a problem more realistic. Third, by allowing the systematic investigation of alternative actions, the range of choices can be expanded, and the relationship of the objectives can be explored.

1.3.4 Checklists, Matrices, and Networks

A number of checklist, matrix and network approaches
have been developed largely in response to NEPA (Hill 1973;
Warner and Preston 1974; Lapping 1974; Canter 1977). A
checklist is a simple enumeration of the possible impacts
of a project (Burchell and Listokin 1975; Planning
Environment International 1975). Galloway (1978) combined
elements of a checklist with a land-suitability analysis
for wetlands. More sophisticated checklists have applied
scaling and weighting techniques to quantified impacts (Dee
et al., 1972; Duke et al. 1977; Solomon et al. 1977).

A matrix lists the potential impacts corresponding to
specific project activities, thus creating a simple model
of causal relationships (Leopold et al. 1971). Networks
use multiple matrices to account for the temporal
interactions of impacts and a full range of possible
interactions (Traveler's Research Corporation 1969;
Sorenson 1971; Thor et al. 1978). Networks may be
computerized to include a larger number of cause-effect
linkages (Thor, Smardon, and Adams 1979).

1.3.5 Modeling and Simulation Approaches

Mathematical modeling and simulation became feasible
for use in environmental assessment with the greater
availability of computers in the 1960s. Their use could
become even more widespread now due to low-cost
microcomputers. Many models of natural systems are based
on the principles of conservation of mass and energy as
well as the factors governing rates of inflows, outflows,
and transformations. These rates may be exogenous,
endogenous, or vary according to operating rules that
depend on the state of the system at the time. A broad
spectrum of natural processes can be modeled including
diffusion, advection, gas or heat transfer, sedimentation
and scour of solid materials, and chemical, biochemical or
photochemical reactions.

Modeling and simulation have been mostly used to
estimate physical, chemical, and biological effects on
water quality (Biswas 1976), air quality (Thom and Ott
1975; Ott 1976), and the structure and functioning of
ecosystems (Russell 1975; Patten 1976; Hall and Day 1977;
Ott 1978). A large number of natural systems models are
summarized in Basta and Bower (1982). A National Water
Quality Network model that simulates the interrelated water
quality changes associated with effluent discharges in the
major rivers, lakes, reservoirs, bays, Great Lakes
shorelines, and seashore segments of the United States have
been developed (Gianesi, Peskin, and Young 1981). The U.S.
Army Corps of Engineers relies heavily on hydrological
models. The U.S. Fish and Wildlife Service (1980) and the

16

U.S. Forest Service (McClure, Cost, and Knight 1979) have adopted modeling approaches to quantify impacts on wildlife. Dynamic modeling has been used in formulating cross-impact matrices (Kane, Vertinsky, and Thompson 1973). A few attempts have been made to broaden the focus of modeling and simulation to include values (Holling 1978).

Mathematical models are useful in environmental assessment because they allow internally consistent testing of alternative policies or projects. Models can trace anticipated effects over time and space and are useful in defining system parts and interrelationships and explicitly delineating assumptions. Modeling is essential when long-term experimentation is unethical because of serious health effects on people or irreversible damage to critical ecosystems. It is also useful in the typical situation of insufficient time, money, or staff to run experiments or collect original data.

1.4 WHERE TO FROM HERE?

Most of the activity in environmental assessment has consisted of ad hoc attempts to deal with specific cases. Few efforts have resulted in generally applicable methods. It is difficult to draw generalizable conclusions when ad hoc methods are used. More progress has been made in redefining techniques for determining physical, chemical, biological, and ecological effects than in incorporating values. Furthermore, some decision makers have unrealistic expectations for the completeness and definitiveness of scientific information (Carpenter 1980). Consequently, some handbooks on these scientific techniques have been prepared for planners and decisions makers. One such handbook is geared to predicting the effects of industrial and municipal pollution (Rau and Wooten 1980). Another handbook emphasizes the selection of suitable sites for agricultural or industrial development (Carpenter 1983).

Many of the proposed methods for placing values on the effects lack a sound conceptual framework and are incomplete or inoperative. In a time of limited public sector resources in both developed and developing countries, it is important to improve the efficiency and effectiveness of environmental assessment methods. Unless a quantitative approach is adopted for measurement of both facts and values, an environmental assessment will be largely descriptive and of limited use to decision makers (Beanlands and Duinker 1983).

Innovative environmental assessment methods are needed because the legal and administrative processes used to collect information for decision making are inherently at odds with the traditional approach to scientific inquiry (Hart, Enk, and Hornick 1984). Many scientists are reluctant to become involved in an environmental assessment because value judgments are involved.

A complete environmental assessment method would (1) ensure that environmental factors are included in an analysis, (2) direct attention to alternatives, (3) assist in quantifying impacts on a common basis, and (4) communicate information to interested parties to facilitate the political process (J. Henderson 1982). In particular, improved methods should be cost-effective, interdisciplinary, and capable of producing timely results. The key environmental attributes that are valued by people should be identified at an early stage in the process so that public participation can be facilitated (Beanlands and Duinker 1983). A more analytical approach to the presentation and interpretation of information on values could reduce conflicts among parties and help decision makers clarify their judgments (Hammond 1978).

Finally, it should be noted that there are many uses and some abuse for analytical tools of any kind. These tools can be used for (1) bringing environmental information into the planning process, (2) adding a remedial step to counteract deficiencies in the planning process, (3) mutual adjustment of positions by various interest groups, (4) environmental advocacy, or (5) perfunctory endorsements (Lim 1984). At times, analytical tools have been used to justify government decisions that have already been made on other grounds. In other cases, scientists have entered the political arena as advocates rather than analysts (Hart, Enk, and Hornick 1984). Nor are environmental assessment methods a substitute for the need to obtain baseline data, strengthen institutions, educate the public on environmental issues, design a system of incentives and disincentives for managing natural resources, enforce or change existing laws, and monitor actual impacts as they occur. Post-hoc audits after project implementation are desirable because they can test the impact predictions made in an environmental assessment, identify new problems, and suggest measures for mitigation or compensation of impacts (Bissett 1981).

2
Pitfalls in Environmental Assessment

2.1 INTRODUCTION

Most environmental controversies are over whose value judgments are represented in decision making and how diverse interests are reconciled rather than being about scientific issues. While environmental assessment methods should clarify the distinctions between scientific facts and value judgments, they often blur them further.

It is expensive to collect and analyze information. Many environmental assessments have compiled large amounts of uninterpreted data which are not geared to the needs of decision makers. This pitfall can be avoided by involving potential users of the environmental assessment in preparation of an information framework for collection of data.

Valid and reliable techniques are available to measure baseline environmental conditions. Mathematical models and statistical techniques can be used, although with considerably less precision, to predict the future impacts of human activities under various states of nature. However, it is much more difficult to obtain good data on people's value judgments and preferences. Particular care must be used in selecting and implementing techniques to elicit values and preferences and in interpreting the findings to avoid systematic biases.

Few environmental assessment methods adequately handle risk and uncertainty. Risk refers to a known probability that a particular outcome will occur. Uncertainty is present when either the nature of the outcome or its probability is unknown. Although experts can estimate actual or subjective probabilities of various outcomes, they do not have special legitimacy in determining what levels of risk and uncertainty associated with human activities should be accepted by society. Techniques exist for measuring the degree of risk aversion that people exhibit, and to a lesser extent, for incorporating risk aversion in an analysis of impacts. However, these techniques are imperfect and have had relatively little influence in government decision making.

19

Another common pitfall of environmental assessments is
the failure to communicate the findings to potential users
in an understandable, concise way. In particular, an
assessment method should facilitate a sensitivity analysis
of objective as well as subjective information. This
chapter discusses the above pitfalls in some detail and
suggests ways to avoid them.

2.2 DISTINGUISHING FACTS FROM VALUE JUDGMENTS

As figure 1-1 shows, environmental assessment
necessarily involves both facts and value judgments. Facts
are objective statements about the existence, magnitude,
and timing of impacts on natural systems. Value judgments
consist of subjective information about whether an impact
is good or bad and how important it is relative to other
effects (Walker 1973).

2.2.1 Scientific Facts and Natural Systems

Because natural systems are complex and interrelated,
the factual investigation must cover important cumulative
effects, synergistic effects, and antagonistic effects.
Cumulative effects are the consequences of separate or
related actions that are minor by themselves, but can add
up to a significant total. Synergistic effects occur when
the total effects are greater that the sum of the separate
impacts due to interactions. For example, the combined
damage to agricultural crops from air containing high
levels of both sulfur dioxide and oxidants is much higher
than the sum of the damage from each of these pollutants
alone. Antagonistic effects exist when one harmful impact
partially cancels out another. Antagonistic effects are
less common than synergistic effects because additional
stress usually disturbs partially degraded natural systems
even more. A possible example of an antagonistic effect
might be reduced eutrophication of a lake receiving
effluent that contains chlorine in addition to phosphates.
The scientific findings of an environmental assessment
depend on the spatial boundaries of the system and the time
horizon of the analysis. The spatial boundaries can either
be based on administrative units such as counties or
states, or on natural systems such as river basins or
forests. There are some advantages in defining the spatial
boundaries of the analysis in terms of natural systems
because water and air pollution, endangered wildlife
species, and recreational travelers cross political
borders. Yet, plans, regulations, and mitigation or
abatement measures must be decided on and implemented by
the responsible administrative authorities. Therefore, it
usually is necessary to use administrative boundaries
unless separate political jurisdictions have set up

effective joint commissions to manage a particular natural system.

The appropriate time horizon of an analysis varies with the objectives of the assessment, the project life, and the kinds of impacts that are expected. Long-run trends may be of primary interest because impacts on natural systems can be persistent. Nevertheless, short-term impacts during dam construction or road-building can cause deforestation, the loss of wildlife species, and a large share of the total erosion and sedimentation associated with a project. Furthermore, the acute impacts of air pollution on human health are mostly associated with short-run, peak concentrations of pollutants. When an environmental assessment adopts a very long time horizon, it is likely to become an exercise in science fiction. Furthermore, if impacts are valued in monetary terms and are discounted (see section 4.2.4), impacts beyond 50 years are given little weight.

The passage of time may also affect the nature of impacts because of changes in other conditions such as the size of the exposed population and degree of exposure to other pollutants. Moreover, new information about the effects of pollutants may be obtained over time. Most environmental assessment methods are static because they assume that the causal relationships in a system are constant. By contrast, dynamic methods allow for interactions between time and other variables. A dynamic analysis is preferable if the scientific data and analytical resources needed to support it are sufficient; otherwise a simpler, static assessment might be more valid.

Factual information can be obtained from scientific principles, past experience under similar conditions, experimentation, and modeling. To save money and time or to avoid harmful impacts on natural systems or people, mathematical models or reduced-scale and reduced-time experimental results from wind tunnels or flumes can be useful in predicting air or water quality under ambient conditions.

Another approach is to rely on statistical associations between the magnitude of environmental impacts and human actions, controlling for differences in the states of nature. States of nature include external conditions such as rainfall, temperature, and hydrological or atmospheric processes that affect the transport and fate of pollutants and the ability of receptors to cope with pollution. States of nature also include actual levels of population, economic activity, and technology that result in the generation of other sources of pollution.

After a model or statistical study has predicted values of environmental attributes under certain conditions, it may be desirable to aggregate the attributes into a smaller number of indices (Landwehr 1974; Inhaber 1976; Orlando and Wrightington 1976; Rosen et al. 1976; Ott 1978a, 1978b; James and Evison 1979). However, there are large differences among these indices, and it is impossible

There is value inherent in fact-finding

to derive a single grand index that captures all of the
attributes of air or water quality.

The acquisition of factual information is not entirely
value-free. The prevailing patterns of thought among
scientists influence the way in which scientific
investigations are conducted and the conventional wisdom is
not always correct. Judgments are also inherent in
translating raw data into intelligible form. In some
cases, scientists may have hidden agendas or political
ideologies that influence their thinking (Conn and Feimer
1985).

2.2.2 Types and Sources of Values

Individuals hold diverse sets of values: attitudes,
preferences, and tastes. Attitudes are global feelings
toward classes of things. Preferences reflect an
individual's specific wants and relate to actual
situations. Unlike preferences, tastes stem from an
individual's views on the needs of society. The fact that
people have certain values does not necessarily cause them
to act on those values because they often hold conflicting
values. Since values are only known to the individuals
themselves, they are not directly observable, but can
sometimes be inferred from people's statements or their
behavior in markets, voting booths, and other social
institutions (see chapters 3, 4, and 5). Values have many
different sources: utilitarian needs, social norms,
ecological functioning, and biocentric ethics (Caldwell
1970; Andrews and Waits 1978; Petulla 1980).

Utilitarian needs encompass material goods and
services whether or not they are sold in economic markets.
In the utilitarian view, forests are resources that provide
wood for construction, paper, and fuel. The degree of
conflict between utilitarian values and other environmental
values depends on population, technology, and lifestyles.

Social norms are broader obligations of kinship,
friendship, and citizenship which are enforced through a
set of shared rewards and sanctions. Social norms are
culturally dependent and can be modified through education.
For example, the emphasis that a particular society places
on cleanliness affects an individual's tendency to litter.

Ecological functioning values stress the importance of
maintaining a balance among humans, other living things,
and the abiotic environment. Ecological functioning values
are expressed in the writings of scientists such as Marsh,
Darwin, and Haeckel in the mid-nineteenth century; Elton,
Tansley, Leopold, Osborn, and Vogt in the early twentieth
century; and Ehrlich and Hardin in the present generation.
In this view, preservation of critical environmental
functions or life-support systems (such as maintenance of
the stratospheric ozone layer) should be given top priority
to ensure the health of the public and the long-term
survival of the human species.

By comparison, biocentric ethics is less human centered because it emphasizes the inherent worth of nature. Philosophers such as Emerson, Thoreau, and Muir wrote about the moral implications of preservation, apart from human evaluations of the usefulness of the environment for meeting utilitarian needs, social norms, or ecological functioning. Since this view implies infinite or very high values for environmental quality, it is not widely accepted.

The "new naturalistic philosophers" argue that humans have an obligation to protect the rights of animals (Marietta 1982). Various rationales have been given for this obligation. Watson (1979) stated that higher animals such as primates, dolphins, and dogs deserve "reciprocal rights" as living things capable of conscious actions that can be judged in moral terms. Warnock (1971) widened the list of animals deserving "moral consideration" to include those that can feel pain or pleasure. An even broader view is expressed by Feinberg (1974) who would grant rights to animals that have interests that can be represented. A few philosophers extend these obligations to plants and even inanimate, natural objects. Goodpaster (1978) contended that the condition of being alive is sufficient justification for "moral consideration", regardless of the ability to act as moral agents or feel sensations. One of the earliest proponents of naturalistic ethics was Leopold (1949) who wrote that, "A thing is right when it tends to preserve the integrity, stability, and beauty of the biotic community. It is wrong when it tends otherwise." This view is echoed by Gray (1979) who argued that the survival of life on earth is threatened by human manipulation of the biotic and abiotic environment. Hunt (1980) also stressed the continuity of living and nonliving things, and notes that the rights of dead people and pets are respected.

The Organisation for Economic Cooperation and Development (1976) rejected the biocentric notion that environmental values exist apart from their implications for human welfare. A balance of utilitarian needs, social norms, and ecological functioning can provide a sensible basis for environmental assessment as long as decision makers have a long time horizon that reflects the needs of future generations, and give sufficient weight to impacts that cannot be quantified easily. An environmental assessment should also recognize differences in the types of values held by people under various contexts.

2.2.3 The Fact/Value Trap

Most environmental controversies are trans-scientific and cannot be solved by scientific arguments alone. The outcomes of these controversies depend on whose value judgments are selected, the types of values included, and the ways in which various values are weighed in the decision-making process. Information on values may be affiliations, or geographic locations.

Although principles of democratic government require representation of a broad set of values, it does not follow that the values of all people in the nation, region, river basin, or locality have to be weighted equally. The appropriate weighting of values depends on the level of government concerned with a decision and the incidence and time pattern of positive and negative impacts.

Another important issue is whether governments should accept values as they are or try to change them. Although an environmental assessment should not rely on uninformed factual information, individuals are often the best judges of their own welfare and each person is entitled to his or her own value judgments. Governments sometimes serve as passive arenas for the resolution of conflicts between groups holding different values, but they frequently adopt an advocacy role to promote social equity or protect the interests of future generations. Where potential hazards are serious, long-lasting, or very uncertain, experts may have a larger role in judging the importance of possible impacts. Yet, it should be remembered that the legitimacy of experts comes from their scientific knowledge, not the ability to make value judgments. In fact, an expert's values may be significantly different from those of the general public. Nevertheless, experts can change people's values through education.

An environmental assessment should keep facts separate from values as much as possible. Many environmental assessments methods fall into a fact/value trap by attempting to derive summary scores that combine indicators of the magnitude of effects with judgments about their seriousness or importance. As a result, decision makers do not know whether a score is high because the magnitude is large or because the effect is judged to be serious. To explain this further, it is necessary to define the four basic types of measurement scales for facts or values: nominal, ordinal, interval, and ratio scales.

Nominal scales refer to the assignment of a label, name, or qualitative description. With a nominal scale, it is possible to count the number of items in each category, but mathematical manipulations should be avoided.

Ordinal scales are based on discrete orderings and thus can indicate whether one item ranks higher than another, but not how much higher. Ordinal numbers cannot be added, subtracted, multiplied, or divided. Preferences expressed on an ordinal scale are not necessarily independent, transitive, or continuous and are difficult to compare because respondents may base them on different points of reference. The Leopold (1971) matrix uses an ordinal scale for the seriousness of impacts. Rankings of the aesthetic quality of the scenes presented in a set of photographs are on an ordinal scale.

Interval scales are calibrated so that each unit represents an equal-sized difference. The origin point on an interval scale is arbitrary. Addition and subtraction are possible on an interval scale, but not multiplication

or division. The ratings produced by the standard gamble
method are on an interval scale (Von Neumann and
Morgenstern 1947).

Ratio scales have equal-sized differences between
units as well as a meaningful origin point. As a result,
multiplication and division make sense on a ratio scale.
The Kelvin temperature scale and monetary units are
examples of ratio scales.

In general, it is best to treat a number at the
highest scale that is supportable without violating the
above definitions and rules. When numbers that are
expressed on different types of measurement scales are
combined, misleading indices that conceal important
assumptions often result. For example, the Environmental
Evaluation System (Dee *et al.* 1972) and WRAM (Solomon *et
al.* 1977) multiply ordinal numbers, blurring facts and
values. Land-suitability map overlays (McHarg 1969) add up
ordinal numbers, implicitly assuming that all factors are
equally critical. The overlay method is valid only when
each factor is derived from an existing legal or technical
constraint that cannot be violated (Hobbs 1980b). In order
to evaluate effects across diverse attributes of the
environment, value weights must be expressed on an interval
or ratio scale. When an evaluation is based on a weighted
sum of the attribute scores, the value functions for each
of the attributes must not depend on the levels of the
other attributes. If the sum of the weights does not equal
one, a multiplicative form can be used instead of an
additive form. Because the weights are meaningless unless
one knows the attributes and value functions, the weights
used in an environmental assessment should not be derived
from a study based on a different set of attributes.

2.3   THE NEED FOR A FOCUSED APPROACH IN DATA COLLECTION AND
      ANALYSIS

The scope of an environmental assessment refers to the
volume, level of detail or disaggregation, and types of
information collected and analyzed. One of the most common
flaws in the first generation of environmental impact
statements is the inclusion of mountains of unnecessary
factual information such as long, uninterpreted lists of
plant and animal species or soil types. It is expensive
and time-consuming to collect and analyze data. Delays can
reduce the usefulness of an environmental assessment to
decision makers, and cost overruns may lower the
credibility of environmental assessment specialists.
Furthermore, too much information can confuse decision
makers and scare away public reviewers.

Therefore, environmental assessments should not
consider all possible impacts, but only the significant
ones (Holling 1978). All other things being equal, the
best assessment method is the one that is most efficient in
the use of time, money, and expertise. The aim of

environmental assessment is to supply the amount of information that is necessary for making rational and timely decisions. The collection of additional information is only justifiable when there is a compensating increase in the validity of the findings and the net benefits of the decisions based on them.   Also, the readiness of an issue for investigation must be balanced against the timing of the information needs of the users.

To avoid producing an environmental assessment with a scope that is too narrow or overblown, an information framework or plan for the collection and analysis of data should be developed. This will help avoid omissions of important data or the acquisition of unnecessary data, and it will make the results easier to interpret. An information framework addresses the following questions:

1. What information should be collected and for what purpose?
2. How much information is needed and at what level or aggregation?
3. What methods and procedures should be used for data collection and analysis?
4. When and how frequently should data be collected?
5. Who should collect, verify, and analyze the data?
6. What is the desired level of precision and accuracy of the data?

To ensure that environmental assessments address the relevant issues efficiently, decisions makers and other potential users of this information should participate in planning the information framework. This framework should be treated as a flexible guide rather than a prescription.

2.4 VALIDITY, RELIABILITY, AND BIAS

Environmental assessment techniques must be reasonably valid, reliable, and free of systematic bias. The concepts described here are applied in chapters 4 and 5 in evaluating specific techniques for eliciting people's values.

2.4.1 Internal Validity

Internal validity refers to how well an environmental assessment method or its component indicators have been designed and executed. Two common problems with internal validity in environmental assessments are the omission of relevant variables and the lack of controls for confounding factors. Indicators are valid when they test the variables of concern directly, and changes in the indicator correspond to changes in the environmental variable. For example, Jackson turbidity units are a valid, objective indicator of the ability of water to transmit light. It is

much more difficult to find perfectly valid indicators of
subjective environmental values.

Since the measurement and valuation of environmental
quality are complex, proxy indicators often have to be
used. Proxy indicators are not completely valid because
they only capture a part of the variables of concern.
Nevertheless, proxy indicators still can be useful by
themselves or in combination. For example, the remaining
land area of a specialized habitat for a small rare bird is
a proxy indicator of the bird's population, which is harder
to measure.

2.4.2 Reliability

Reliability, also known as external validity, refers
to the consistency of findings across different random
samples or with changes in measurement procedures.
Reliability can be tested by applying statistical tests to
find the strength and significance of associations in
replicated studies. For example, one study found that two
alternative techniques for valuing impacts (weighted
ratings and indifference tradeoffs) implied significantly
different siting patterns for a power plant although the
same set of respondents was involved (Hobbs 1980a).
Reliability is also affected by sample size.

Even if an assessment method or indicator is
internally valid and reliable, the findings should not be
accepted automatically. The findings should be compared
with similar studies by other researchers and with
different types of studies on the same subject. It is more
reasonable to accept objective findings if they are
plausible in terms of known physical, chemical, or
biological relationships, and there is a gradient between a
human activity and the levels of the environmental effects.
Similarly, the subjective findings on values should be
consistent across disciplinary perspectives and theoretical
approaches.

2.4.3 Systematic Bias

Systematic bias consists of non-random distortions in
the findings of an assessment method or its component
indicators. Techniques based on expert values are prone to
different types of bias than techniques that examine a
broader set of social values. Subjective techniques are
susceptible to instrumental bias, informational bias,
hypothetical bias, and strategic bias.

Instrumental bias occurs when investigators create,
use, or interpret techniques in a way that does not mirror
the objective conditions or subjective values that they are
investigating. Researchers can unwittingly or deliberately
push the outcome in a particular direction. Instrumental
bias in surveys or interviews may be very subtle and often

crops up in the phrasing of questions or in the relationship between the interviewer and the respondent.

Experts consciously or unconsciously introduce a variety of biases into their objective analyses and subjective evaluations of impacts. Experts working in government agencies, consulting firms, or academia have their own special interests and motivations. In addition, experts are prone to certain cognitive patterns as a result of the ways that they have learned to think about a problem.

Informational bias is a result of uncertainty in (1) future human activities, (2) the effects of human activities on natural systems, and (3) the values placed on a set of impacts. Informational bias may cause experts to anchor onto particular kinds or sources of information that they are familiar with due to their disciplinary perspectives, professional contacts, and access to information. Experts may give relatively too much attention to current controversies compared with long-standing ones as a result of pressures from the media or public to address prominent issues.

Hypothetical bias occurs because respondents give hypothetical answers to hypothetical questions. People's behavior shapes their preferences and vice versa as new circumstances are created. Thus, a hypothetical question "reveals preferences only within the constraints of its context and provides no evidence of what the preferences would be if those constraints were changed" (Andrews and Waits 1978).

Strategic bias reflects the fact that individuals may hide or distort their true preferences out of self-interest. For example, people might understate their demand for an environmental amenity if the same amount is provided to everyone and people expect to be taxed or charged user fees equal to their stated demand. Conversely, when individuals believe that the supply of the good will be financed by an income tax or head tax which is unrelated to their preferences for the good, they have incentives to exaggerate their true demand in order to have access to an expanded supply of the good at no extra cost (see section 4.3.1).

Strategic behavior may vary systematically with socioeconomic status, education, or group affiliation. Thus, people who favor small governments for general ideological reasons or who expect poor government performance might understate their true preferences for a collective good. If a systematic relationship between strategic behavior and these other variables can be estimated, the analysis can correct for strategic bias, but this may open a greater risk of manipulation of the results.

2.5 RISK AND UNCERTAINTY

Failure to account for risk and uncertainty is one of the largest pitfalls of most environmental assessment methods because natural systems are affected by random factors. Usually, it is only possible to estimate a range of probabilities for impacts because some key factors may be unknown. In the long run, the range of probabilities can be narrowed through scientific research or experimentation, but environmental assessment specialists rarely have the luxury of being able to gather much original data.

The term "risk" has been used in many different ways. Confusion can arise when risk is defined as a compound measure of both the probability of harm and its magnitude (Lowrance 1976). Consequently, this book defines risk as a known probability that a particular outcome will occur.

Certainty means each action is associated with only one possible outcome. The certain case is not necessarily a trivial one because there may be a large number of alternative actions to consider and the costs and benefits of some of the outcomes might be unknown.

With uncertainty, either the nature of the outcome itself or its probability is unknown (figure 2-1). Five major sources of uncertainty in environmental assessment may cause impacts to be larger or smaller than expected. First, there is uncertainty about the quantity or type of residuals that will be generated, the area of land to be developed, or the amount of natural resources that will be consumed. These factors depend on future siting decisions and levels of population and economic activity.

The second source of uncertainty relates to the kinds of environmental management strategies and controls that will be adopted in the future. New technologies that are more effective or cheaper may be developed in the future. Third, uncertainty exists over how controlled emission rates translate into ambient environmental quality. The actual concentration of residuals depend on the states of nature and the timing of the discharges.

Fourth, estimates of impacts on receptors introduce additional uncertainty. Residuals do not become actual pollutants until natural systems are damaged. The health effects of a pollutant vary within a particular population of humans or animals. The degree of damage also depends on the cumulative dose; the means and duration of exposure; the length of time lags before damage is evident; the possibility of defensive actions by receptors; synergistic and antagonistic effects; and the ability to measure subtle changes in physical or mental functions. For some pollutants, there may be dose-response thresholds below which no damage occurs or there are no cumulative effects. Fifth, there is uncertainty over how a certain impact should be valued, given the expectation that it will occur.

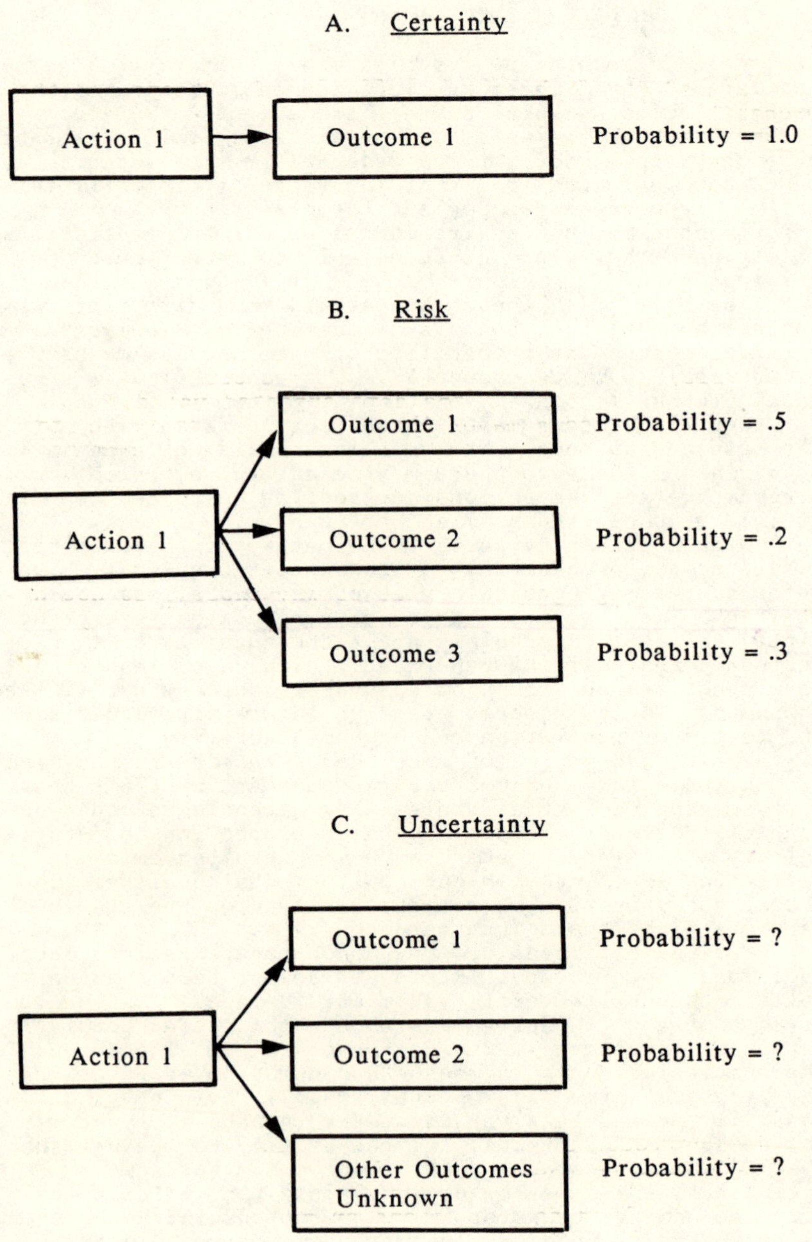

A. <u>Certainty</u>

B. <u>Risk</u>

C. <u>Uncertainty</u>

Figure 2-1 Certainty, risk and uncertainty

2.5.1 Risk

The simplest way to handle risk is to choose the action with the highest expected value. An <u>expected</u> <u>value</u> is the product of the net payoff of each outcome and the probability of its occurrence. The use of expected values assumes that the payoffs can be quantified and decision makers are risk neutral. A person who is risk neutral would be willing to pay $1 for a chance to participate in a lottery that yields $1,000 at a probability of 0.001.

In contrast, a risk-averse decision maker would prefer an action with a lower expected value provided that the most probable benefits are higher or the most probable costs are lower. Society commonly differentiates between certain types of hazards with the same expected values. In general, most people rate a catastrophic event with a low probability more negatively than a more probable event with smaller consequences and the same expected value. Furthermore, since a major disaster is a rare event, there is more uncertainty about its probability of occurrence. As a result, it may be prudent to assign higher subjective probabilities to these rare events for the purposes of decision making.

Determining the likelihood of a hazard is an objective task, but deciding on the acceptability of the risk involves value judgments. That is why experts do <u>not</u> have the right to dictate the levels of risk that society should accept. Experts are only qualified to estimate the probabilities of risk that correspond to various magnitudes of effects. There are serious ethical considerations in imposing risks on unwilling people who do not have a say in the matter. Probabilities are averages over an infinite number of trials, but in most development decisions there is only one event and certain effects may be irreversible. Consequently, some risk aversion is appropriate in judging the acceptability of environmental impacts.

Lowrance (1976) noted that acceptability of a hazard depends on whether the hazard

1. Is assumed voluntarily
2. Has immediate or delayed consequences
3. Is well understood by the scientific community and by members of the public
4. Has alternatives or can be reduced through technology
5. Is associated with an essential good or a luxury
6. Is encountered occupationally
7. Brings a common or a dread hazard
8. Affects average people or only sensitive people
9. Will be used as intended or misused
10. Has reversible consequences
11. May lead to intrusions on personal freedom in the pursuit of safety.

Starr (1969) attempted to determine what society thinks is an acceptable level of risk by examining the risks that individuals accept in daily living. This approach is misguided because it focuses on currently encountered risks which are not necessarily optimal future levels of risk. For one thing, society's awareness of potential hazards changes over time as more information is discovered and disseminated. For example, more is understood today about the hazards of cigarette smoking than was known three decades ago. Starr's approach also assumes that people are aware of the risks they face. People perceive familiar, day-to-day activities to be less risky than they really are due to psychological avoidance, incomplete information, and a false sense of security (Fischoff, Slovic, and Lichtenstein 1978).

Many studies indicate that people have trouble making rational decisions in the face of high risk and uncertainty. Their decisions are very sensitive to subtle changes in the context or framing of a problem. Probability judgments are based on people's past experience which is quite limited in dealing with small samples of events that are not representative of the universe that they are drawn from (Tversky and Kahneman 1974). As a result, people usually overestimate the risk of low-probability events and underestimate the risk of high-probability events. Media coverage provides a high profile for low-probability events. In addition, Starr ignored social equity and differences in the ability to avoid risks. Yet, people tend to have too much confidence in their abilities to judge risks (Lichtenstein et al. 1981). Furthermore, it is difficult to change their initial impressions because contrary evidence tends to be dismissed (Slovic et al. 1982).

Do people try to maximize their expected utilities under conditions of risk and uncertainty? Most decisions are made in a decomposed fashion through relative comparisons rather than with comprehensive information. People's decision strategies vary with the complexity of the task. If there are a large number of attributes to consider, screening rules or intuition are often used. The expected utility model approximates reality best when the decisions concern well-structured, repetitive tasks. Such problems typically are treated in isolation from other risks, and options are assessed with regard to reference points and aspiration levels (Schoemaker 1982).

In an environmental assessment, the probabilities of significant hazardous impacts should be quantified to the extent feasible. However, it is best to leave value judgments about risk acceptability to decision makers who are in contact with the full range of public opinion.

2.5.2 Uncertainty

Uncertainty can never be eliminated because it is a characteristic of dynamic, natural systems (Holling 1978).

Nevertheless, people make decisions all the time, often
without explicitly analyzing their implications.
Development decisions are not deferred until cautious
scientists are able to reach unanimity. The best that an
environmental assessment can do about uncertainty is
indicate ranges of uncertainty about key causal
relationships, estimate risks, and include a sensitivity
analysis to explore the effects of alternative assumptions.

Some experts argue that assumptions should be
conservative to leave a margin of safety in case later
scientific findings indicate that the hazards are greater
than was expected. Others believe that environmental
assessment professionals should adopt the most likely
assumptions in the objective analysis and let decision
makers choose whether to introduce conservatism in judging
the acceptability of risks. When uncertainty is high,
development decisions could be kept flexible and made in
stages so that impacts can be monitored, activities can be
changed, and new information on effects or abatement
technologies can be introduced. If potential impacts on
critical environments or human health are serious or
irreversible, it might be best to avoid actions with highly
uncertain outcomes (Krutilla and Fisher 1975; Lowrance
1976). In less extreme cases, an environmental assessment
can handle uncertainty explicitly through the use of (1)
game theory strategies, (2) subjective probabilities, or
(3) decision analysis.

Game Theory Strategies. Game theory strategies can be
useful when the probabilities of possible outcomes are
unknown or the degree of risk aversion is large. The first
step in applying game theory strategies is to frame the
problems in a payoff matrix. A payoff matrix is a
rectangular tableau of numbers representing the gains or
losses associated with the alternative actions listed in
the rows and the possible states of nature across the
columns. In the case of certainty, there is only one
column because the state of nature is known.

Table 2-1 contains a payoff matrix for a hypothetical
example of the impacts of a decision to issue, deny,
or place conditions on a license for a nuclear power plant.
After the payoff matrix has been constructed, one of five
basic game theory strategies may be adopted: (1) the
Laplace strategy, (2) the maximin strategy, (3) the maximax
strategy, (4) the coefficients of optimism strategy, or (5)
the strategy of regrets. The choice of which strategy to
adopt depends on the attitudes of the decision makers
toward uncertainty.

If all the possible outcomes yield positive net
benefits and do not have serious negative impacts, the
Laplace strategy may be appropriate. The Laplace strategy
assigns equal probabilities to each state of nature when
there is no information on the actual risk probabilities
(Luce and Raiffa 1957). In this example, each state of
nature would be given a probability of one-third. Then,

TABLE 2-1
Payoff matrix for economic and environmental impacts
of a nuclear power plant siting decision

| | | | States of Nature | |
Actions		S_1	S_2	S_3
		Stable	Earthquake	Major Fire
A_1:	Issue unconditional plant license	+25.0	-20.0	+3.0
A_2:	Issue conditional plant license	+17.0	-15.0	+10.0
A_3:	Deny license	-8.0	-8.0	-8.0

the analyst would maximize the expected value of the
returns.

The maximin strategy is appropriate when the decision
maker is risk averse or some of the potential outcomes are
dangerous or irreversible. This strategy assumes a
malevolent world in which the worst possible state of
nature for each action will always occur. Under the worst
possible circumstances, the best that can be done is to
maximize the minimum payoff (Wald 1948).

The maximax strategy (1951) is the opposite of the
Wald criterion because it is based on the assumption that
the best possible state of nature for each action will
prevail. Under those conditions, the rational strategy
would be to maximize the largest possible payoff (Hurwicz
1951).

The maximin and maximax strategies may be combined in
a way that allows for intermediate conditions based on the
degree of optimism. Coefficients of optimism represent the
decision maker's degree of confidence in how favorable the
state of nature is likely to be. The coefficient of
optimism is the lowest probability (expressed in decimal
form) that the decision maker would be willing to accept in
a lottery between the maximum payoff and the minimum payoff
(Hurwicz 1951). When the coefficient of optimism equals
unity, it is equivalent to the maximax strategy, and when
it equals zero it is the same as the maximin strategy.
Suppose that this probability is 60 percent. Then, for
each action, the analyst multiplies the maximum payoff
under the most favorable state of nature by 0.6 and adds
this product to 0.4 times the payoff under the maximin

assumption. The alternative with the highest score represents the best choice under this strategy.

The strategy of regrets may reflect human attitudes toward decision making as well. After having selected an action, the decision maker may regret knowing that a different alternative might have been more profitable or less costly if they had known in advance what the state of nature would have been. A regret is the difference between the payoff received and the payoff that would have been possible in the absence of uncertainty. The first step in applying this strategy is to construct a matrix of the regrets associated with each outcome (Savage 1951). Table 2-2 displays the regrets matrix for the example in table 2-1. Then, one of the four above strategies has to be applied to the new matrix. Table 2-3 lists the likely payoffs associated with each action under the game theory strategies discussed above. The optimal action in each case is the one with the highest positive gains or least losses. If two alternatives have the same payoff under a particular strategy, a decision maker would be indifferent between them. Note that the various strategies imply different choices. Also, combining the criterion of regrets with the maximin strategy implies a different decision than using the maximin strategy alone.

Subjective Probabilities. Subjective probabilities can be estimated for uncertain outcomes through the judgment of an expert. If estimates from a group of experts are available, their estimates can be averaged, fitted into mathematical distributions or left as an array of different predictions. The latter approach has the advantage of allowing decision makers to see the variation in estimates and to use their own judgment in choosing the estimates of a particular expert. Experts also can be asked to estimate the degree of confidence that they have in their own subjective probability judgments (Feagans and Biller 1981; Merkhofer 1981; Winkler and Sarin 1981).

Subjective probabilities can be used in calculating an expected value. Alternatively, it may be better to display both the subjective probabilities and the impact magnitudes or outcomes in an event tree. An event tree is a technique for analyzing problems that involve an ordered sequence of decisions and chance outcomes which depend on earlier decisions or chance outcomes. The branches of the event tree represent the choices available to decision makers at each decision node or the likely states of nature that may follow from each chance node. An event tree helps in structuring a problem by representing a complex sequence of events by a series of discrete events. However, decision makers still may find it difficult to think in terms of probabilities for a problem with many variables. Figure 2-2 shows an example of an event tree in an air quality assessment in which there are twenty-four likely concentrations of ambient air pollutants over an area.

TABLE 2-2
Regrets matrix corresponding to Table 2-1

States of Nature

Actions	S_1	S_2	S_3
A_1	0.0	-12.0	-7.0
A_2	-8.0	-7.0	0.0
A_3	-33.0	0.0	-18.0

TABLE 2-3
Comparison of the decisions implied by various
game theory strategies

				Strategies	
Actions	Laplace	Maximin	Maximax	Coefficient of Optimism =0.6	Regrets With Maximin
A_1	+2.7	-20.0	(+25.0)	(+7.0)	-12.0
A_2	(+4.0)	-15.0	+17.0	+4.2	(-8.0)
A_3	-8.0	(-8.0)	-8.0	-8.0	-33.0

[a]The circled payoff is associated with the selected action shown in the corresponding row.

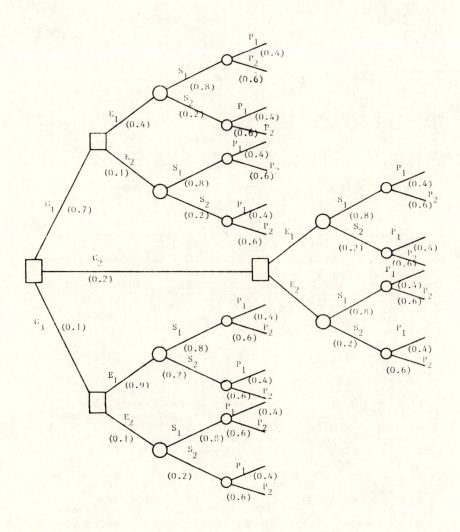

Key

    –Decision node   G – Residuals generation rates
                     E – Emission rates after abatement
                     S – States of nature
    –Chance node   P – Physical transport or chemical
    processes

Figure 2-2 An event tree for an air quality analysis

38

Decision Analysis. Several approaches are available to estimate the amount of risk that people are willing to accept. The basic approach, known as the standard gamble method, can be used when the payoffs have not been quantified in dollar or utility terms (Von Neumann and Morgenstern 1947). In a standard gamble, decision makers are asked what chance of getting the preferred outcome A (getting nothing if they lose) they would be willing to exchange for getting outcome B with certainty. Similar pairwise comparisons are made for each alternative. Given the preference rankings of decision makers, these ordinal rankings can be converted to an interval scale if preferences are transitive. Transitivity implies that if A is preferred to B and B is preferred to C, then A must be preferred to C.

Suppose that a decision maker would accept a two-thirds chance of getting A rather than receiving B for certain. Similarly, the decision maker would accept a probability of one-half for A over certain receipt of C. The preferred outcome, A, is arbitrarily assigned a value of 1.0. Outcome B would be assigned a value of 0.67 and C would be given a value of 0.5. Each risky, quantifiable gain or loss may be replaced by its certainty equivalent. These numbers may be used as subjective probabilities and then the expected value criterion can be applied (Sinden 1974; Keeney and Raiffa 1976). Keeney and Raiffa's method specifically designed for environmental assessment is described and evaluated in Chapter 7.

2.5.3 Applications of Risk and Uncertainty Analysis

Techniques for analyzing risk and uncertainty have been used in diverse environmental applications: regulation of carcinogens and toxic substances (Leape 1980; Moreau 1980), development of ambient air quality standards (Feagans and Biller 1981), health impacts of fossil fuel combustion (North and Merkhofer 1976; Morgan et al. 1978a, 1978b; Wilson et al. 1981), comparative impacts of alternative energy technologies (Philipson et al. 1974; Comar and Sagan 1976; Holdren 1978; Dossani, Watson, and Weygart 1979; Inhaber 1979; Spangler 1981), environmental hazards (Kates 1978), and nuclear power plant accidents (U.S. Nuclear Regulatory Commission 1975; Spangler 1980).

Yet, government agencies in the United States and other countries have not advanced very far in evaluating risk and uncertainty. As the U.S. Toxic Substances Strategy Committee (1980) observed,

A shortcoming in federal regulation of toxic substances is the failure to improve analytical methods for developing cost-benefit information and using it, as appropriate, as one of several tools in regulatory decision making. Despite inherent limitations of cost-benefit analysis and the practical difficulties frequently encountered, improved

analytical methods will help the agencies select
consistent and cost-effective ways to reduce risks.

The development and use of these techniques in the United
States have been inhibited by laws that reflect
congressional hesitancy to delegate decisions to the
executive branch or to allow explicit tradeoffs between
health effects and economic costs and benefits.   In
addition, these techniques have not yet gained the
confidence of many decision makers although there seems to
be growing acceptance of the need for this type of
analysis.

2.6   PRESENTATION AND COMMUNICATION OF FINDINGS

The real test of the success of an environmental
assessment is how well it is integrated into decision
making.   Lack of sufficient attention to the presentation
and communication of findings is one of the reasons for the
limited usefulness of the first generation of environmental
impact statements. Decision makers do not have time to
plow through huge documents. Furthermore, poorly presented
documents scare away potential reviewers.
        An environmental assessment has to be concisely
written to attract the attention of decision makers. The
presentation of the findings should recognize the different
levels and possible uses of assessments such as: (1)
selection of alternatives, (2) justification of decisions,
(3) public participation, (4) defense against lawsuits, and
(5) design of corrective or mitigating measures. The
presentation should contain a summary as well as a complete
record of the analysis. Pictures, graphs, and maps can
simplify and summarize important information.
        The key assumptions must be clearly shown so that
users will understand what was done and can have confidence
in the results. The findings should be disaggregated in a
way that allows regrouping of facts or reweighting of
values. This type of "open-book" record allows decision
makers or users to conduct a sensitivity analysis combining
different sets of values with a given set of facts to
determine how the choice of values affects the conclusions
of the analysis. Suppose that two of the potential users
of the analysis disagree on whether environmental quality
benefits ought to be weighted two or three times as
important as the private economic benefits of a proposed
development. A sensitivity analysis might show that this
difference in values does not affect the implications of
the analysis for the development decision. In short, an
environmental assessment should be viewed as a process
rather than a product. Consequently, it should be designed
with the expectation that the professionals who prepare
them will be asked to explain and modify their work.
        Chapter 7 draws on the pitfalls discussed in this
chapter to develop and apply seven criteria for evaluating

environmental assessment methods. The SAGE method,
presented in chapter 8, deals with many of these problems,
especially the fact/value trap, the validity and
reliability of elicited values, as well as the presentation
and communication of findings to facilitate a sensitivity
analysis.

3

Incorporating Representative Values Through Public Participation

3.1   INTRODUCTION

As stated in chapter 2, one of the most difficult
tasks in environmental assessment is obtaining information
on the values that people place on environmental resources
and amenities, and combining that subjective information
with scientific facts. Information on values can be
obtained by relying on experts or through direct
participation of the public. These two approaches are not
mutually exclusive and the strengths of one approach may
complement the weakness of the other.

Expert-based methods represent, elicit, or simulate
people's attitudes and preferences. Examples of these
methods include the extramarket valuation techniques,
public opinion surveys, and energy analysis techniques
discussed in chapters 4, 5, and 6, respectively. Although
expert-based methods generally provide useful information,
decision makers may find them incomplete or unreliable in
some cases because they do not address the political
ramifications of a decision and the need to build consensus
to implement the decision.

By contrast, public participation methods allow people
to take a more direct and active role in the decision
making process. In addition to clarifying facts and
values, public participation can support other societal
goals such as making all participants feel that they have
been treated fairly and maintaining the perceived
legitimacy of governing authorities in a democratic state.

Methods to carry out a participatory approach include
advisory committees, public meetings, and group process
techniques. These methods may be particularly well suited
for conflict resolution when the key parties to the
dispute can be easily identified. This chapter reviews the
reasons why public participation is important, discusses
the advantages and disadvantages of this approach and
compares the main types of methods for facilitating public
participation.

3.2 POLITICAL AND ADMINISTRATIVE PROBLEMS IN ENVIRONMENTAL ASSESSMENT

Controversy over the purpose of environmental impact statements and the appropriateness of the methods used to obtain information on values has limited the effectiveness of environmental assessment as a decision-making tool. In the United States, there has been confusion over whether an EIS is a procedural requirement or a type of analysis. Environmental assessments often have not adequately taken into account effects that are difficult to quantify, social impacts, and political implications (Schramm and Burt 1970; Ortolano 1976). These analyses have seldom involved the full range of affected segments of the public (Borton *et al.* 1970; Warner 1971; Ragan 1975; Pierce and Doerksen 1976). Yet, the choice of whose values are represented and how these values are combined is a key stumbling block in the development of more useful environmental assessment methods (Andrews and Waits 1978; McAllister 1980). Because this political question is often neglected, the information from environmental assessments frequently is not well used in decision making (Andrews 1976; Ortolano and Hill 1976; Socolow 1976).

Administrative problems in environmental assessments also have arisen from the segmented and mission-oriented structure of agencies in the natural resources sector. This fragmentation makes it difficult to conduct comprehensive, interdisciplinary analyses. In addition, the lack of coordination among agencies allows special-interest groups to gain disproportionate influence (McConnell 1966).

Agencies sometimes displace important societal goals with internal goals of organizational survival or expansion and the personal achievement goals of their staff (Etzioni 1964; Downs 1967). These problems are increased by the vague wording in many laws and conflicting views in the legislative history. Agencies have a great deal of discretion in interpreting their direct responsibilities toward the chief executive, the legislature, and the courts, as well as their indirect responsibilities to the general public, special interest groups, political parties, and professional organizations. Nevertheless, political pressure from the public can lead to more open decision making, as was the case with many federal agencies in the United States during the 1970s.

Environmental quality issues have special political problems because property rights for natural resources often are poorly defined. Many decisions on the use of these resources provide significant benefits to a small segment of the population and spread the costs over the entire population. As a result, the individuals and groups who take the time and effort to organize and influence decisions usually are those who would benefit such as farmers who want inexpensive water for irrigation, industrial or municipal polluters, and construction contractors and labor. User groups, such as the National Rivers and Harbors Congress and the National Reclamation Association, have had disproportionate influence in government decision making (Ingram 1969; Morgan 1971; Rosenbaum 1977). These special-interest groups find it economically worthwhile to muster political clout, while the rest of society lacks the incentive and resources to effectively counteract these groups. This "collective action" problem leads to a decision making environment in which each actor claims concern for the "public interest," but the values of a substantial part of the public remain underrepresented (Davidoff and Reiner 1962; Friedrich 1966; Hardin 1982).

3.3 INTEREST GROUP DOMINANCE OF GOVERNMENT DECISION MAKING

In response to autocratic governments, Utopian democratic theorists such as Rousseau and More urged active political involvement by the masses. On a local scale, mass participation can be very successful, as with New England town meetings. However, it is much more difficult on a larger geographical scale or where the issues are complex or extensive.

Pluralism is an alternative view that sees the role of the citizen in a modern democracy as one of choosing among competing representatives rather than getting directly involved in decision-making processes. Potential representatives battle for votes and political contributions in a process that can enable the peaceful resolution of conflicts in a society. The smooth functioning of government requires a working agreement on which issues are to be addressed first; yet, mass participants mobilized around particular issues generate conflict that can disrupt the decision-making agenda (Schumpeter 1950; Lipset 1960; Almond and Verba 1963; Dahl 1963; Milbrath 1965; Kneese and Schulze 1985).

A political interest group is a collective unit that shares certain values on existing conditions and makes prescriptions for public policy (Truman 1951). These groups form on the basis of common interests and the members of a group are willing to support it to ensure that their views are heard (Olson 1965; Moe 1980; Walker 1983). Because there are many different interest groups, the term "publics" is often used to indicate the diversity of values in society. Political interest groups may represent special interests such as businesses or the ideologies of certain public groups.

Pluralists also claim that the public interest or at least some stable equilibrium is achieved through a balance among competing political interest groups (Downs 1957). Interest groups provide information on technical matters and values, although the information may be selective. It is assumed that those interest groups that are successful in influencing policy represent large enough segments of

the public to justify their influence. Coalitions of
political interest groups with legislators or bureaucrats
can result from (1) shared perceptions or constituencies,
(2) personal friendships, (3) routine channels of
communication, and (4) a need for apparent unanimity in the
political arena.

Many studies substantiate the dominant role of certain
interest groups in government decision making in the United
States. As a result, legislative decisions often are made
through "log-rolling"-- the trading of votes on different
issues to provide pork barrel benefits to the
constituencies of key legislators (McConnell 1966). For
example, there has been a strong correlation between the
location of federal water resources projects and the
districts of senior legislators and committee leaders
(Ferejohn 1974). In addition, client groups have often
dominated the deliberations of federal government agencies
in a variety of different programs (Freeman 1955; Lowi
1969; Bachrach and Baratz 1970). This has been
particularly true in the area of natural resources (Ingram
1971; Wandesforde-Smith 1974).

There are many problems with the pluralist notion of
the public interest. As Schattschneider (1960) notes, "The
flaw in the pluralist heaven is that the heavenly chorus
sings with a strong upper class accent." The needs and
interests of the silent majority and the silent minorities
are left underrepresented, biasing public decisions toward
selective private goals. Many potential interest groups
never get organized and thus are unable to influence
government. Small interest groups, especially business
lobbies, usually organize more effectively than larger
groups that represent a broader segment of the population.
The evidence contradicts the pluralist assumption that a
political interest group will form wherever there is common
interest (Schattschneider 1960; Olson 1965; McConnell 1966;
Lowi 1969). Perhaps most important, pluralism is incapable
of producing a moral consensus because many conflicting
views of ethics can be used at the same time to justify
incompatible policies (MacIntyre 1981).

As a result, Haefele (1973) concluded that under the
strong influence of political interest groups, government
has "lost the ability to ... choose among conflicting
priorities [and] to make judgments across substantive
fields." Pluralism may also move government policy away
from effective regulation toward distribution of income
through taxes and spending (Lowi 1966; 1970). Sometimes,
the battling among interest groups can increase conflict
and reduce communication. For example, in an environmental
dispute in the Florida Everglades, developers and
conservationists were at odds over false issues because of
mutual suspicion and the failure to define the areas of
agreement and disagreement (Socolow 1976).

The disproportionate influence of political interest
groups may have other undesirable side-effects, such as
encouraging apathy or polarization by reinforcing the

belief that individuals cannot influence public decisions
and reducing the commitment of diverse groups to successful
implementation of the policies that are adopted. At some
point, the long-term stability of a political system that
excludes mass participation may be jeopardized.

3.4 PUBLIC PARTICIPATION AS A SOLUTION

The dominance of political interest groups in
government could be reduced by creating a countervailing
power either through expanding the power of the legislature
or increasing public participation in administrative
processes. The strength of the legislative branch could be
increased by reducing the amount of discretion that the
legislature gives up to regulatory and administrative
agencies (Lowi 1969; Haefele 1973).

Arguments for stronger legislative control overlook
several important considerations. First, the legislative
process is imperfect as a means of determining the values
of the public in a democracy because officials are elected
on the basis of a "package of issues" so that voters are
unable to register their preferences on each policy issue.
Futhermore, elections may be won through the approval of a
scant majority of the few people who actually vote.
Second, legislatures themselves are affected by interest
group pressures at least as much as the administrative
agencies because these groups provide financial support,
easily accessible information, and grassroots organization
of vocal individuals. For example, although the expressed
opinions of legislators may show a striking similarity to
public opinions from surveys, other incentives may prevent
legislators from taking effective action (Ingram, Laney,
and McCain 1980). Third, there is substantial evidence
that the administration of legislative directives cannot be
divorced from policy making. Fourth, an increased role for
any branch of government can reduce the spirit of
democracy.

The better alternative is to encourage greater or more
representative public participation through programs aimed
at opening up political conflicts to broader segments of
society (Verba 1967; Wilson 1967; Arnstein 1969; Wengert
1971). However, the way in which a public participation
program is designed can affect how the findings are used.
For example, when the U.S. Army Corps of Engineers began to
open up its decision making processes in the 1970s, it
accepted public participation as a means to speed up plan
implementation, but not as a means to question the
desirability of the projects (Mazmanian and Nienaber 1979).

There are two rationales for public participation:
efficiency and legitimacy. The efficiency rationale
suggests that participation will result in better-designed
government services and a greater ability to gain the
support of diverse groups in fulfilling policies after
their adoption. The legitimacy rationale sees
participation as a way to increase people's confidence in

officials and make government more stable and accountable
(Cole 1975). Government administrators usually accept
efficiency more readily than legitimacy as a rationale.
When care is taken to ensure the representation of all
concerned groups through an extensive media and outreach
campaign, public participation can broaden the range of
values considered in an environmental assesment (Warner
1971; Pierce and Doerksen 1976). However, if public
participation results in an unbalanced representation of
values, the efficiency goal may be served in the short run,
but the legitimacy goal will not be achieved. A public
participation program can be designed to obtain a broad
range of values, but the representativeness of the values
that are expressed should also be verified. Some social
scientists believe that advocates are needed to express the
interests of the least articulate segments of society
(Davidoff 1965) or to represent the environmental interests
of future generations (Page 1977). One problem with the
advocacy approach is that it is difficult to ensure the
legitimacy of individuals who claim to be advocates for
other groups.

People may have several reasons for participation,
beyond conveying their values on a specific environmental
issue. They may see an opportunity to participate in an
administrative decision as a chance to advance larger
causes, promote themselves, or interact with other
participants. Thus it is important to keep the
participants focused on the task at hand.

Public participation programs are generally more
successful when combined with a public education program
that summarizes the technical analyses and the legal and
institutional issues in an easy-to-understand way. People
can make a more effective contribution to policy making
when they have some grasp of the decision environment and
technical issues, including the available alternatives.

Although public relations is not the primary goal of a
true participation program, any such program does have
public relations ramifications because a participation
program may provide the only direct contact that many
people have with government agencies. People who have no
particular inclination to provide input for a decision may
become aware of an environmental issue through the outreach
component of a participation program. This increased
awareness can lead to changes in public opinion or media
attention and may stimulate political activity.

The timing of participation should be coordinated with
the schedule of decisions to be made, and the participation
activities should contribute directly to the various
decisions. Participants generally will know when they are
being asked their opinions only to justify decisions that
have already been made, and they will resent it.

3.5 METHODS FOR PUBLIC PARTICIPATION

Because of the complex interplay of goals and actors
in public participation, the methods used should be
selected and executed carefully. It is not satisfactory to
announce a public meeting and then simply take notes on
what the people who happen to show up will say. Methods
are available that are tailored to specific purposes and
settings.

After listing the decision points, the next step is to
identify and inform the publics that need to be involved if
the participation program is to be successful. Geographic,
demographic, social, and equity factors should be
considered in targeting groups for participation. There
are three ways to identify publics: (1) self-
identification through petitions, lawsuits, protests,
requests for information, and attendance at prior public
hearings; (2) third-party identification by citizen
committees; and (3) staff identification using lists of
associations, demographic studies, historical analysis of
reports, files, newspaper and magazine articles, and field
interviews (Willeke 1976).

Targeted publics may include businesses potentially
affected, professional organizations and labor unions,
public interest groups, various branches and levels of
government and the general public (Godschalk 1975).
Specific methods of participation have to be geared to the
capabilities and resources of the targeted publics. For
instance, businesses may be willing to release personnel
for participation on "company time," and organized
political interest groups may have skilled lobbying staff.
By contrast, the general public faces time and financial
constraints. Local government agencies may be limited by
budget funds and legal or informal restrictions on their
political activities (Schunk 1977; Gormley 1983).

Two important decisions in designing a public
participation program are the duration of the methods used
and the direction of communication. The duration may be
one time or ongoing. One-time activities are scheduled for
a particular purpose and are not expected to last beyond
completion of that purpose. Ongoing activities begin early
in a program and continue on a regular basis.
Occasionally, one-time activities lead to ongoing ones
(Godschalk 1975).

The direction of communication flows may provide
input, output, or interaction. Input is the expression of
information and values by the publics. Output refers to
the planners' stated definitions of the participation
program, and the associated public education and public
relations activities. Interaction implies both input and
output (Warner 1971). Figure 3-1 shows the two dimensions
that characterize public participation methods.

Ongoing output methods are designed for disseminating
information. They include newsletters, library
depositories, recorded phone messages, speakers' bureaus,

48

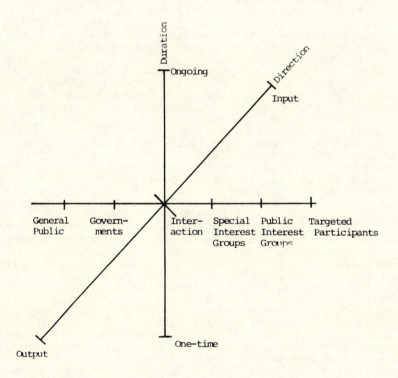

Figure 3-1 Typology of methods of participation

and media relations programs. These methods have limited roles in environmental assessment because they do not contribute directly to the determination of public values. Nevertheless, they can inform a wide spectrum of targeted participants about the assessment process so that people can become further involved if they so desire.

One-time output methods include public presentations, training seminars, newspapers supplements, and radio or television documentaries. As with the ongoing output methods, they play no direct role in the completion of an impact assessment, except for alerting potential participants.

The telephone hotline is the principal ongoing input method for the expression of public opinion. A hotline can facilitate the entry of new participants and increase the effectiveness of continuing participants. Knowledgeable staff can help participants cut through agency red tape and direct their input to the proper place.

One-time input methods such as public hearings, public meetings, and public opinion surveys are commonly used in environmental assessment. Public hearings are often institutionalized in legal requirements for due process, but their formality intimidates the general public. Moreover, the time and place of hearings often restricts participation to a small proportion of the publics. Participants can only get involved in hearings superficially, except through submission of written statements for the record, because it is difficult to probe comments in a detailed way. Often, hearings are held too late in the assessment process to influence the way issues are formulated. Although this mode of participation minimizes overt conflict, its authoritarianism and elitism can increase public frustration and impede real communication. Although hearings may seem to be efficient, they hinder open participation.

Public meetings are less formal than hearings. A wide variety of techniques for facilitating input at public meetings are described elsewhere (Jordan *et al.* 1976; Creighton 1980). Two are mentioned here--brainstorming and the nominal group process. Brainstorming is a relatively unstructured group process for generating new ideas on a problem (Osborn 1963). It emphasizes avoiding premature criticism of ideas so that spontaneity can be encouraged. Brainstorming is most effective in a group of seven to ten people who know each other and are motivated to solve the problem (Bouchard 1971). It is possible that authority relationships within the group may affect the free exchange of ideas or that a few people will dominate the discussion.

When the emphasis is on input for judgmental decisions, a nominal group process may be appropriate. This technique produces a group decision through the expression of individual rather than group opinions. The first step consists of the silent generation of ideas in writing by individuals working independently, but in each other's presence. In the second step, the ideas are recorded and discussed by the group. The third step begins with a preliminary vote to rank the importance or priority of items. After further discussion, a final vote is taken. A nominal group process may be used to determine the elements of a problem, rank goals or priorities, identify experts or skills, and increase the involvement of key individuals in decision making.

A nominal group process has some advantages. It can help separate ideas from personalities by decreasing the likelihood of domination by a few people or interference from poor interpersonal relations. It minimizes the disruption of the participants' thinking and avoids premature narrowing of ideas. Thus, it may produce more creative solutions and give more attention to opinions of minorities or quiet personality types. It can be efficient because it focuses attention on the tasks and reduces rambling in the discussions. However, it decreases interchange in the formulation of ideas and is unsuitable for groups much larger than ten people. It can also be expensive to gather the group together if the members are in distant locations (Delbecq *et al.* 1975; Delp *et al.* 1977).

Public opinion surveys are sometimes used in environmental assessments to determine values (Webb and Hatry 1973; Milbrath 1981). These surveys can be targeted at various groups of participants and may be conducted in person, through the mail, or by phone.

Personal interviews allow questions to be explained or adapted through immediate feedback. Face-to-face interaction can increase the respondent's interest. A skilled interviewer can pick up nonverbal cues to assess the validity of the responses. However, the cost of data collection and analysis in personal interviews can be high. The format of the questionnaire is often inflexible and does not encourage creativity in the responses. Moreover, respondents might not feel sure about the confidentiality of their answers.

Mail questionnaires allow respondents time to think about the question, which may reduce hypothetical bias and increase strategic bias. The responses can be kept confidential. They are usually less costly than phone surveys or personal interviews. Unfortunately, the response rate on a mail survey is selective and low, leading to sampling bias. The lack of an interviewer to judge whether the questions are understood or require elaboration is a serious drawback in a mail survey (Delp *et al.* 1977). Survey techniques for the economic valuation of environmental services are discussed in chapter 4 and techniques based on the psychology of individual preferences are covered in chapter 5.

Ongoing interaction methods provide for both dissemination of information and expression of public opinion. They include the use of advisory committees, task forces, and the Delphi process. These methods are an effective means of acquiring information on values from participants who possess technical knowledge or represent key publics. They also have potential in conflict resolution. By providing a setting for discussing values, these methods can encourage movement toward a consensus through negotiation or meditation (Ozawa and Susskind 1985).

Advisory committees are used in many environmental assessments, especially for comprehensive planning or large-scale projects (Rodgers 1977; Widditsch 1977). Membership on advisory committees and task forces is usually at an agency's discretion, but may be through self-nomination by participants or appointment by elected officials. Often, some committee members who have relevant professional expertise are chosen. Usually, there is some attempt to balance the representation of key affected groups or appoint advocates for that group.

The Delphi process is a technique for facilitating group interactions which does not require that the group meet in person. A Delphi process consists of several rounds of mail questionnaires. The responses are kept anonymous and analyzed so that the results can be reported and used in developing the next round of questions. Successive drafts of documents are circulated among group members for comment until agreement is reached through unanimity or a voting process.

A Delphi process can be used to set goals and priorities, identify the attributes of a problem, make forecasts, and develop a consensus or at least an understanding of the basis of disagreement. It can expand the number of alternatives and viewpoints considered because it relies on separate generation of ideas by individuals. The process can allow a large group of people to participate and express their opinions openly. Like a nominal group process, a Delphi reduces the dominance of vocal individuals and the "bandwagon effect" of peer pressure. It may be useful in consensus building by pressing people to reexamine their assumptions and because it encourages a democratic aggregation of responses.

Multiple rounds of collecting and analyzing information in a Delphi process can be time consuming since several iterations through the mail may be needed. A Delphi requires a large amount of commitment by the participants, especially in the later rounds. Furthermore, the benefits of instant, face-to-face communication and intellectual stimulation from interaction in the group are lost in the process. Also, the values expressed in a Delphi process are only as representative as the participants that are selected (Dalkey 1967; Pyke and North 1969; Delbecq *et al.* 1975; Delp *et al.* 1977).

Conflict resolution in ongoing interaction methods may be facilitated by using a neutral third party as a helper. Helpers vary in their responsibilities, as is reflected by the variety of terms used to describe them--facilitators, mediators, and arbitrators. Facilitators only concern themselves with logistical arrangements such as meeting times, places, and supplies. Mediators actively try to assist parties in reaching agreement through negotiations, single-party conferences, and analytical work to create innovative solutions that the parties might not be able to develop on their own. Arbitrators listen to the various positions and arrive at a finding that may or may not be binding on the parties (Clark and Cummings 1981; Susskind and Madigan 1985).

One-time interaction methods may involve scaled-down versions of the ongoing interaction methods. A method specifically designed for one-time interaction is the "charette." A charette is an intensive session to find a solution to a policy problem. Charettes often last several days and take place in a laboratory-like setting in which technical assistance is provided on the impacts of proposals and the feasibility of alternatives (Batchelor 1971). All parties are on an equal footing in a charette, unlike in public hearings. A charette differs from a nominal group process because it places a time constraint on the participants and does not discourage group interactions in the preliminary rounds.

3.6 IMPLICATIONS FOR ENVIRONMENTAL ASSESSMENT

The effectiveness of environmental assessments has been hindered by excessively narrow views of how to go about doing them. One such view is that environmental impact statements are a product generated by bureaucracies to resolve issues through the use of "objective" observers and expert opinions obtained from scientific measurements and quantitative models. The opposing view is that the preparation of an EIS is a process of conflict resolution that is mainly concerned with the subjective perceptions revealed through participation of key actors. In actuality, neither of these polar views is acceptable in practice. Scientific approaches are needed to collect and analyze factual data, while subjective methods of understanding values are important for adhering to democratic principles and facilitating pragmatic implementation of plans.

Policies made without broad public awareness and debate run the risk of causing delays through protests, litigation, and lack of compliance. Organized publics can stop or ruin a project with truth or rhetoric. Therefore, assessment methods should be capable of identifying the agreements that exist and sharpening the points of disagreement so that they may be worked out.

Most existing environmental assessment methods neglect public participation and depend on expert opinions. Environmental assessment practitioners need to rethink the weights given to the values of experts versus the general public. The values of experts may not be representative of those held by the overall population. In addition, experts frequently disagree over "trans-scientific issues." These issues are couched in scientific language, but are

unsolvable through science alone because of uncertainties
in casual relationships, analytical criteria, future
conditions, or determinations of impact acceptability
(Ozawa and Susskind 1985). Experts should not be able to
impose their personal views of what level of environmental
risks society should accept or what society's aesthetic
preferences should be. An appropriate role for experts is
to assess the physical, chemical, biological, ecological,
economic, and social consequences of human actions. In
addition, experts can help people clarify their values and
improve the consistency of their stated or implied
preferences.

Three changes in the practice of environmental
assessment will improve the likelihood that the analysis
will contribute to equitable and effective policy. First,
assessments should increase the scope and number of publics
who directly contribute to decision making. In this
manner, better information may be available for more
creative solutions, and the degree of cooperation in
implementation of the decision might increase. Second,
input from participation by organized publics should be
balanced by the use of some other means for representing
the values of unorganized publics, such as the use of
advocates or surveys of broader samples. Finally,
assessment methods should display the range of views of
various groups, rather than aggregating the information on
facts and diverse values into a grand index. Such a
display can help decision makers design policies and
projects that are sufficient, equitable, and democratic.
The SAGE method, discussed in chapter 8, takes this
approach.

4
Estimating the Monetary Benefits and Costs of Environmental Quality

4.1 INTRODUCTION

Economic theory plays an important role in explaining the behavior of households and firms, and in developing and evaluating government policies. Conventional benefit-cost analysis, which often is used in environmental assessment, has its roots in welfare economics. Because it focuses on the single criterion of economic efficiency, conventional economic analysis cannot capture the full range of societal values for environmental quality. This chapter reviews the basic concepts of welfare economics and examines the usefulness of new techniques for extending benefit-cost analysis to include the value of environmental goods and services.

4.2 WELFARE ECONOMICS AND CONVENTIONAL BENEFIT-COST ANALYSIS

The importance of comparing the benefits and costs of federal government investments was recognized in the United States as early as 1808 by Secretary of the Treasury Gallatin in a report on transportation infrastructure. The Federal Reclamation Act of 1902 specifically required an economic analysis of the direct impacts of irrigation projects (Kneese 1984).

Welfare economics is concerned with how a society should use or conserve its resources to maximize economic well-being. Benefit-cost analysis hypothesizes the existence of a social welfare function that permits society to judge whether economic conditions are better or worse (Mishan 1976). However, welfare economics does not specify exactly which indicators should be included in a benefit-cost analysis nor how they should be defined and combined. Although welfare economics rests on some fundamental characteristics of human behavior, it contains some implicit value judgments. This review of welfare economics concentrates on (1) individual utility maximization, (2) consumer's surplus as a measure of individual utility, (3) the relationship between individual utility and social welfare, and (4) the tradeoffs between the welfare of present and future generations due to the discounting of net benefits over time.

4.2.1 Utility

Utility is a measure of the satisfaction individuals receive from the consumption of goods and services. This concept grew out of hedonistic psychology (the theory that normal human behavior is motivated by the desire for pleasure and the avoidance of pain) and the utilitarian philosophy of Bentham and Mill in the nineteenth century. Prior to Pareto in the late 1920s, many economists thought that utility could be measured in discrete units. Modern welfare economics recognizes that (1) utility can only be compared in ordinal units, (2) any interpersonal comparisons of utility involve value judgments, and (3) utility is not an inherent quality of an object, but a matter of subjective tastes and preferences. Welfare economics is not concerned with the ultimate sources of these tastes and preferences.

Economists assume that people are rational consumers who maximize utility in the face of a budget constraint by choosing the goods that offer them the highest utility at a given price. Consumers have to make tradeoffs among goods because resources are limited. An individual's preferences are considered stable at an instant, but they may change over time.

The total utility derived from most goods increases with the amount consumed. Marginal utility is the change in total utility associated with a small unit change in consumption of a good. Over some range of consumption, marginal utility may increase at an increasing rate. For example, a person might enjoy wilderness recreation more after improving backpacking skills through experience. Over a certain range, marginal utility typically increases at a decreasing rate; this phenomenon is known as the law of diminishing marginal returns. Economic "bads," such as nuclear waste and raw sewage, provide negative marginal utility.

4.2.2 The Price System and Consumer's Surplus

Costs are reductions in output or increases in the consumption of inputs that could have other productive uses. Benefits are increases in the output of goods and services that satisfy human wants. An individual's demand for a good originates in that person's impressions of the marginal utility of the good relative to its price. A demand curve is defined as the maximum quantity of a good that will be consumed at a given price, holding other factors constant such as the price and availability of substitutes or complements, real income, public preferences, and population. Short-run supply is the

maximum quantity of a good that sellers are willing to
provide at a given price, holding other factors constant
such as the price and availability of production inputs and
technology.

Under perfect competition, market prices of goods and
services are determined by the simultaneous interaction of
demand and supply in a society. A society's demand for an
ordinary economic good can be found by horizontally summing
the demand curves of the individuals in that society so
that the short-run supply of a good is allocated to the
highest bidders. Since income affects an individual's
willingness to pay for a good, the rule of the market is
not "one person, one vote", but "one dollar, one vote".
Thus, market prices give greater weight to the values of
the wealthy.

To the extent that imperfections exist in markets, the
use of market prices in valuing economic goods and services
has some serious limitations:

1. The possibility that market prices can be
   manipulated when there is only one seller of a
   good (monopoly), just a few sellers (oligopoly),
   a single buyer (monopsony), or a small number of
   buyers (oligopsony)
2. Collusion between certain buyers and sellers due
   to friendship or kinship ties or corrupt
   practices
3. Imperfect information about quantities and
   qualities of goods and resources
4. Trade barriers and regulatory restrictions
5. Indivisibilities or immobilities of inputs and
   final goods

Although their absoluteness as a measure of value is
subject to question (Loebl 1976), market prices often
provide a relatively objective way of evaluating costs and
benefits. In cases where market prices do not exist or
might not reflect societal values accurately, they may be
adjusted by shadow pricing (Margolis 1977; Haveman 1983).
Shadow pricing is used most often in impact assessment to
value environmental services that do not have market prices
and to compensate for distortions in the costs of capital,
foreign exchange, labor, and land.

Net social benefits are the difference between gross
social benefits and costs. Consumer's surplus is the proper
measure of social benefits because total revenues (the
product of output and market price) underestimate the gross
social benefits of a good (Dupuit 1844). Gross consumer's
surplus is the sum of total revenues and net consumer's
surplus. Net consumer's surplus is the excess over market
price that people are willing to pay in order to avoid
doing without a good. This amount is the area below the
demand curve that is above the market price line, (AP(o)C)
figure 4-1. Since P_o is the equilibrium price and Q_o is the

the in equilibrium quantity, (P(o)OCQ(o)) is the total
production costs of the good while (AOQ(o)C) represents
gross consumer's surplus. Suppose that a new technology
lowers the costs of producing solar electric cells. The net
benefits of this to society equal the increase in
consumer's surplus (P(o)P(1)DC) caused by the fall in price
to P(1) and the increase in consumption to Q(1) (figure
4-2).

There are two complications in the definition of
consumer's surplus. The first complication is that when the
price of a good decreases, consumers have more money to
spend on other goods and this effectively increases their
incomes. Since demand curves are defined over a constant
level of real income, a fall in prices results in a
different demand curve. In practice, this difference can be
ignored as long as the good is a small part of the
consumer's total budget or if the price decline is small
enough to make the income change insignificant.

The second complication is that there really are four
variations of consumer's surplus (Hicks 1943). The
variations depend on whether consumer's surplus is defined
in terms of willingness to pay for a gain or willingness to
accept compensation for a loss and whether individuals
remain at the original level of utility or are allowed to
reach a new level of utility. In theory, the differences
between these four measures are small and can be explained
by income effects (Willig 1976). However, these
differences could be large because of risk aversion or
differences in the way people view receiving or paying an
equivalent amount of money (Gordon and Knetsch 1979). In
practice, the differences between these measures can be
large when surveys are used to estimate people's values
because respondents might have incentives to distort their
true demand for extramarket goods.

4.2.3 Decision Rules for Evaluating Changes in Social Welfare

Some decision rule must be selected in order to
determine whether an action that affects individuals
increases or decreases social welfare. Three common
examples are (1) Pareto optimality, (2) the Kaldor-Hicks
decision rule, and (3) Little's decision rule.

The most accepted decision rule, Pareto optimality,
states that in order to be unequivocally desirable, an
action must increase the welfare of at least one individual
without leaving anyone worse off. The Pareto rule does not
require any interpersonal comparisons of utility.
Unfortunately, since most governmental actions result in
gains for some individuals and losses for others, the
Pareto rule is rarely applicable.

The Kaldor-Hicks rule (sometimes called the potential
Pareto rule) states that an action increases social welfare
if the gainers are made sufficiently better off so that the
losers could be compensated and some of the gains

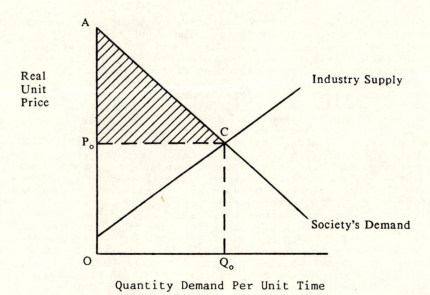

Figure 4-1   The definition of consumer's surplus

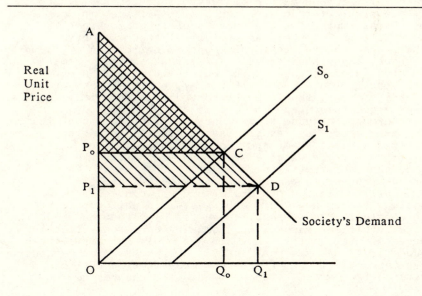

Quantity Demand Per Time Unit

Figure 4-2   Partial equilibrium analysis of an
increase in supply

would still be left over. This rule does not require that
compensation actually be paid, only that it could
potentially be paid. Decisions on whether or not to pay
compensation are political rather than economic because
compensation is a redistribution of the slices of the
economic pie rather than a change in the size of the pie.
The Kaldor-Hicks rule makes no economic distinctions
between who gains and who loses since it only focuses on
whether society as a whole is better or worse off.

The Kaldor-Hicks rule was institutionalized into
benefit-cost analysis for water resources by the Flood
Control Act of 1936. This law states that projects are
justified if their total benefits exceed their costs "to
whomsoever they accrue." The Kaldor-Hicks rule also forms
the basis of Executive Order 12291 of 1981, which requires
federal agencies to conduct benefit-cost analyses before
issuing major regulations or legislative proposals.

Little's rule placed an additional condition on the
Kaldor-Hicks rule to account for the social welfare effects
of changes in the distribution of income. The additional
condition is that society or its designated decision makers
must approve of the resulting redistribution of income.
Little's rule is a reasonable alternative, although
arguments can be made on ethical grounds for a different
rule that requires actual compensation of the losers by the
gainers. The SAGE method discussed in chapter 8 adopts
Little's rule for judging the social welfare implications
of fiscal impacts on the budgets of local governments.

Some philosophers and political theorists have
challenged the conventional economic definition of social
welfare. Many people would agree that there is some
"public interest" apart from the sum of the interests of
individuals (Colm 1966). For example, the rights of
minority groups should be protected even when it is against
the personal interests of the majority to do so.
Furthermore, because of the unequal distribution of income,
social justice may require paying special attention to the
interests of the poor and the handicapped. There are
other humanistic value systems that emphasize the
importance of the fairness of social decisions (Rawls 1971)
or due process in making the decisions (Nozick 1974).

Utilitarianism centers around the consequences of
actions on humans. Some ecologists and philosophers (e.g.
Ehrenfeld 1978) have challenged the view that human welfare
is a sufficient yardstick for making decisions affecting
environmental quality. A small group of ecologists led by
Odum (1971) believe that a value system based on net energy
can internalize the effects on ecosystems better than a
utilitarian system based on money (see chapter 6).

4.2.4 Discounting and Welfare Maximization Over Time

Because of the time value of money, economists
conventionally discount future benefits and costs to a

common point in time so that they can be compared in present value, future value, or annual equivalent terms. Table 4-1 illustrates how quickly the present value of net benefits declines as the discount rate increases or the time period lengthens. For example, a project yielding $1 of net benefits each year would produce $50 of net benefits after 50 years and $100 after 100 years when there is no discounting. When discounted at 10 percent, the percent value of net benefits (PVNB) after 100 years is just $9.99, only $0.08 more than the PVNB after 50 years. There are two alternative views on what the discount rate should represent: the opportunity cost of capital and the social rate of time preference.

TABLE 4-1
How the discount rate and time horizon affect the present value of net benefits (PVNB) of an annuity of $1.00 per year

Discount Rate (%)	Time Horizon of Project (years)			Change in PVNB between 50 and 100 years
	20	50	100	
0.0	20.00	50.00	100.00	50.00
2.5	15.59	28.36	36.00	8.20
4.0	13.59	21.48	24.50	3.00
6.0	11.47	15.76	16.62	0.86
10.0	8.51	9.91	9.99	0.08

The opportunity cost of capital is the amount of income foregone by not investing the capital in its highest-value alternative use, accounting for risk. The opportunity cost of public investments varies with the source of the capital: public debt, taxation, or inflationary finance (Hirshliefer, DeHaven, and Milliman 1960; Baumol 1977). The cost of public debt is the interest rate on long-term government bonds. Although market factors affect this interest rate, it can be manipulated by the government. The economic production foregone as a result of taxation depends on whether the burden of the tax falls on consumers or directly displaces corporate investments. In theory, market interest rates on business loans reflect the productivity of corporate investments. Although taxes may reduce consumer spending and this affects corporate profits, the opportunity cost is lower than when taxes displace consumption rather than productive investments. By increasing the money supply, the federal government can take advantage of inflationary finance, but each dollar in circulation is worth less than before. Since all of the above methods may be used at the same time to finance public expenditures, determining the opportunity cost of capital can be quite complicated.

The social rate of time preference is based on an entirely different principle -- not what the opportunity cost is in the economy, but what society thinks the discount rate should be for reasons of intertemporal equity. A society may be concerned about the distribution of wealth between present and future generations, and the private sector will not automatically take care of this in the desired way. Thus, governments might need to use a modified discount rate that differs from the myopic time preferences of individuals (Pigou 1929). Or, people might have different time preferences in their roles as individuals versus citizens in society, so that the amount of money that one person wants society to invest for future generations may depend on the willingness of others to contribute as well (Marglin 1963b). Also, society may recognize that market interest rates weight different people's time preferences unequally according to the number of "dollar votes" they can invest. Another factor affecting the social rate of time preference is the expected effect of changes on technology or the availability of natural resources on real incomes over time.

The social rate of time preference is harder to determine than the opportunity cost of capital. One method of estimating it is to examine the tradeoffs between present and future generations implicit in government decisions. However, the political process may be poorly suited for determining a social discount rate because (1) the time horizon of politicians might be limited by election terms; (2) future generations cannot vote; and (3) organized interest groups dominate policy in accordance with their wealth, power, and bargaining ability (Lowi 1969).

Although discounting is necessary to ensure economic efficiency in allocating resources over time, some economists have criticized the practice on the grounds of intergenerational inequity. When all effects on social welfare are evaluated from the point of view of present consumers, the values of future generations are ignored (Ramsay 1928). As shown above, the costs of long-term resource and environmental problems are downplayed by high discount rates. To treat each generation equally and encourage long-term investments in environmental quality, Page (1977) recommended that discounting only be used to allocate resources within a generation and not across generations, except to account for improvements in technology over time.

The use of low or zero discount rates has two types of effects on natural resources and environmental quality. First, a low discount rate stimulates investments which may accelerate the depletion of nonrenewable resources. Therefore, use of a low or zero discount rate in the public sector might not help future generations. Indeed, it might result in investments in inefficient government projects that cost more than the value of their benefits. As more investments are made in long-term projects, fewer resources are left for future generations to decide how to use themselves. In addition, there may be a tradeoff between the state of technical knowledge and the state of unused resources left to future generations (O'Toole and Walton 1981).

Second, with low discount rates, long-term investments in sustaining environmental quality become more attractive. For a persistent environmental hazard such as nuclear waste, Schulze, Brookshire, and Sandler (1981) recommended using a zero discount rate to avoid inflicting damage on future generations. Since it is unlikely that cross-generational payments will be made to compensate for the risks of long-term environmental hazards, the question of the discount rate for determining the amount of compensation needed becomes moot. However, discounting is generally used in benefit-cost analyses of measures to prevent or mitigate possible hazards. If compensation is not paid, a decision to proceed with a hazardous activity will not be Pareto optimal, but it might satisfy the Kaldor-Hick rule criterion.

Fisher and Krutilla (1975) concluded that a different rate should be applied in managing nonrenewable resources than in making decisions affecting environmental quality. Nevertheless, there may be better ways of maintaining the resource base and the quality of the environment than by altering discount rates. Other possibilities include laws and regulations, severance taxes, more research and development, reduced population growth, or maintenance of unforeclosed options for the future.

4.3 BASIC CONCEPTS OF ENVIRONMENTAL ECONOMICS

Except for Pigou (1920) and Kapp (1950), few economists before 1960 wrote about the relationship between human activities and environmental quality. Most economists considered pollution to be a market imperfection with little policy significance for economic stability and growth. By the 1960s, environmental pollution had become pervasive and began to receive increasing attention from economists. The sixth Resources for the Future Forum was a milestone in the study of environmental quality in a growing economy (Jarrett 1966). The main concepts of environmental economics relevant in impact assessment are externalities, pure public goods, and materials balance. In addition, a number of techniques for the valuation of extramarket benefits and costs have been developed.

Externalities are spillover effects of someone's production or consumption that affect the well-being of other producers and consumers. Because these effects are not directly reflected in market transactions, there can be a big difference between the private and social benefits and costs of free market activities. Environmental economics deals extensively with the use of charges and subsidies to induce an efficient allocation of resources to pollution control (Dales 1968; Kneese and Bower 1968; Baumol and Oates 1975; Anderson *et al.* 1977; Committee on Environment and Public Works 1977; Dasgupta 1982).

The concept of pure public goods was introduced to justify government expenditures on certain collective goods such as national defense (Samuelson 1954), but other economists later applied it to environmental quality. Pure public goods are characterized by zero marginal costs of providing them to an additional user once they have been produced and high exclusion costs. These characteristics result in a "free-rider problem" that makes it difficult to prevent people from using the goods free of charge. Since pure public goods often are indivisible, it is not possible to supply them in the different quantities that various groups would prefer to consume. In fact, it is difficult to determine the true demand for a pure public good. If individual demand curves for pure public goods can be identified, they should be summed vertically (rather than horizontally as for an ordinary good) in order to find society's maximum total willingness to pay.

The application of the principles of conservation of mass and materials balance to the problem of wastes was an important conceptual connection between the natural resources use and environmental quality (Kneese, Ayres, and d'Arge, 1970). A materials balance accounting of the interrelationships of residuals (consumption or production wastes), environmental media, economic activity, and recycling provides a systems basis for environmental quality management that is superior to the conventional single-pollutant, single-medium approach (Kneese and Bower 1968). Materials balance accounting also offers a convenient classification for environmental damage at various stages of economic activity. This approach has been applied to a number of different industries (Bower and Basta 1973; Russell 1973; Spofford, Russell, and Kelly 1975; Russell and Vaughan 1976).

A related technique, input-output analysis, can model the consumption of natural resources and the associated pollution on a regional or economy-wide level. The addition of pollutant transport and transformation models to an input-output analysis permits the study of ambient pollutant concentrations in time and space. The economic impacts of various emission standards also can be simulated in an input-output model for water quality and, to a lesser extent, for air quality (Isard 1969; Leontief 1970; Ayres and Gutmanis 1972; Victor 1972; Cumberland and Korbach 1973; and Muller 1979). The greatest obstacle to use of the technique is lack of the pollution coefficients for economic activities at the regional level. As a result, none of these input-output models is fully operational, although a good attempt has been made in the case of a nuclear power plant (Johnson and Bennett 1979).

Because the production and distribution of most environmental goods and services fall outside of market processes, market prices for making rational decisions on their use and preservation are unavailable. Yet, it is important to be able to make tradeoffs between benefits and costs in environmental quality, economic efficiency, and other societal objectives. Money provides a convenient measuring rod for comparing these tradeoffs on a common scale. The "Green Book" (U.S. Federal Interagency River Basin Committee 1950) was an early attempt to consider environmental "intangibles" in water resource planning. Kneese (1964), Krutilla (1967), and Kneese and Bower (1968) were among the first to place economic values on physical measures of environmental quality.

Much of the recent research in environmental economics focuses on ways to impute demand curves or estimate shadow prices for extramarket goods and services in order to conduct a benefit-cost analysis. If the economic benefits of pollution abatement are not estimated, an analysis is limited to cost effectiveness -- determining the cheapest way to achieve a particular level of environmental quality without trying to identify the optimal level of pollution abatement.

Some environmental benefits are easy to analyze in a benefit-cost analysis because they directly affect production processes or consumption. Benefit-cost analysis works best for perceptible, short-term effects that pass through markets. For example, water pollution can decrease the value of fishing catches and sedimentation of a dam reduces its economic life. The public sector often provides outdoor recreation services for free although they could easily be priced.

Pollution can cause large economic losses from decreased yields of agricultural, silvicultural, and livestock products. Air pollution can cause large economical losses in agricultural production. One study estimated that ozone levels in four areas in Central and Southern California resulted in annual losses of $45,000,000 for 14 vegetable crops. About four-fifths of this loss was in producer profits and one-fifth in net consumer's surplus (Adams, Narongsdakdi, and Crocker 1979). These losses are significant, but are much smaller than than the urban nonagricultural losses associated with property value decreases in the same areas. There has been relatively little quantification of the effects of air pollution on materials although the economic losses involved may be significant (Kneese 1984).

Air quality studies have mostly focused on acute health impacts due to measurement problems and the difficulty of showing that ambient exposures cause chronic health impacts. Yet, the economic losses from chronic health impacts may exceed those form the acute impacts (Kneese 1984).

Use value is difficult to evaluate for scenic, historic, cultural, or scientific resources that are collective goods. It is also difficult to value services associated with the environment's capacity to assimilate the residuals of human activities such as a forest's ability to reduce erosion or the atmosphere's dispersion of pollutants. It is even more difficult to analyze long-term, extensive, and global effects or irreversible impacts on ecosystems (such as losses in the size and diversity of gene pools). The value of nonreproducible environmental amenities might increase over time because of increased scarcity and changes in preferences due to income growth and lack of close substitutes for the amenity. At the same time, the value of economic goods relative to environmental services might decrease over time due to technological progress (Krutilla 1967). Moreover, attempts to estimate the costs of risks to human health and safety are loaded with ethical value judgments.

In addition to use value, option value may be relevant in valuing environmental amenities (Weisbrod 1964; Krutilla and Fisher 1975). Option value refers to benefits that people place on the availability of a resource or good even if they do not use it at present. This term has been used to mean five different concepts:

1. Risk aversion -- Potential users of a resource are not sure about whether they will use the resource in the future or whether it will be available.

2. Quasi-option demand -- Potential users may defer decisions until more information is available.

3. Existence value -- Nonusers can derive value from knowing that an area is preserved in its natural state.

4. Vicarious use value -- Nonusers can receive pleasure from having other people enjoy an amenity.

5. Bequest value -- Individuals can feel some moral responsibility or altruism toward leaving amenities for future generations.

Option value could be negative or zero since there is risk in buying an option will not be used, and the desirability of doing so depends on consumers' marginal utilities of income (Schmalensee 1972). However, even if

people are risk-neutral, there is likely to be a positive
option value for environmental resources that can be
irreversibly destroyed. To date, most environmental
assessments have neglected option demand even though it may
be significantly larger than the consumer's surplus from
user demand. It may be double counting to include a risk
aversion or quasi-option value for the future and the use
value for those who actually use the resource later (Bishop
1982). It would not be double counting to include the
other three types of option value together with use value.
Bequest value is not completely altruistic because it is
based on the utility that someone gets from knowing that an
environmental amenity is passed on to the next generation.
Some critics urge that environmental bequests be treated as
an ethical obligation to preserve the options of future
generations, rather than as a voluntary source of utility
(Page 1982).

An environmental assessment should address impacts on
natural resources as well as environmental goods and
services. Natural resource economics help us understand
the causes of the depletion of nonrenewable and critical
zone resources and the overexploitation of renewable
resources. Nonrenewable resources, such as copper or
petroleum, exist in fixed stocks although they often can be
reused or recycled. The proportion of these stocks that is
economically accessible depends on technology, and the
location and market prices for the resources. Renewable
resources such as a fishery or forest can be replenished
through growth and reproduction.

A critical zone resource can be renewed only until a
threshold of irreversible depletion has been reached;
beyond that level it may be lost forever. The best example
of a critical zone resource is an endangered species, which
can expand its population provided that its numbers do not
fall below a minimum viable level. However, the minimum
viable level often is uncertain. For this reason, a few
economists advocate a safe minimum standard approach in
dealing with a critical zone resource. This safe minimum
standard would be maintained unless the social costs of
doing so were unacceptably high. This approach is different
from the standard benefit-cost framework.

Natural resource scarcity and environmental quality
are closely related because excessive depletion of
resources leads to more intensive resource extraction or
harvesting processes and an accelerated substitution of
synthetic inputs that degrade the environment. Therefore,
resource management plans should discuss environmental
quality and an environmental assessment needs to consider
natural resource issues. (See Hyman (1984) for an overview
of the usefulness of economic models for determining
optimal rates of use of natural resources.) Figure 4-3
summarizes the relationships between welfare economics,
environmental economics, and natural resource economics.

A wide range of techniques are available for
estimating the use value of environmental goods and

68

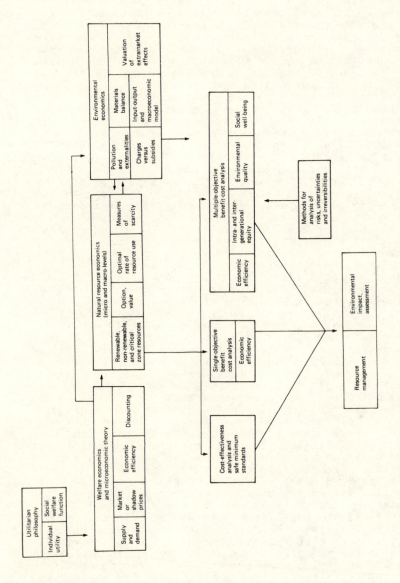

Figure 4-3 The relationship between welfare economics, environmental
economics, and natural resources economics
(Source: Hyman 1984, p. 175)

services. Most of these techniques ignore option values; one exception is hypothetical valuation, which relies on survey measurement of demand. Section 4.4.1 describes hypothetical valuation techniques. There are potential problems with the validity, reliability, and systematic biases of hypothetical valuation, as is discussed in section 4.4.2. As a result of these problems, three types of nonsurvey techniques have been proposed: (1) revealed preference measures, (2) the human capital approach for valuing lives saved or lost, and (3) threshold analysis. Section 4.5 discusses these nonsurvey techniques for valuing extramarket benefits and costs.

Many techniques for valuation of extramarket goods and services are based on the hedonic price theory of consumer choice (Becker 1965; Lancaster 1966). According to this theory, goods are not valued in and of themselves, but as a collection of attributes. For example, a house consists of a roof for shelter, a certain number of rooms of various sizes and functions, and a whole set of social and cultural implications. Similarly, a wilderness site has many attributes: topography, flora and fauna, water bodies, and other features of utilitarian and aesthetic importance (see section 5.3.2). The utility provided by a good also depends on the other inputs used with it, and the characteristics of the user. For instance, the quality of a recreational experience depends on the availability of food, backpacks, hiking shoes, as well as an individual's survival skills, knowledge of nature, and companions.

Hedonic price theory has two basic principles. The first is that individuals choose a consumption pattern that maximizes utility subject to constraints of time, income, and the production technology. The second is that a value can be inferred for each major attribute of a good by working backward from the cost or value of the whole good. These principles allow the derivation of a demand curve for each attribute from comparisons of actual expenditures or survey preferences for closely related goods that differ marginally in the quantity or quality of their attributes. A hedonic price analysis assumes (1) indivisibility of the attribute bundle, (2) availability of a continuous choice of products, (3) perfect competition, and (4) perfect knowledge. It also assumes that utility functions are weakly separable so that the prices of substitutes and complements can be ignored. In practice, there are statistical problems in estimating hedonic prices because the production functions may be joint, nonhomogeneous, or subject to increasing or decreasing returns to scale (Pollak and Wachter 1975).

4.4 HYPOTHETICAL VALUATION OF EXTRAMARKET GOODS AND SERVICES

4.4.1 Description of the Techniques

Hypothetical valuation techniques simulate markets for extramarket goods through interviews with potential consumers. The purpose of hypothetical valuation is to derive shadow prices or a surrogate demand curve that can be used to estimate aggregate consumer's surplus. To use these methods, there must be a well-defined good, even if it is not bought or sold in the markets. There are four types of hypothetical valuation methods: (1) direct questioning, (2) bidding games, (3) use estimation games, and (4) tradeoff analysis.

Direct Questioning. In direct questioning, respondents are asked to state their maximum willingness to pay (WTP) for various quantities or qualities of hypothetical environmental goods. This may be done through a single question in personal interviews or by mail or phone surveys. Alternatively, respondents could be asked about the smallest amount of money that they would be willing to accept as compensation (WTA) for a decline in the quality or quantity of an environmental good.

If implicit property rights are given to polluters, the WTP measure should be used to determine the value of pollution abatement. On the other hand, WTA is more appropriate if consumers have a "right" to a pristine environment. Generally, WTA measures produce higher dollar values than WTP because willingness to pay is limited by the respondent's disposable income. However, gamesmanship is more likely to be a problem with the WTA measure because a few excessively large or infinite WTA bids can skew results.

The interviewer should suggest some neutral means of collecting or disbursing the money such as a payment or credit on lump-sum taxes or utility bills. The interviewer should emphasize that this money would be placed in a trust fund to provide or maintain the amenity, or pay compensation. The problem of differences in respondents' personal discount rates is circumvented since, in theory, respondents consider their desired tradeoffs between present and future consumption in deciding on their bids.

Meyer (1976, pp. 39-40) tested for differences in values associated with the wording of four types of direct questions on public recreation and preservation benefits to residents located near the Fraser River in Canada:

1.   What would you pay?
2.   What would I have to pay you to give it up?
3.   If you were making a community decision, how would you reallocate the budget for recreation on the Fraser River?

4. If you were a judge and someone had
been arbitrarily excluded form the
activity listed below for one year,
what dollar damages would you award?

The four types of questions addressed different
concepts of values. If the amenity is publicly owned and
has been supplied at a zero or nominal price, the WTP bids
tend to be lower than respondents' true valuations. This
is common because of respondents' perceptions that they
have paid taxes to maintain the site or that the amenity
should be free because it is part of their birthright. The
WTA question implicitly recognizes the time, utility, and
opportunity costs of substituting other sites or
activities. The third question focuses attention on public
values and priorities for society as a whole and is less
affected by an individual's income than is WTP. The fourth
question has a social justice and equity slant. Each type
of question also had a separate option demand part similar
to the following:

Some people associate a value with environmental
resources even though they don't expect to use them,
simply because they feel they should be preserved. If
you are one, what annual payment would you agree to
accept for the permanent loss of these recreational
opportunities? (Meyer 1976)

Table 4-2 compares the results of these four types of
direct questions. Except for the differences between the
judicial award and community decision-making questions, all
of the differences were statistically significant at the
.05 level. In each case, WTA was much higher than WTP.
The social-oriented measures were roughly halfway between
WTP and WTA. For the most part, option value exceeded use
value. The large confidence interval shows a high degree
of individual variation in response. The same rankings
across question types held for the evaluation of specific
activities such as swimming, boating, fishing, and viewing.
Relatively high values were placed on simply viewing the
environment.
Some of the more recent applications of the direct
questioning approach have relied on payment cards
containing a list of monetary amounts from zero to some
maximum in even increments. Sometimes, payment cards with
different ranges of values are used for respondents in
different income groups. The respondents are asked to
choose one amount from the payment card rather than
participate in an iterative bidding process. Like
starting-point bids, payment cards may introduce
instrumental bids because they give respondents some idea
of the range of responses expected by the analyst.

TABLE 4-2
A comparison of four direct questioning methods

| Question Type | Use Value | | Additional Option Value | |
	Mean	95% Confidence Interval	Mean	95% Confidence Interval
Annual amount you would pay	$ 1,099	$\pm$ 993	$ 2,894	$\pm$1,698
Annual amount you would accept	$20,961	$\pm$6,028	$27,079	$\pm$4,744
Community decision making, annual budget	$11,833	$\pm$4,793	$14,833	$\pm$3,858
Judicial award per annum	$11,683	$\pm$5,559	$10,519	$\pm$3,013

Adapted from: Meyer (1976, pp. 12 and 15)

When a random sample of respondents is stratified into people who currently use a river or lake for boating, fishing, or swimming and those who do not, the difference in expressed willingness to pay by these two groups can provide some indication of the relative magnitude of use values compared to option and existence values. The responses of users include a mixture of use, option, and existence values, while responses of nonusers only include option and existence values. If it is assumed that users and nonusers have a similar willingness to pay for option and existence values, the two types of values can be calculated separately (Mitchell and Carson 1985). For example, suppose that the total WTP per household per year is $100 for users and $40 for nonusers, and there are 1,000 users and 2,000 nonusers in an area. Using the assumption above, the annual option and existence values would total $120,000 ($40 x 3,000), and the annual use value would be $60,000 (($100 - $40) x 1,000). However, users of nature-based recreation may have different tastes and preferences than nonusers and the responses of nonusers, in particular, may be subject to hypothetical bias.

Bidding Games. The bidding game approach is similar to direct questioning except that instead of a single question, an iterative process is used to estimate the values (Bohm 1972). It is supposed to be easier for respondents to handle a bidding game than direct questions about the monetary value of environmental quality.

The maximum WTP is found through an iterative bidding process in a personal interview. Mail surveys cannot be used efficiently for a bidding game. First, the interviewer describes the quantity, quality, timing of availability, and location of the amenity, and defines the right to use the good. Next, the interviewer gives the respondent a starting-point bid and asks whether the respondent would pay that amount for the good. If the answer is yes, the interviewer raises the bid. The bid is increased until the respondent is no longer willing to pay. Next, the interviewer lowers the bid to fine-tune the exact amount the respondent is willing to pay. A similar process is used to find the minimum WTA for loss of a use right. As a check on the bids, respondents could be asked to rank their values for several alternatives (Desvousges, Smith, and McGivney 1982).

For marketable goods, the individual bid curves would be summed horizontally to estimate society's demand curve. In the case of pure public goods, the individual bid curves are added vertically to obtain an aggregate bid curve because the marginal cost of providing these goods to an additional user is zero once they are supplied to anyone. When bidding games are conducted for several environmental attributes in the same analysis, the implied tradeoffs among the attributes can be derived.

Zero bids should be probed to analyze whether they represent an individual's true valuation or a protest against the format, payment vehicles, or personality of the interviewer. Further questioning should be done to follow up on zero bids, using such questions as (1) "Do you believe X would not be worth anything to you?" (2) "Do you believe taxes (or utility bills or another vehicle) are already too high?" and (3) "Do you think X is valuable but it would be unfair for a certain group (e.g., local area residents or campers) to have to pay for it?" The U.S. Water Resources Council (1979) recommended revising the format of a question if it leads to more than 15 percent protest bids. Otherwise, protest bids should be recorded separately, but do not have to be eliminated from the sample. The analyst can exclude protest bids form respondents who reject the idea of placing a monetary value on environmental goods or who do not take the exercise seriously. Data form respondents who appear to misunderstand the questions or demonstrate significant starting point bias may be excluded (Desvousges, Smith, McGivney 1983).

A good way to estimate option value in hypothetical valuation is to ask respondents about their option price-- the maximum amount they are willing to pay for a change in environmental quality for actual and potential use. Then, the respondents are asked about their willingness to pay for the actual use of the good. The option value is the difference between the option price and the expected consumer's surplus. Any additional existence value may be added to the option value. However, it is difficult to

separate option value from existence or bequest value in
hypothetical valuation because most respondents do not
understand the distinction and often just repeat their
option value bids (Desvousges, Smith, McGivney 1983).

Bidding games have been tried in valuing reductions in
pollution, particularly for visibility (Barrett and Waddell
1973; Randall, Ives, and Eastman 1974; Brookshire, Ives,
and Schulze 1976; Blank et al. 1977; Rowe d'Arge, and
Brookshire 1980), wildlife management (Hammack and Brown
1974), impacts from geothermal development (Thayer and
Schultze 1976), industrial water pollution (Gramlich 1977),
and risks affecting human health (Cooper and Rice 1976;
Jones-Lee 1976; and Needleman 1976).

One bidding game study found that option and existence
values comprised a large part of the total value of
visibility at key vistas in three major national parks in
the United States. The respondents placed a higher value
on a small, initial decrease from clear conditions than on
subsequent decreases (Schulze et al. 1981). Although the
majority of the population does not visit one of these
parks in a given year, most people still place a high value
on visibility there. Even if they place a low individual
value on visibility in the parks, the aggregate value would
be high because of the larger number of concerned people.
The value would be even higher if the preferences of
foreigners were included. The conclusions of this study
might not apply to all environmental amenities equally
since the parks that were included in the study contained
dominant features like the Grand Canyon, which are
recognized by most of the population and evoke strong
feeling of national pride. A subsequent experiment also
indicated the possibility of hypothetical bias in the
earlier results because when people were asked about their
willingness to pay for closer environmental amenities
first, they placed lower values on more distant scenic
features. Other studies have confirmed that option and
existence values can be large relative to use value and
substantial in the aggregate (Brookshire et al. 1979;
Randall, Hoehn, and Tolley 1981).

Hypothetical valuation can be used to value health
risks including incremental morbidity and mortality, moving
costs and income losses due to migration induced by a
desire to avoid health effects, anxiety costs, and the
values placed on the lives of friends and relatives. The
future timing of the risk matters because it reflects the
person's personal discount rate and it affects the
potential for technological change in medical care. The
bids also depend on people's prediction of life
expectancy, which may be inaccurate. The application of
hypothetical valuation methods to health risks requires the
tenuous assumption that individuals treat longevity like
other goods and are willing and able to make rational
tradeoffs in this area.

Use Estimation Games. Some responses to a decline in environmental quality are reflected better through behavior substitution rather than price changes. For example, people may watch television instead of jogging if air pollution levels are high. Although respondents cannot adjust the available quality or quantity of some environmental amenities, they can modify their activities to maximize their own utility under the circumstances. In such cases, use estimation games are more appropriate than bidding games.

With use estimation games, the investigator asks about the quantity or quality of a good that would be demanded at a constant price, instead of inquiring about WTP or WTA. The investigator also asks questions about attitudes toward substitution of other leisure and work activities. Use estimation games are most appropriate when a site is one of several visited on a single trip and when a proposed project will cause a small change in environmental quality.

Use estimation games are the flip side of the bidding game approach. At equilibrium, the marginal rate of substitution between any two environmental attributes is related to the ratio of the prices of the two attributes. Given a cost function, the analyst can estimate the marginal rate of substitution among attributes. Then, by choosing a set of attributes as the output level and by varying the prices of the attributes, the analyst can derive a demand curve for the good.

Tradeoff Analysis. Tradeoff analysis is used to elicit expressions of preference in a way that recognizes the scarcity of resources and opportunity costs. People may find it easier to make choices on packages of goods than to place dollar values on the goods.

The priority evaluation approach is a good example of tradeoff analysis (Hoinville 1975). This is a structured method for determining tradeoffs among different types of goods subject to a set of prices and a budget constraint. It simulates a situation in which there are no market failures, so it can be especially useful for extramarket environmental goods and services. Yet, the hypothetical nature of the exercise may be a problem because people are not accustomed to making comparisons between consumption of economic goods and environmental quality and other goods and services.

The priority evaluation approach begins by asking individuals to describe their current consumption of selected attributes on established scales. The interviewer then tallies up the points according to a schedule previously assigned to those levels of each attribute. Next, the respondents are asked to maximize their utility by reallocating the total number of points that they currently have if they wish to purchase a different quantity or quality of any attributes. Later, the interviewer changes the total number of points available and asks for a reallocation of points among attributes.

For greater realism, respondents could be allowed to defer present consumption for future consumption by saving points.

Careful construction of the tradeoff scales is crucial. Each scale should have four or five quality and quantity levels marked with increasing point values. Points are preferable to real money prices so that the numbers can be smaller, but they should have some basis in supply costs. The lowest position on each scale is assigned a zero price. The logical order for the scale is not always from worst to best. For example, a small amount of sound may be preferred to absolute silence even though silence may be preferred to a lot of noise. The scales should be marked off in discrete increments whether or not the variable is continuous. For example, noise as measured in decibels is a continuous variable, but people perceive noise in discrete thresholds. Pretesting is important to set the range of the scales because at the extremes on a scale, it is impossible to tell whether people would prefer to remain at that level or consume a bundle of goods that is off the scale.

The attributes must be statistically independent; this may require combining some variables or explaining how they differ from one another. Broad attributes should be broken down so that tradeoffs can be useful in policy making; for instance, traffic has several components--noise, fumes, safety, and crowding. Tradeoffs should reflect relative differences, such as a 20 percent savings in travel time rather than a 1-hour savings because of differences in the absolute amount of commuting time. People should have to trade equivalent items to move to a different position on the scale.

Because pure public goods can be provided at only one quantity or quality level, the analyst manipulates the prices of these goods until an equilibrium is reached. This is done by estimating aggregate WTP for that level and comparing it with supply costs to fix the optimal quantity. For ordinary goods, the analyst examines the tradeoffs and the portion of the total budget spent on each attribute.

The priority evaluation approach can be improved by using either opportunity costs or values established in previous studies as first approximation values. The proportion of the budget allocated to an attribute under optimal conditions can be compared with the existing budget to determine the shadow price of the budget constraint. A display with electrical switching can be used to allow for quick, visual analysis of current positions and options. Respondents could move pegs or switches on the display board and lights would indicate their new positions.

In the example in table 4-3, respondents would pay up to 1.5 points to obtain an increase in the stocking of trout and they are willing to have fewer miles of marked trails in return for more fish. In this case, decision makers should not spend the bulk of the park's budget on traffic control or trail marking.

TABLE 4-3
Hypothetical example of tradeoff analysis

Attributes	Units	Existing Score	Optimal Choice	Percent Change	Average Points Invested Per Respondents
Trout biomass	Pounds of fish per mile of river	1.5	3.0	+100	0.5
Traffic at site	20 vehicles per hour	4.0	4.0	0	0.0
Marked	Miles	5.0	3.5	+ 30	1.5

An individual's consumption bundle is optimal when no reallocations can be made that would boost satisfaction (in other words, when the marginal utility of each good divided by its price equals the same ratio for all goods). This condition can be translated into a test that indicates the changes in prices necessary to reach equilibrium. If prices are set at willingness to pay, one would expect each feasible combination of factors to occur just as frequently. The probability of choosing bundle "x" would equal the probability of choosing bundle "y" and the events would be random variables.

At equilibrium, $\dfrac{O_x}{E_x} = 1,$

where O_x is the observed frequency of choice x and E_x is the expected frequency of choice x

If $\dfrac{O_x}{E_x} > 1,$ price underestimates willingness to pay because the quantity or quality supplied is less than the optimum.

If $\dfrac{O_x}{E_x} < 1,$ price overestimates willingness to pay because the quantity or quality supplied is less than the optimum (Pendse and Wyckoff 1974, 1976).

A chi-squared test can be used to determine whether a ratio is close enough to 1 to represent an equilibrium for that sample size, given an acceptable probability of error. However, this ratio only indicates the direction of the needed change, not the relative magnitude of the change. Thus, an iterative series of tradeoff games is necessary (Sinden and Worrell 1979). In addition, the ratio can only be used in adjusting a single price at a time.

Other techniques of tradeoff analysis have been developed. In the Cassandra method, respondents are given a short list of scenarios representing existing conditions, and regression coefficients are used to identify the most important attributes. The responses are then transformed into estimates of the marginal rates of substitution across attributes -- the coefficient of each attribute's importance is divided by the coefficient of its cost (Coughlin 1976).

The costless choice method asks respondents to rank their preferences for different bundles of goods rather than locating points of indifference in consumption (Romm 1969). As a result, it can only provide ranges of dollar values. For instance, the investigator may ask a respondent if he or she would prefer a free car or a television set to specific improvements in environmental quality. If the answers are yes and no, respectively, and the dollar equivalents for the two goods are $5,000 and $100, the respondent values the improved environmental quality somewhere between $100 and $5,000. Inclusion of a larger number of alternatives can decrease the distance between the upper and lower bounds. This method is simpler for respondents than the priority evaluation approach, but both methods share the drawback that respondents may find it meaningless to compare environmental quality to economic goods.

4.4.2   The Validity, Reliability, and Bias of Hypothetical Valuation

One way of judging the validity of hypothetical valuation in environmental assessment is to examine the experience with market research surveys for new consumer goods. In practice, the validity of surveys for new market goods is disappointing. For example, Theil and Kosobud (1968) found that only 32 to 43 percent of respondents who said they intended to purchase a good actually did so, compared with 6 to 9 percent of non-intenders. Many new products tested by market research quickly disappear from the marketplace for lack of demand. The correlation between stated intent to purchase new consumer goods and actual behavior usually is low because interviewers are told what they want to hear, and respondents often hope to receive free samples (Spindler 1975). More fundamentally, behavior of people often does not match their attitudes (Schuman and Johnson 1976).

It is even less likely that consumers can understand and explain their preferences for extramarket goods. People are not used to thinking about environmental goods and services in monetary terms and may have incentives to distort their true preferences for collective or pure public goods in a survey. Although bidding games are not supposed to reveal maximum willingness to pay, one-third of the respondents raised their top bids when told that they were not high enough to achieve their desired pollution reductions (Blank *et al.* 1977). Moreover, some responses to a change in environmental quality are reflected in behavior substitution rather than in dollar bids.

There is less consensus on monetary evaluations of an environmental amenity than on site attractiveness ratings (see section 5.4). For example, in one direct questioning of WTP for recreation and preservation, the 95 percent confidence interval stretched from $106 to $2,092 per year (Meyer 1976). Some of the variation in individual environmental preferences stems from education, cultural background, income, and other characteristics. For hypothetical valuation to be valid, a survey sample either must be representative of the population as a whole, or multiple regression analysis used to control for socioeconomic differences. Since the demand for visibility may be evenly distributed among people living near a proposed power plant and nonresidents, it is important to include nonresidents in the sample (Blank *et al.* 1977).

In bidding games involving environmental quality, most people bid about 0.5 percent of their disposable income and environmentalists bid around 1.0 percent of their income (d'Arge 1983). This high degree of consistency raises the question of whether people are uniformly responding incorrectly. For example, are people really identifying the values that they place on environmental quality or just expressing the minimum that they are willing to pay for anything? Respondents may view the amount of money that they bid as loose change that could be committed to any miscellaneous purpose, or people may have "mental accounts" for environmental improvement. One study asked a set of respondents to estimate their willingness to pay for a certain improvement in water quality. It then asked a similar question on the value of the same improvement in water quality plus an improvement in air quality to a different set of respondents. The average WTP estimates were similar in both studies (Kneese 1984). This result either implies that the perceived benefits of cleaner air were zero (which is unlikely), or that the respondents had a set amount of money that they were willing to say they would devote to environmental quality.

Tradeoff analysis might yield more valid results than bidding games because respondents are forced to give something up to get more of a good so that they are unable to express unlimited wants. Still, a tradeoff analysis does not require the people to give up something real. The validity of a tradeoff analysis depends on the consumer's

skill in making hypothetical decisions and the
investigator's skill in setting up the starting prices.

Hypothetical valuation assumes that individuals are
the best people to make the necessary value judgments,
believe they are the best persons to do so, and are willing
and able to make them (Mooney 1978). That may not be the
case, particularly for health risks. People often have
little knowledge of their present (let alone future) health
status, and consumer sovereignty is not a characteristic of
medical services. In addition, respondents generally find
it difficult to make judgments about risk possibilities. Ex
ante bids (when people are confronted with an additional
risk of dying) might be very different from ex post bids
(that they would make after having acquired the disease)
because people tend to discount their chances of dying
below the actual probability of risk (Burton, Kates, and
White 1978).

The willingness to accept risks is nonlinear; it
changes over the range of risk magnitude. It varies with
the nature of the illness, perceived benefits from the
risky activity, amount of information, certainty of risk,
and whether the risk is everyday or extraordinary and
voluntary or involuntary (Lowrance 1976). Expected values
are not a sufficient basis for decision making since
low-probability, catastrophic events might be less
acceptable than high-probability, less serious events with
the same expected value (see section 2.3.1.).

For social equity reasons, hypothetical valuation is
less relevant for health and safety risks than for
environmental amenities. Because bids are influenced by the
current distribution of income, hypothetical valuation
places a higher value on the lives of the rich. Since the
poor have little disposable income, their WTP bids would be
relatively low. Moreover, an individual's own bid might be
very different from society's valuation of the life of that
individual, and it can be difficult to identify the
affected parties in advance.

Section 2.4 defined the types of bias that may be
inherent in techniques used for environmental assessment.
Hypothetical bias is a serious problem in survey
measurement of demand because respondents are asked to
pretend that perfect markets exist for intangible
environmental goods. Respondents may find it hard to place
monetary values on environmental quality because they are
not used to thinking about these goods in economic terms.
Consequently, stated willingness to pay for existing public
amenities that historically have been supplied at zero or
nominal cost might be much lower than the real value of the
amenity to the user. Thus, a better understanding is needed
of the relationship between property rights for
environmental goods and hypothetical valuation measures.
Habituation to changes in environmental quality over time
also may distort expressed hypothetical values.

Another type of hypothetical bias occurs when the
respondents are asked to place a value on a good that they

are not consuming at present. To reduce this problem, a
survey of WTP for a recreational site could be limited to
people involved in the recreational activity (Knetsch and
Davis 1966). However, that strategy could disturb some
respondents, and it ignores the values of future users and
option values. To reduce hypothetical bias, comparisons
from different bidding games or tradeoff analyses should be
confined to respondents starting from similar initial point
levels because choices are influenced by the available
opportunities.

Because their stated preferences are not tied to
market purchases, respondents have no incentives to give
correct answers in a survey. In fact, they may have
strategic incentives to bias their responses. For example,
respondents might understate their wants if they expect
their bids will not change the supply of a collective good,
but might affect their own payment obligation (Wicksell
1896). Or, if respondents believe that their supply costs
for the good are fixed and a particular quantity and
quality of the good will be provided somewhere, then they
might overstate their preferences to increase the
probability that the goods will be provided in their area
without risking higher taxes or user fees. Respondents who
feel threatened by a possible real loss also are likely to
misrepresent their preferences.

The potential for strategic behavior may be analyzed
in terms of the expected payoffs to individuals who bias
their true preferences (Freeman 1979). Strategic bias may
be a larger problem for WTA surveys than for WTP surveys
because a few infinite or exceptionally high WTA bids will
skew the averages. Tradeoff analysis is less subject to
strategic bias than bidding games or direct questions
because respondents are not allowed to express unlimited
preferences since they must give up something to increase
their consumption. To reduce strategic behavior,
respondents could be told that their answers will not
affect the pricing or supply of the good and that the
interviewers are not associated with public officials. On
the other hand, such an admission would increase
hypothetical bias and respondents know that unofficial
surveys can influence general policy.

Bidding games also are prone to information bias
established by the level of the starting-point bid. To
elicit yes or no answers, interviewers suggest an initial
bid which is then adjusted depending on the answer to the
first question. The starting point can give respondents
some idea of the expected range of answers. Conversely, if
the starting bid is too far from the respondents'
equilibrium values, they may become bored with the lengthy
bidding process. Without a starting point, people find it
difficult to estimate the value of extramarket goods
because they do not know how much they pay for them in
taxes or what it costs to provide and maintain the goods
(Kneese 1984).

Hypothetical bias may be reduced if the respondents are told the current amount spent by the public sector on the extramarket good. The initial prices and consumption levels may also present problems in a tradeoff analysis because respondents may choose bundles of goods that do not reflect their true utilities. Some respondents might stick too closely to the status quo while others might feel that they have to make a lot of changes as part of the exercise. Information bias can be reduced by randomly assigning different starting bids or initial prices to respondents.

Instrumental bias derives from the survey or interview instrument itself. This problem may be caused by leading questions, the desire of the respondents to say what they think the interviewer wants to hear, or anger with the interviewers or formats. Instrumental bias can be associated with the financing vehicle used to collect fees or pay compensation. Possible vehicles include entry fees and user charges, property taxes, income tax charges equal to the individual's bid, share of total costs proportional to the bid, or lump-sum taxes). Arrangements that restrict consumption choices through income and substitution effects will decrease WTP and increase WTA bids.

Instrumental bias depends a great deal on the phrasing of the questions. For instance, the question "How much are you willing to pay for a clean environment?" is too vague, while "What are you willing to pay for an increase in dissolved oxygen content from 3-4 milligrams per liter in this 1-mile stretch of the Potomac River?" is too specific. It is important to make sure that respondents understand the questions. The interviewers should write down their judgments of each respondent's perceptual and cognitive ability and sincerity afterwards on the questionnaires.

People might avoid expressing zero values in a bidding game, knowing that the interviewer wants to hear some positive value expresses. In fact, small bids might not be significantly greater than zero. The aggregation of many small bids over a large population can yield a large total value, but that is not the case if the values are really zero (d'Arge 1983).

Tradeoff games are subject to a conflict between validity and instrumental bias. Validity requires a continuous range of varied options. Yet, as the number of choices to be made increases, instrumental bias might increase because the respondents may get confused or bored. With four-point scales for each of eight variables, there are 4,096 possible combinations of choices.

A few studies have tried to assess the relative magnitude of various types of bias in bidding games, but it is difficult to separate the effects of each type of bias. Blank et al. (1977) claimed a low level of strategic behavior in one bidding game, except for one respondent who was an economics professor. This conclusion was based on the hypothesis that if strategic bias had been present, a bimodal distribution would occur with high bids from environmentalists and low willingness to pay from the

development-oriented respondents. However, the absence of a
bimodal distribution also could be attributed to
hypothetical bias if the respondents believed that the
experiment's results would not affect any real situation.
Nevertheless, strategic behavior is often less important
than one might expect, and steps can be taken to minimize
its effect (McKinney and McRae 1978).

Blank *et al.* (1977) did find significant starting-
point bias and some instrumental bias. The willingness to
pay bids were higher for payroll taxes than for entrance
charges because user fees reduce opportunities for
substitution of other goods. Information bias might be more
important than strategic bias. Thayer and Schultz (1977)
noted no significant information or strategic bias in a
bidding game evaluation of geothermal development impacts.
Thayer (1981) observed no significant starting-point bias.

At this stage of their development, hypothetical
valuation techniques should be used with care in an
environmental assessment in developed countries. Although
tradeoff analysis offers some promise, it is more
appropriate in finding out general values toward
environmental quality rather than in making specific policy
choices because it requires environmental attributes to be
in simplified, discrete form. Hypothetical valuation is
especially questionable in less developed countries where
education levels and incomes are low (Hufschmidt and Hyman
1982). Other techniques that are not based on survey
measurement of demand are available and are discussed
below.

4.5 NONSURVEY TECHNIQUES FOR VALUING EXTRAMARKET GOODS AND SERVICES

4.5.1 Revealed Preference Measures

Economists generally prefer to observe people's
preferences through their behavior rather than relying on
what people say they prefer. Revealed preference studies
examine such things as replacement costs and defensive
actions against environmental damage, the alternative cost
of supplying an environmental good, actual expenditures on
related economic goods, travel behavior, property values,
or wage differentials. The conceptual validity of revealed
preference measures is relatively well established, and
they are less subject to systematic biases than
hypothetical valuation techniques. However, revealed
preference measures do not address social equity because
they give inadequate weight to the preferences of the poor
who have little disposable income, and because of the
divergence between private and public benefits and costs.
Revealed preference approaches also place little weight on
the traditional rights of a small number of users, and they
ignore option demand and the values of nonusers.

Replacement Costs and Defensive Expenditures. The
costs of replacing or cleaning up environmental damage can
be saved if pollution or resource depletion is prevented.
If society is willing to pay these costs, then it must
value environmental quality or resource availability at
least as much as the defensive expenditures (Michelson and
Tourin 1966). This method assumes that the efficient level
of cleanup has been reached through a political consensus.
Since environmental quality has aspects of a pure public
good, the chosen cleanup level represents the preferences
of the median voter (Bowen 1943).
    Individuals can alleviate risks to human health
through defensive expenditures on preventive or curative
medical care, insurance premiums, safety equipment, air
conditioners, and water filters. Indoor noise levels can be
reduced by adding double-glazed windows, although this does
nothing for noise levels outside (Starkie and Johnson
1975). Some damage to residential amenities or human
health can be avoided by moving from a polluted area. The
costs of moving include shipment of goods, higher prices
for equivalent housing, housing search costs, income losses
due to changing jobs, "psychic costs" of dislocating, and
anxiety on the part of the movers and their friends and
relatives (Walters 1975; Pearce 1978).
    Society also spends money on prevention of premature
deaths and accidents and extension of longevity through
medical care standards and subsidies, traffic speed
controls, seat belts, home smoke alarms, and occupational
health and safety regulations (Blomquist 1979; Dardis
1980). By estimating the value of time spent in buckling
seat belts, a WTP estimate of $260,000 was made of the
value of a life saved (Blomquist 1979). That study
assumed that people make rational decisions about whether
or not to buckle seat belts even though this may mostly be
a matter of habit.
    However, studies of the implicit values society places
on lives in its resource allocation decisions for curative
and preventive health care, insurance, and safety show
little consistency in implied values for human lives. For
example, relatively little is spent on highway safety
programs where many lives are at stake, but a large amount
is spent on a small number of aircraft pilots (Freeman
1979). Safety expenditures often are higher for new risks
than old risks (Cohen 1980). Furthermore, political factors
may override informed analysis.
    The replacement costs and defensive expenditures
approach can sometimes yield higher values than the travel
cost method (Bockstael and McConnell 1981). Damages are
monetary losses that are only incurred above some threshold
level of effects. In estimating defensive costs to avoid
damages, one needs to know the extra expenditures needed
for maintenance or replacement of equipment, materials, and
products as a result of pollution. Examples of replacement
costs and defensive costs include the present value of
incremental costs for health care for livestock and pets;

cleaning costs for materials, buildings, autos, clothing and people; accelerated replacement or repair of equipment and materials; replacement of damaged crops and trees; rehabilitation of the nutrients and structure of soils; cleanup of contaminated aquifers; substitution of alternative sources of water; and restoration of game habitats and restocking of fish. (Fink *et al.* 1971; Bell and Canterbury 1976; Hodge 1976; Heintz, Hershaft, and Horak 1976; Maler and Wyzga 1976; Kim and Dixon 1986). The population of some endangered species can be increased through a breeding program. The costs of a breeding program depend on the difficulty of obtaining breeding stock or eggs, the availability of suitable habitat, the frequency of breeding, and the number of offspring per cycle (Yang, Dower, and Menefee 1984).

Some expenditures may require several simultaneous adjustments by producers and consumers; for instance, in materials composition of products, replacement frequency, component redundancy, production processes, or tolerances for deterioration or soiling. The cost of the cheapest acceptable adjustment should be used. In some cases, there will be no producer response, just direct effects on household well-being such as people's dissatisfaction with the flavor or odor of drinking water. Double counting can be a problem with the related expenditures approach. For example, when a duck species is used for hunting, that may preclude bird watchers from receiving benefits at least for very long, so values should not be assigned for both purposes (Yang, Dower, and Menefee 1984).

Defensive costs often are underestimated because of measurement problems, and they also exclude consumer's surplus. Methods based on defensive expenditures and replacement costs neglect the real issue of determining the optimal level of abatement. The benefits do not necessarily equal the cost of facilities, especially when municipalities and industries can pass on external costs and waste discharges to other users. Typically, only part of the damage is alleviated or compensated so remaining damage costs should be added to defensive expenditures. Replacement costs and defensive expenditures are most useful when an impact affects private industry and there are no substitutes for the good or service. Replacement in kind is impossible for extinct species and many environmental amenities once they are destroyed.

The perspective of an economic analysis affects what is counted as a defensive expenditure or damage cost. The perspective may be the national, state, or local economy; households; individual firms, farms, or the industry as a whole; or federal, state, or local government budgets (fiscal impacts). Some costs to consumers or producers also are social costs, but certain financial costs are balanced by corresponding benefits to others within the same economy. Fiscal impacts may be important because they can cause damaging budgetary dislocations for governments, particularly when they are the result of emergencies that cannot be anticipated. However, public decisions should be based on the costs and benefits to that level of society rather than on fiscal impacts.

Two categories of costs not previously mentioned are expenses for legal and administrative expenses and compensation of damaged parties. Legal and administrative costs do consume real economic resources, but they are not necessarily proportional to the amount or type of pollution. Since compensation is a transfer payment between groups in a society, it is only a redistribution of funds and not a social cost. Nevertheless, compensation is important for equity reasons and may be counted as a cost in financial analyses from the perspective of governments, certain producers or consumers.

Table 4-4 shows how one might structure an analysis of the costs of groundwater contamination from various perspectives. It includes both the costs of remedies and damage costs. The table should be viewed as a checklist of what items might be relevant since many contingencies and complexities may be present in any particular case. For example, a firm might be able to shift its costs to consumers, depending on the market structure of the industry, the price elasticity of demand for its products, and the regulatory framework. The costs incurred by a single firm or farm might not affect the whole industrial or agricultural sector because other firms or farms may gain from the losses of their competitors. Also, costs can be shifted to governments (and thus to all other tax-paying consumers and producers) through favorable tax treatment or subsidies.

Alternative Cost. The alternative cost approach is applicable when other means of providing the same good or service are available but are more expensive. This approach does not require estimation of a demand curve for the good. Consumers will buy a good if the benefits exceed the costs. If the benefits cannot be determined directly, the costs of the good can be used as a lower bound estimate of the benefits. The alternative cost approach uses the costs of the next cheapest means of providing the good as a proxy for the benefits. For instance, if a hydroelectric plant provides 1,000 megawatts of electricity at a cost of $5 million, and the cheapest alternative means of supply is a coal plant that costs $10 million, the $10 million can be used as a proxy for the gross benefits of the hydroelectricity.

The alternative cost approach is only valid when the demand for the good is price inelastic so that the same quantity is consumed regardless of the price. In addition, all of the other characteristics of the alternatives (including environmental and social impacts) must be identical. In some cases, the benefits of public works such as reservoirs may be less than the costs of construction, operation, and maintenance because legislative decision making is often based more on political than economic grounds (Ferejohn 1974). This approach has been misused by development advocates trying to avoid a criterion more stringent than cost effectiveness.

The alternative cost approach has also been misused by environmentalists. Gosselink, Odum, and Pope (1974) attributed a very large annual value to a Georgia tidal marsh by assuming the marsh could perform the functions of tertiary treatment and hypothesizing a level of waste dumping equal to the current advantage for four northern estuaries. They counted the costs of a similar capacity of waste disposal through capital-intensvie sewage treatment plants as the benefits of the marsh. However, if the marsh is not receiving the waste load, it cannot be given a value for that function. Also, a sewage treatment plant might not be the least-cost alternative in comparison with land treatment and process or product modification. Nor does a marsh provide the same quality and quantity of service as a treatment plant.

Related Expenditures. Some inferences about the value of environmental services that are not sold in economic markets can be made from data on related expenditures on complementary or substitute goods. Complementary goods are used together with another good, for example, maple syrup and pancakes. Substitutes are goods that partially or completely take the place of another good, for example, margarine and butter. Sometimes the expenditure may be time that could otherwise be spent in productive activities. For example, the long hours spent in the collection of fuelwood by rural women in less developed countries has an opportunity cost in foregone agricultural or cottage industry production (Hyman and Dixon 1986).

Weak complementarity exists when an individual receives no marginal utility from the consumption of an extramarket good unless a certain amount of a marketed good is also consumed. With this association between the two types of goods, transactions for the marketed good can be used to estimate the demand for the extramarket good. The assumption of weak complementarity is not necessary for the property value and travel cost approaches (Smith and Krutilla 1982).

Proxy values from similar sites can be used to evaluate an environment of known characteristics if the benefits of the site to an individual are not affected by changes in environmental quality at other sites that the individual does not visit. However, an improvement in environmental quality may increase use of the site by generating new recreational demand and transferring demand from other site, in addition to increasing expenditures at previous sites. The related expenditures approach has been applied most frequently to recreational activities by estimating how much money is spent on fishing, hunting, and camping equipment and trips or on birdseed, bird feeders, wilderness gear, memberships in environmental organizations, and nature books and magazines (Crutchfield 1982; Morgan 1966; Payne and DeGraaf 1975).

TABLE 4-4
Checklist of social, financial, or fiscal costs and damages from groundwater contamination

Type of Cost/ Damages	Perspective of Analysis								
	National Economy	State Economy	Local Economy	Households (Consumers)	Firms or Farms	Industrial or Agri- cultural	Federal Govern- ment	State Govern- ment	Local Govern- ment
Determination of the extent and degree of the contamination	L	L	L	L	L	P	P	P	P
Decreased value of industrial or agricultural production	L	L	L	N	L	P	P	P	P
Avoidance of impaired uses through relocation	L	L	L	L	L	P	N	P	P
Decreased prop- erty values	N	N	L	L	L	P	N	P	P
Dissatisfaction with the taste or odor of water	N	N	P	L	P	P	N	N	N
Legal and admini- strative costs	L	L	L	L	L	P	L	L	L

Compensation payments or receipts	N	P	P	L	P	P	L	L
Confinement of the spread of contamination	L	L	L	P	P	P	P	P
Cleanup of contaminated plumes	L	L	L	N	P	P	P	P
Incremental costs for replacement of contaminated water	L	L	L	L	L	P	N	P
Reuse, recycling, or down-shifting of water	P	P	P	P	P	P	N	P
Incremental costs of pretreatment of water before use	L	L	L	L	L	P	N	P
Damage to materials	L	L	L	L	L	P	L	L
Effects on human health	L	L	L	P	P	P	L	L

Source: Hyman (1985). Reprinted by permission.

L = likely to be relevant

P = possibly relevant, depending on situational, geographic, or institutional factors

N = not likely to be relevant

The expenditures approach is of little help when it is
difficult to express the values of substitutes and
complements in dollar terms or where certain expenditures
are prohibited by law or social custom. For example, since
it is illegal to hunt endangered species, the use of
hunting expenditures data would imply a zero value for
these species. Also, data on expenditures may be
unavailable because people often underestimate their total
costs, and companies are unwilling to release proprietary
data on sales (Pearse and Bowden 1966). Expenditures
generally underestimate benefits because they measure what
is paid for environmental amenities rather than the
consumer's surplus. In fact, two amenities may provide
very different amounts of utility even though it costs the
same to take advantage of them (Sinden and Worrell 1979).
This method also is difficult to apply when expenditures
for a good support several different activities or purchase
durable goods that can be used for many years.

Travel Cost. The travel cost approach is a commonly
used method for evaluating the benefits of an unpriced
recreational site. It was suggested by Hotelling, who
proposed estimating how much money a price-discriminating
monopolist could extract from travelers originating from
concentric zones around the site (Prewitt 1949). The
travel cost from each zone is used as a surrogate for
price. The quantity consumed at that price is determined
by counting the number of visitors from each zone. A
demand curve for the site can be derived accounting for
differences in populations across zones and variations in
length of stays. The rate of visitor-days per 1,000
population is used as the quantity measure (Clawson 1959).
This method has been applied to the valuation of sport
fisheries (Brown, Singh, and Castle 1965; Shucksmith 1979);
wildlife areas (Everett 1978); water-based recreation
(Tussey 1967); and damages from an oil spill (National
Oceanic and Atmospheric Administration 1983).

Even where use of the site is free, the travel cost
method derives a relationship between the total number of
visitor-days and a hypothetical set of entry fees equal to
the difference in transportation costs between each pair of
zones. It is assumed that after imposition of the fee,
residents of the closer zone would reduce their visit rates
to that of people from a more distant zone who spend the
same total amount of money for transportation and entry.

A simple example shows how this method works for an
existing site. First, the park ranger tabulates
information on the number of visitors from each zone, how
long they stay at the park, and how far they traveled to
get there (table 4-5). Table 4-6 shows the expected change
in visit rates at various hypothetical admission fees as
calculated from travel behavior in different zones. Next,
the visit rates per 1,000 population are multiplied by the
population in each zone and this product is summed

TABLE 4-5
Sample data for the travel cost method

Zone	Average Distance Traveled (km)	Estimated Average Transportation Cost ($)[a]	Visitor-Days Originating in the in the Zone per 1000 Population
A	20	1	80
B	40	2	60
C	60	3	40
D	80	4	20
E	100	5	0

[a] Assuming $0.05 per kilometer

TABLE 4-6
Expected declines in visit rates when admission fees are charged

	Visitor-Days Per 1000 Population				
Zone	Fee=$0	Fee=$1	Fee=$2	Fee=$3	Fee=$4
A	80	60	40	20	0
B	60	40	20	0	0
C	40	20	0	0	0
D	20	0	0	0	0
E	0	0	0	0	0

separately over the zones at each admission fee (table 4-7). In this example, the population of each zone is 10,000, but it is not necessary for each zone to have the same population. Then, a demand curve is derived from this information (figure 4-4). Finally, the consumer's surplus associated with use of the site for free can be calculated. Since the area of a triangle is (0.5)(base)(height), the net consumer's surplus is $4,000 in this example.

Only the variable costs of round-trip travel should be counted since the fixed costs of auto ownership do not affect decisions to drive further. A travel cost demand curve is very sensitive to estimates of the operating costs of automobiles. If a trip has multiple destinations or purposes, the cost must be prorated. The related expenditures approach can be combined with the travel cost method by including the money spent in travel plus the costs per visit of recreation supplies, fees for camp or trailer rental, boat launchings, fish bait, and the costs of food beyond those that would be incurred at home. However, the U.S. Water Resources Council (1979) recommended against including equipment costs or lodging since these costs are not tied specifically to the site.

Park user surveys often are available for an existing site. The surveys usually cover the trip origin, average visit length,and activities chosen. Survey data should be adjusted for seasonal variations in use. For sites that have not been developed yet, there are two approaches. The first relies on a regression model to relate visit rates to distance, site characteristics, and socioeconomic characteristics of the zone. The second approach uses data from existing similar sites. The second approach is less costly, but might not be valid when the proposed site is not exactly the same as the similar site. The potential for substituting other recreational facilities in the vicinity of the proposed site must also be considered (Burt and Brewer 1971; Krutilla and Fisher 1975).

The travel cost approach assumes that recreational preferences are constant across regions. Alternatively, the analysis could be based on samples of individuals rather than zones, but this requires more data on each individual's income, recreation budget, age, education, and outdoor activities. The sampling of individuals has the advantage of decreasing the statistical problem of multicollinearity from the simultaneous inclusion of travel cost and travel time by increasing the sample size.

It is more likely that visitors from a given income class share common preferences than travelers originating from a zone based on distance. If the socioeconomic characteristics in the zone are not homogeneous, a travel cost demand curve will not be valid unless some adjustments are made (Pearse 1968; Reilling, Gibbs, and Stoevener 1973). For example, one could define the marginal visitor as the person with the highest travel cost within an income class. After assuming that this marginal visitor receives no consumer's surplus, one can calculate the maximum

TABLE 4-7
Total number of visits expected

Zone	Fee=$0	Visitor-Days Fee=$1	Fee=$2	Fee=$3	Fee=$4
A	800	600	400	200	0
B	600	400	200	0	0
C	400	200	0	0	0
D	200	0	0	0	0
E	0	0	0	0	0
Total	2000	1200	600	200	0

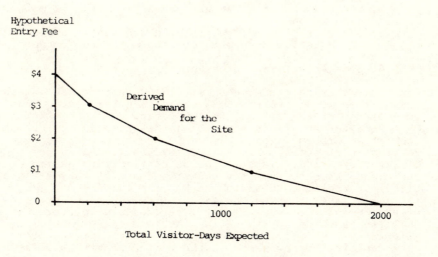

Figure 4-4 Demand curve for a recreational site
imputed by the travel cost method

entrance fee that could be charged other visitors within that income class so that the total travel cost and entry fee from each visitor matches that of the marginal visitor (Pearse 1968). To avoid statistical outliers, the marginal visitor can be defined as the person whose travel costs are two standard deviations above the mean (Chowdhary 1977).

The travel cost method has been refined to include costs of travel time, which may be more important than the transport costs (Knetsch and Davis 1966). The value of time varies depending on whether it is used for work, leisure, or travel. Economists usually value travel time in terms of the money that people would have earned during that period of time. This approach is most valid for sales representatives or casual workers with flexible hours and less valid for workers who have little or no opportunity for paid overtime. If overtime is not available, the appropriate wage would be the rate paid for part-time moonlighting, which may be lower than the wage for a worker's main job. Since people enjoy leisure travel, one component of travel time is a cost and the rest is a benefit (Wilman 1980).

Most applications of the travel cost method have valued time at the minimum wage or the mean wage, but the median may be a better measure if incomes are distributed unequally. Cesario (1976) suggested using one-fourth to one-half the mean wage as the value of time because

1. Some willingness-to-pay studies indicate that the value people place on their time falls within that range,
2. Second jobs often do not pay as well as the main occupation,
3. Some travelers are unemployed spouses or children who have lower opportunity costs for their time, and
4. Some travel is a pleasant use of time.

The U.S. Water Resources Council (1979) recommended valuing travel time at one-third the average wage for adults and one-quarter of that amount for children.

An alternative way of valuing this time is to look at the actual tradeoffs people make between time and money. For instance, people often spend more to ride a faster mode of transportation. Yet, it can be difficult to estimate the tradeoffs between money and time costs if they are too closely correlated (Cesario and Knetsch 1976).

The travel cost method can provide separate estimates of the demand for recreational experiences of different qualities such as sport angling for warm water game fish, cold water game fish, and rough fish. One estimate of water quality improvements in the United States associated with "best practical control technology" is an increase of 100,000 acres in the 30 million acres suitable for sport fishing, and a more significant increase in the gamefish share of the sport fishing catch from 89% to 96%. By incorporating information on the number of people fishing for sport, the average number of days per year that they spend fishing, and a travel cost per day of fishing at different quality sites, the benefits of improving water quality for recreational purposes in the United States were estimated at $307 million from expenditures on fuel, restaurants, and lodging. When travel time was valued at the average wage rate, it increased the benefits by $376 million (Vaughan and Russell 1982).

The travel cost method has some drawbacks. It may underestimate benefits when a dense population of users live close to a site (Meyer 1975). Many residents choose to locate near a scenic area because of the environmental amenities. As a result, their recreational travel costs are low, but they pay higher commuting costs to work. Also, if most users live within a short radius of the site, travel costs are roughly uniform and one cannot generate enough data points for a demand curve. In addition, there are many environmental amenities that people enjoy spending their time on whether or not they have to travel far. Expenditures of time could be used as a proxy for the price of these amenities. On the other hand, that may overstate benefits when a trip has multiple purposes or destinations (Haspel and Johnson 1982).

The travel cost method assumes that people treat travel costs and site fees identically, which might not be so (Gibbs 1974). People frequently underestimate the costs of private automobile travel (Common 1973). In addition, the current pattern of population dispersion, the distribution of income and leisure, location of transport facilities, and preferences for recreation area use are taken as fixed in this method. Other assumptions behind the method are that (1) the sole purpose of the trip is for recreation, (2) the amount of time spent at the site does not vary with the distance traveled, and (3) the same mode of transportation is used for all trips. To make it more likely that these assumptions are realistic, a cut-off should be set for the distance of the farthest zone (Smith and Kopp 1980).

Nor does the travel cost approach reflect the quality of the recreational experience. The approach is less applicable in evaluating wild rivers because it does not reflect enjoyment of the site, and wilderness is preserved best when few travelers visit a site (Sonnen and Davis 1979). Since the perceived recreational benefits of wilderness are strongly affected by congestion, the travel cost method must be modified to account for the reduction in recreational quality associated with crowding. Otherwise, the highest values will be placed on the most crowded sites. One possibility would be to exclude the travel costs of additional users beyond the number compatible with the carrying capacity of the site, but that still does not reflect the decrease in benefits caused by additions to congestion below the limit.

A travel cost analysis could be combined with willingness-to-pay surveys for crowded and uncongested sites to establish the connection between the site quality and the benefits (Cicchetti and Smith 1976). The travel cost method probably underestimates actual benefits since it does not capture maximum willingness to pay. In theory, the travel cost approach should produce lower values than hypothetical valuation because the former assigns a zero value to the preferences of individuals whose willingness to pay is positive, but less than their travel cost. This theoretical difference may be partly offset by the income effects associated with cash bids. Despite these problems, the travel cost method is well accepted, and its validity is relatively high because it is site specific.

Knetsch and Davis (1966) noted approximate agreement between a bidding game and a travel cost application. Bishop and Heberlein (1979) cross-tested results from bidding games with a simulated market for goose hunting permits by sending checks ranging from $1 to $200 to a group of goose hunters. The hunters were instructed to either return the check or send the hunting permit in exchange. The average size of the accepted check was $63. Of course, this average depends on the range of sizes of the checks that were sent out. In contrast, a WTP bidding game produced an average value estimate of $21 and a WTA bidding game indicated that owners would only sell their permits for an average of $101. The travel cost method with time valued at one-fourth the average wage produced a value of $28. The travel cost value increased to $43 when travel time was charged at one-half the average wage. A combination of strategic, informational, and hypothetical biases may explain these differences.

Another study compared five methods of estimating the willingness to pay for avoiding the total loss of a recreational area or obtaining an improvement in water quality from a boatable level to the fishable level or the swimmable level. The WTP values for avoiding the loss of an area varied greatly across the methods: $20 from a direct questioning or payment card, $7 from a bidding game with a $25 starting point, $36 from a bidding game with a $125 starting point, and $83 from a generalized travel cost model that included the opportunity cost of travel time at the wage rate (Desvousges, Smith, and McGivney 1983). That study concluded that hypothetical valuation is sensitive to the starting-point bid and the format of bidding versus direct questions. It also concluded that hypothetical valuation is not directly comparable to the travel cost method because the methods are based on different assumptions, and the true value of the environmental amenity is not known.

Unit-Day Value. The unit-day value method relies on experts to estimate the values of various categories of recreational sites to the average user. It does not consider the benefits of a specific site to particular users. However, these values may be classified into general and specialized recreation. General recreation

attracts the majority of users and has convenient access
and adequate facilities. Specialized recreation is more
inaccessible or appeals to a more limited segment of the
population often because it requires special skills (e.g.,
rock climbing in the wilderness). The U.S. Water Resources
Council (1979) proposed a schedule of unit-day values for
general and specialized recreation on several categories of
site quality although it is now dated. This schedule rated
site quality numerically according to five criteria:

1. Types of activities
2. Availability of recreational alternatives
3. Carrying capacity
4. Accessibility
5. Environmental quality

The change in unit-day value is calculated by multiplying
the number of points corresponding to the type and quality
category of the recreation by the change in the number of
visitor-days resulting from a proposed environmental
change. The gains and losses in visitor-days should be
listed separately to facilitate sensitivity analysis.
    The unit-day value method has serious limitations
compared to the travel cost method. Since it does not
focus on site-specific demand, it may assign a high dollar
value to a site that has little actual value, or vice-
versa. Nor does it account for seasonal use patterns
affected by climate and culture, the opportunity cost of
time, or risk and uncertainty. The U.S. Water Resources
Council (9180) recommended using the unit-day value method
only for federal water resource projects with relatively
low recreational benefits and costs.

    Property value. In theory, the value of a parcel of
land equals the present value of the future net benefit
stream associated with that site. When the future net
benefit stream deteriorates, the sale price of the land
decreases. To the extent that prospective buyers agree
that environmental damages reduce the desirability of the
land, these costs will be reflected in property values.
Technically, changes in economic rents would be the proper
measure, but property values are easier to observe,
especially for owner-occupied property.
    Many studies have found a relationship between
property values and environmental quality. For example,
Lind (1973) noted that after cleanup of a polluted lake,
aggregate residential land rent increased relative to a
similar area with a polluted lake. Freeman (1979) examined
eighteen studies relating air pollution and property
values; only three of these did not show a significant
correlation between these two variables. Other
applications have focused on pollution of residential lakes
(Lind 1973); noise pollution (Pearce and Edwards 1979);

damages to neighborhood parks, farmland, and licensed commercial fisheries (Armstrong 1974; Polinsky and Shavell 1976; Abelson 1979); and health effects of pollution (Portney 1981). Conversely, there can be benefits in property values resulting from pollution abatement (Freeman 1980). However, there may be a weak relationship between property values and experts' evaluations of water quality (Dornbusch 1975). In the aggregate, property values in the Los Angeles region would increase by $1.5-3.0 billion if ambient air quality standards were achieved and this could be accomplished at a cost of $0.6-1.32 billion (Brookshire *et al.* 1979).

The use of changes in property values in environmental assessment is only valid if there are competitive market conditions, perfect information, and all economic surpluses and losses accrue to the landowner in control when the net benefit stream changes. Land markets in the United States are reasonably competitive, but that is not the case in developing countries that are still influenced by colonial land distribution policies. In both developed and developing countries, some of the surplus or loss accrues to the public in the form of changes in property tax payments. If the reduction in taxes associated with the decline in property values is ignored, the method underestimates the costs of pollution (Niskanen and Hanke 1977). The opposite is true when property values increase. Renters under long-term contracts may also absorb some of the loss or gain (Yang, Dower, and Menefee 1984).

Averting behavior unrelated to site characteristics also presents a problem. For example, if local residents substitute other recreational opportunities for swimming, property values might not capture the full willingness to pay for water quality. Similarly, some of the consumer's surplus that would result from cleaner air might have gone into the purchase of air conditioners. If people expect that there is a possible risk of damage from a disamenity such as a nearby nuclear waste facility, the perceived probability of the risk will be incorporated in property values before an accident occurs.

If land is used as an input in a production process, some of the economic surplus from environmental quality changes may be passed along to consumers of the products, depending on the amount of competition in the industry and the price elasticity of demand for the produced good. For example, if photochemical smog is reduced in California, the yield of fruits and vegetables will increase, and a smaller fraction of the crop will be damaged. Some of this benefit will go to the farmer as higher profits, but food processors and consumers may capture some of it through lower prices. If the property value approach is used, care must be taken to avoid double counting caused by including the improvements in productivity, reduced damage, or stated willingness to pay for environmental quality along with the corresponding increase in property values.

A property value analysis should include only the rent of the land and not the housing on it because environmental quality is a characteristic of the site rather than the structure. Also, the analysis must control for all other factors affecting land values, some of which may be correlated with the amount of pollution in an area. These factors include transportation facilities, accessibility to employment, noise, quality of schools, and cultural amenities. For example, some coastal areas in the Los Angeles region have relatively low air pollution levels due to sea breezes and the same beach properties are also desirable for their scenic and recreational advantages (Brookshire *et al.* 1979). However, this is not the case in the San Francisco Bay area, where the beachfront offers fewer amenities and is less accessible to the main centers of employment (Loehman, Boldt, and Chaikin 1980).

Segmentation of residential property markets by income, social class, or ethnic group also distorts property values because it restricts intraurban mobility (Freeman 1979). If income or social class segmentation corresponds to areas of high air quality, high-income households might be unwilling to pay more for reducing air pollution because they already enjoy high air quality. Multiple regression analysis can be used to control for various socioeconomic factors (Ridker and Henning 1976).

Since owner-occupied housing is sold relatively infrequently, it may be hard to obtain the data needed for the property value analysis. Tax appraisals should be used with caution as a substitute for actual prices because these appraisals are often obsolete or are kept below market values for political reasons. Owner estimates of property values tend to be exaggerated in comparison with professional appraisals. The method also requires that all other prices and levels of other economic activities remain constant, but corrections can be made for general inflation.

Maler (1977) criticized seven assumptions embedded in the property value approach:

1. Relative land rents reflect the marginal valuation of environmental quality.
2. The method uses historical data for environmental quality to determine current and future land prices.
3. People can perceive differences in environmental quality.
4. People are only willing to pay for environmental quality improvements in the communities where they are now living.
5. Perfect information exists on real estate prices.
6. Households continuously reevaluate their locational decisions.
7. People cluster in a location for no social or geographic reasons other than environmental quality.

Nevertheless, because the property value approach is based on actual market data, it is less prone to systematic biases than hypothetical valuation measures. However, there are questions regarding its validity. It is doubtful that all households have identical utility functions or that they equate the marginal costs and benefits of every housing attribute, including environmental quality. In general, people have imperfect information and inaccurate perceptions of pollution. Also, there might not be a sufficient range of sites and structures in many geographic areas to suit preferences. If the marginal willingness to pay for improved environmental quality is declining, the method may overstate actual benefits. Yet, it is more likely that the method underestimates benefits because property values only reflect the benefits to landowners near the amenity, while there are also benefits to other users. Nor can the method capture externalities, the option demand of nonusers, or the preferences of future generations.

In theory, a property value estimate of the costs of air pollution would be larger than a WTP estimate from a bidding game because property values reflect the preferences of the most sensitive individuals while the bids reflect the average preferences. This hypothesis was confirmed in a study of the Los Angeles region. The average WTP bid was $29 per household, and the difference in property values amounted to $42 per household per month on area with poor or fair air quality. The authors of that study concluded that bidding games can produce reasonable estimates at a relatively low cost, although they did note that residents of the study area have a relatively high awareness of air pollution problems (Brookshire *et al.* 1979). Another study confirmed these findings (Loehman, Boldt, and Chaikin 1980).

Wage Differential. The wage differential approach is based on the premise that extra earnings are required to induce people to work in risky occupations or locate in polluted areas, all other things being the same. Consequently, wage differentials can be used as a willingness-to-accept compensation (WTA) measure of the value of occupational health risks (Meyer and Leone 1977; Thaler and Rosen 1976; Dillingham 1979; Viscusi 1979; Portney 1981; Sharefkin, Schechter, and Kneese 1983). One study used this approach to estimate a WTA value of $340,000 per life saved (Thaler and Rosen 1975). This approach should be extrapolated with caution because workers in risky occupations may be more willing to accept risks than the rest of the population.

This approach assumes that people make free choices under perfect information in the absence of barriers to mobility, discrimination, monopsony, union market power, involuntary unemployment, or other labor market imperfections. The wage differential approach has many of the same drawbacks as the property value approach, but the labor market is more imperfect than the real estate market. Since the poor are more likely to reside or work under more hazardous conditions with fewer environmental amenities, the wage differential approach fails to address social equity because of the divergence between willingness to pay and ability to pay. The attitudes of the poor toward environmental amenities and health risks might not be representative of other social and economic groups. The wage differential approach applies to only marginal changes, and the results cannot be extrapolated beyond the range of money and longevity tradeoffs in the data. Nor does the approach discriminate between risks of death and risks of nonfatal accidents or chronic illnesses.

The evidence is less clear on the relationship between wage differentials and residential location than for occupational hazards, although some studies have estimated large costs in this way (Ben-David et al.,n.d.; Brookshire et al., n.d.). Concentrations of air pollutants at the relatively small number of monitoring stations may be very different from those at homes and workplaces. When aggregate data are used, it is difficult to correct for differences in the types of employment and employers across areas. Moreover, many people commute long distances to their place of work to avoid living in polluted areas, and polluted areas often have inferior social services.

4.5.2 Human Capital Approach for Valuing Human Lives

In order to quantify the costs of environmental hazards, values must be placed on human deaths and illnesses. Many people oppose this quantification on the grounds that it dehumanizes life, which they argue has an infinite value. In practice, however, individuals place values on lives through everyday decisions on preventive and curative health care, safety, and the purchase of insurance. Society also implicitly places a finite value on human lives in budgetary, regulatory, and judicial decisions. Most people agree that society places a higher economic value on the remaining life of an average 30-year old father of three than on a centenarian.

The human capital approach can be used to estimate some of the welfare lost to society as a result of premature illness or death (Schelling 1968; Zeckhauser 1976). This approach focuses on the foregone future earnings of an affected individual. Society loses the individual's economic output, which is worth the discounted expected value of these future wages.

$$V = \sum_{t=a} \frac{(L_t)\ (W_t)\ (E_t)\ (Y_t)}{(1+r)^{t-a}}$$

where   V   is the economic value which society places on a human life;

L_t is the probability that an individual of age a will live to age t;

W_t is the probability that an individual of age a will be in the workforce at age t;

E_t is the probability that an individual of age a and in the workforce at age t will be employed at age t;

Y_t is the annual pretax income in year t of this individual, and

r   is the discount rate (Ridker 1967).

    The human capital approach places a low value on the lives of the elderly, the poor, the unemployed, and people such as housewives who are not paid cash wages for their work. Nevertheless, it is possible to estimate a shadow wage that reflects the value of the productive activities of these people. For example, the value of housework must be at least as much as a housewife could earn in the labor market if family decisions are rational. The average wage can be used as an estimate of a child's unknown future earning capacity. The present value of people's consumption should not be subtracted from the value of their production because social welfare is the sum of the well-being of each person. The discounted value of early burial costs or hospitalization costs can be added to production losses.

    The human capital approach makes no attempt to deal with lost personal happiness, the costs of pain and suffering, or the noneconomic values of people to their families and friends. Nor does the approach discriminate between risks of death and permanent disability. Obtaining the data necessary for the economic valuation is complex because of the scientific uncertainty in estimating the magnitudes and probabilities of environmental hazards. The main sources of this uncertainty are in measurement of the actual exposure of individuals to the hazards, the relationship between human behavior and health, interaction effects with other pollutants, time lags, and random factors or statistical problems.

    Estimating the causal relationships between environmental hazards and lost work-days from illnesses is difficult because effects may be multiple or subtle. Various definitions of morbidity, such as "restricted activity-days," "bed disability-days," and "work-days lost," confuse the health condition with people's varying responses to ill health (Freeman 1982).

An aggregate epidemiology approach based on city-level statistics has been used to estimate the effects of air pollution on human health (Crocker *et al.* 1979). Crude estimates of differences in diet, smoking habits, and access to medical care across cities can be incorporated in a regression analysis. A better way to handle differences in health risks is to use a disaggregate epidemiology approach, which is based on survey data or health records for particular individuals (Portney and Mullahy 1983).

One problem with many epidemiology studies of air pollution effects is that they rely on pollution data from dispersed monitoring stations rather than the actual exposures of people to pollutants. Ambient air pollution concentrations may vary a great deal within the locale of monitoring stations, and indoor pollution concentrations differ from outdoor levels. In recent years, portable, personal air pollution monitors have been developed to measure actual exposures.

Although important noneconomic factors are ignored in the human capital approach, sometimes economic information alone is sufficient for decision making. Consider the case where cleanup of a toxic chemical spill will cost $5 million, and the human capital benefits of saving an estimated ten lives amount to $10 million. Obviously, the more difficult cases are those where economic costs exceed the benefits. In those instances, economic information is still useful, but it is only one consideration.

Court awards in accident causes could be used as estimates of the societal value of a reduction in quality-adjusted life-years. However, since court awards only represent a judge's guess of the economic worth of a life, they vary a great deal across judges. Approaches that rely on the implicit value of societal decisions affecting mortality have produced estimates ranging from $9,000 to $9,000,000, while the human capital approach has yielded estimates between $100,000 and $400,000 (Foster 1982).

All methods for valuing human lives involve ethical judgments. Although it is less difficult to quantify the social value of lives in general than the value of a particular life, neither can be accomplished objectively or scientifically. The ethical issues in valuing lives must be settled by some social consensus. Neither the market system nor the political system provides a perfect mechanism for making these decisions. Thus, agreement on the legitimacy of the process for reaching decisions is important.

4.5.3 Threshold Analysis

Krutilla and Fisher (1975) turned the valuation problem around. Instead of trying to infer values and derive a demand curve for environmental amenities, they employed a threshold analysis. A threshold analysis begins with the calculation of the net present value of development benefits, B(d). A development decision would only be rational if the development benefits exceed the environmental amenity losses, B(p). Thus, the question for the decision makers is: "If the preservation benefits are unknown, how large would they have to be to leave you indifferent between development and preservation?" In other words, what value of B(p)* sets (B(d)-B(p)) equal to zero? After answering this question, the decision makers are asked whether they think the actual amenity benefits are likely to be more or less than B(p)*. Often, it is easier for decision makers to place some monetary value on the amenity directly.

Krutilla and Fisher applied threshold analysis to a proposed hydroelectric power project at Hell's Canyon in Idaho. They found that the benefits of preserving Hell's Canyon would have to be worth between $40,000 and $150,000 in the initial year for the difference between development and preservation benefits to be zero. In that case, the decision makers agreed that the canyon benefits were worth at least that amount and decided against the hydroelectric development. The Hell's Canyon analysis also recognized that the relative value of environmental goods may increase over time due to greater security. Threshold analysis is a good technique for accounting for extramarket effects when there is a clearly defined development alternative to preserving a specific amenity.

4.6   THE USEFULNESS OF EXTRAMARKET VALUATION TECHNIQUES

Table 4-8 compares each of the main techniques for evaluating extramarket effects. Since environmental assessments are often done under tight time and resource constraints, ease of data collection is a particularly important criteria in choosing among these techniques.

Some people argue that it is morally undesirable to put monetary values on natural environmental amenities. In the past, many environmental professionals were unwilling to think of amenities and natural resources as anything other than intangibles rooted in personal values, which could not be measured on a monetary scale. As a result, environmental quality variables generally were either ignored or discussed in emotional arguments about their infinite value. Consequently, decisions often were made in an unsystematic, judgmental way that contained implicit tradeoffs between dollars and environmental goods. Decision makers tend to give more credence to quantitative analysis and monetary values than to checklists of physical, chemical, or biological impacts.

Most techniques for simulating market values underestimate actual values and some groups oppose quantification for this reason. Fortunately, in many instances, lower bound values are all that is needed to prove that a resource is more valuable preserved than developed. However, in cases where the benefits and costs are nearly equal, lower bound values are not sufficient. One of the major problems with using economic techniques to estimate environmental values is that people might not be able to think in terms of complex economic tradeoffs and contingencies. Critics of the economic approach complain that:

> Human beings have a variety of diverse motivations which do not lend themselves to maximization of utility -- at least so long as utility is defined in terms of the satisfactions resulting from marketplace phenomena. . .[Consider] the enormous influence of social institutions, habit, and tradition on the choices and decisions made by individuals (Millar and Starr 1967).

Neoclassical economic presumes a high level of rationality, knowledge, and ability to make evaluations under uncertainty. Since these conditions are not likely to hold, there are difficulties in imputing values to environmental goods and services by either revealed preference or hypothetical valuation methods. In particular, people are not used to making tradeoff comparisons among market goods, environmental quality, and other pure public goods. Although people can give valid reasons for environmental protection, they may be unable to quantify these values in terms of dollars or other cardinal units. When applied to aesthetics, economic valuation approaches force people's thinking into a narrow model. The use of these approaches raises serious moral questions when applied to health and safety. Also, since it is impossible to create new natural wonders to replace developed ares, environmental assessments should pay special attention to possible irreversible damage to environmental quality because preservation decisions can be reversed.

Revealed preference and expressed willingness-to-pay bids are molded by the current distribution of wealth because behavior and perceived opportunities depend on ability to pay. Thus, these methods have a status quo bias and do not allocate resources in an equitable manner. Environmental amenities can be considered equity goods which all people have an inherent right to enjoy, or merit goods which individuals would not buy in large enough quantities to suit society's values. Measures based on willingness to accept compensation can be just as valid as those based on willingness to pay and can produce very different results in evaluating environmental impacts. More work needs to be done in comparing the validity, reliability, and biases of techniques for extramarket valuation. For example, multiple questions can be used to check responses for internal consistency, and values can be correlated with income and education (Sinden and Worrell 1979).

TABLE 4-8
Summary of methods for the valuation of extramarket benefits and costs

Approaches	Hypothetical Valuation	Revealed Preference	Related to Willingness to Pay	Related to Willingness to Accept Compensation	Inclusion of Option Values	Theoretical Validity in Measuring Use Value	Freedom from Problems of Reliability and Bias	Ease of Data Collection	Overall Applicability and Usefulness of EIA
Bidding games	C	N	C	C	P	H	L	M	2
Use estimation games	C	N	N	N	P	M	L	M	2
Tradeoff analysis	C	N	C	N	P	H	M	L	2
Replacement costs and defensive expenditures	N	C	N	C	N	H	H	H	1
Alternative cost	N	C	C	N	N	L	H	H	2

Related expenditures	N	C	C	N	N	L	H	L	3
Travel cost	N	C	C	N	N	H	H	H	1
Unit-day value	N	N	P	P	N	L	L	H	3
Property value	N	C	C	C	C	M	H	M	1
Wage differential	N	C	N	C	P	L	H	H	2
Human capital approach to valuing lives	N	N	P	N	N	M	M	H	2
Threshold analysis	N	C	C	N	P	M	H	H	1

Source: Adapted from Hyman 1981, pp. 250–251. Reprinted by permission.

Key: C – characteristic of the approach
P – possible characteristic of the approach
N – not a characteristic of the approach

H – high
M – medium
L – low

1 – very useful
2 – useful
3 – possible useful

Some externalities are so broad in scope or diffused in the natural setting that they are difficult to quantify in physical terms, and economic characterization of these is nearly impossible. There usually will be a substantial residual of these effects that must be brought into an analysis as constraints (e.g., standards for ecosystem tolerance or health-related pollutant concentrations). Nevertheless, the economic opportunity cost of the constraints should be determined.

Techniques for valuing extramarket effects are most relevant in formulating projects or resource management plans and identifying specific impacts of large projects. These techniques work best for short-term effects that can be perceived directly. They can be useful for environmental impacts that affect production or when consumption values for amenities are reflected in markets, as in real estate and recreation. The techniques are less suited to generalized natural system values and long-term, extensive, or global effects.

4.7 CONCLUSIONS

The purpose of welfare economics is to determine the most economically efficient allocation of market and extramarket goods and services for society. The concepts of utility and consumer's surplus form the basis for benefit-cost analysis, which can be an important tool in impact assessment.

Environmental economics offers insight into the causes of environmental degradation and also possible solutions. Market-oriented techniques can suggest efficient means for governments to attain environmental quality goals where the market has failed to do so. Still, the following limitations of these techniques must be recognized:

1. Imperfections that distort prices observed in real markets
2. Omission of equity considerations
3. Problems with the validity of measures of benefits and costs
4. Insufficient availability of empirical information
5. Failure to account for risk and uncertainty

The first of these limitations is well recognized in economic models based on perfect competition. Market prices might not reflect changes in the scarcity of natural resources over time in a smooth transition (Hyman 1984). Some opponents of economic analysis are unwilling to accept market information when it implies outcomes that differ from their political preferences. Still, market prices do provide a relatively objective way of estimating social

values and shadow prices can be used where market prices
are clearly inadequate.

Second, economic evaluation often fails to account for
equity and social justice. The initial distribution of
income affects market prices and estimates of willingness
to pay. Because the rich have greater influence on
preferences revealed in the market, they also have greater
weight in market-based indicators of social values.
Nevertheless, before one can reject such measures, it is
necessary to determine the effect that changes in the
distribution of income have on the indicators. More
fundamentally, social welfare might be more than just the
summation of the utility of individuals.

Conventional benefit-cost analysis is indifferent to
the incidence of benefits and costs across different
groups. As a practical matter, the environmental impacts
of many actions might not have important distributional
implications, but when they do, techniques are available to
weight the marginal social utility of income across
socioeconomic groups. Intergenerational equity is another
consideration omitted in most economic models. The
discounting of benefits and costs that occur at different
times might discriminate against the economic well-being of
future generations relative to present generations.
Discounting reduces the consumption of nonrenewable
resources in public investments, but it also results in
insufficient attention to long-term conservation measures.
Because intergenerational equity is an ethical issue and
the future is uncertain, there are no value-free ways to
make this concept operational.

The third problem is the most difficult to resolve.
Many environmental use values cannot be expressed in
unarguable economic equivalents. Currently, the ability of
existing valuation techniques to fully reflect
environmental values is limited, but growing. Still,
empirical studies using accepted techniques are limited in
number and geographic specificity. In particular, there
are no suitable techniques for measuring the value of
irreversible changes in the ecosystems or gene pools,
unique aesthetic landscapes, and effects on human health.
Human values might not be a sufficient yardstick for making
decisions that affect the long-term operation of
ecosystems. The concept of option demand may encompass a
portion of these values, but it is usually ignored, and
methods for quantifying option values remain undeveloped
even though they may exceed use values.

Fourth, inadequate treatment of risk and uncertainty
is a serious limitation. Despite significant advances in
handling risk and uncertainty in systems analysis and
decision theory (see section 2.5), there have been only
limited advances in applying these concepts in
environmental impact assessment.

More research is needed to refine techniques for
valuing extramarket effects. In particular, research is
needed on the effect of the order of the questions, the

payment vehicle, and the information contained in the
questionnaire (Desvousges, Smith, and McGivney 1983).
Meanwhile, several alternative techniques can be used in an
environmental assessment as cross-checks, and a sensitivity
analysis could be performed using the different estimates.
Since serious and persistent impacts may be occurring,
decisions may have to be made immediately even without
perfect information on economic costs and benefits. Since
many techniques for estimating the benefits of remedies for
environmental pollution are likely to underestimate actual
damage costs, a sound case can be made for undertaking the
remedy if these lower bound estimates of the benefits
exceed the costs. Furthermore, it may be obvious from even
a crude economic analysis that prevention of pollution is
often cheaper for society than after-the-fact remedies. In
any case, the assumptions behind the use of the techniques
should be well documented so decision makers can assess
their validity and separate facts from value judgments.

Although economic considerations are important, they
are not the only consideration. Public decisions are also
based on social acceptability, political processes, and
legal principles. Since society has other objectives
beside economic efficiency (e.g., the distribution of
income and political feasibility), some method is needed
for summing up the accounts within each of the objectives.
Then, a scaling and weighting procedure can be used to
compute a multiple-objective score to rank alternatives.
The SAGE method described in chapter 8 is one way of
determining the scaling and weighting factors implicitly
applied by diverse, representative groups of individuals.

5
Perception and Evaluation
of Scenic Environments

5.1 INTRODUCTION

Chapter 3 states the case for a participatory approach to environmental assessment that incorporates information on the values and preferences of various publics. The economic model, discussed in chapter 4, provides some information about societal values, but is not completely satisfactory because it takes a narrow view of the components of welfare, overlooks the sources of values, and fails to address social equity.

Psychology yields some insight into how people experience and understand scenic environments and how they form and express their values. Human behavior is not solely concerned with the maximization of material well-being. Other needs such as love, friendship, knowledge, status, justice, freedom, responsibility, security, and beauty also motivate people (Foa 1971; Ward 1976). Generally, it is impossible to substitute greater fulfillment of one of these needs for another type without a loss in well-being.

The first part of this chapter draws upon two schools of thought within psychology that offer explanations for the interaction between humans and their environments: information-processing theory and social judgment theory. The second part of this chapter focuses on theories of aesthetic preferences toward natural environments. The third part examines a variety of perceived environmental quality indicators for measuring values and discusses their validity, reliability, and susceptibility to biases.

This chapter does not deal directly with mental responses to environmental pollution or catastrophes such as nuclear power plant accidents (Edelstein 1982; Finsterbusch 1982). The psychological impacts of such manmade disasters exceed those of natural disasters of similar magnitude, but victims are not uniformly affected (Gleser, Green, and Winget 1981). Traditionally, courts have been hesitant to compensate for emotional injuries in the absence of physical injury to person or property.

Exceptions were made if physical injury were threatened and the defendant's actions were negligent or willfully inflicted emotional harm (Hartsough and Savitsky 1984). In 1983, the U.S. Supreme Court ruled that psychological impacts may be considered under NEPA when they arise from direct sensory impacts in the physical environment rather than just a perception of risk (Metropolitan Edison Co. v. PANE 1983).

5.2 TWO THEORIES OF PERCEPTION AND EVALUATION

5.2.1 Description of Information-Processing Theory

Information-processing theory, one of the most widely accepted schools of thought within psychology, divides environmental knowing into two separate processes: perception and reaction (Ittleson 1973; Proshansky, Ittleson, and Rivlin, 1976). Perception is the process of receiving and becoming aware of sensory information. Perception is characterized by the ability of the human mind to orient, filter, categorize, and manipulate information. Reaction consists of the recall of stored data as well as physical, logical, and emotional responses to the perception of stimuli. Reaction necessarily follows perception, but prior reactions can influence perceptions.
Perception and reaction are influenced by cognition and affect (Posner 1973). Cognition is the ability to reason and solve problems logically. It derives from the experience, learning, intellectual aptitude, and intuitive awareness of people. Affect comprises the feelings and expectations people bring to specific perceptions and reactions, such as emotions and symbolism (Appleyard 1979). Affect balance, the net result of an individual's general positive and negative feelings, also colors specific perceptions and reactions. Affect balance is highly influenced by expectations. For example, two individuals living under identical conditions might not be equally satisfied because they have different expectations of success (McKennell 1978). Expressed satisfaction with an environment may reflect either goal attainment or accommodation to conditions that appear unchangeable (Strumpel 1974).
Because of personal differences, individuals may perceive and react differently to a particular stimulus (Rosenberg 1960; Moore and Gollege 1976). Responses also vary with culture and education. There may be systematic differences between the perceptions and reactions of experts and those of the general public. The objective or physical, chemical, and biological attributes of environments may be quite different from people's subjective impressions of these attributes.
Information-processing theory views people as active individuals who care about their environments and are

capable of expressing their preferences effectively and
acting upon them. In this model, people

1. Crave information and want to learn, but only
    seek a certain amount of information,
2. Do not want information that conflicts with what
    they already know,
3. Prefer to discover things rather than being told,
    and
4. Handle concrete examples and visual images better
    than abstract words (S. Kaplan, 1978b, p. 123).

Information-processing theory also recognizes that the
capacity of the human mind for processing information is
limited (Miller 1956; Simon 1957).
    Information-processing theory has five main
implications for environmental assessment. First, although
some generalizations can be made about environmental
preferences, experts cannot give people the environments
they want without public input. Second, if people are
given the opportunity, motivation, and background for
expressing their values, they can do so effectively. Third,
techniques for tapping the values of the public should be
kept simple and easily understandable. Fourth, people's
preferences toward environments are intuitive and rooted in
images rather than verbal analysis. Fifth, close attention
should be paid to the presentation and communication of
factual information to publics and decision makers in order
to avoid information overload. Most of the perceived
environmental quality indicators discussed in section 5.3
are based on the assumptions of information-processing
theory.

5.2.2 Description of Social Judgment Theory

    Social judgment theory is less global in its attempt to
explain perception and evaluation than information-
processing theory. It is based on the "lens model of
decision making" (Brunswick 1952). This model holds that
choices for an outcome are formed from preferences for a
composite of attributes that comprise the outcome, and
valid information on preferences for these attributes
cannot be obtained through direct questioning. Instead,
questions must focus on potential decisions, and then the
value weights can be inferred indirectly (Rappaport and
Summers 1973; Kaplan and Schwartz 1975; Stewart and Gelberd
1976).
    Social judgment theory does not hypothesize any
particular model by which individuals or groups combine
values associated with specific attributes in arriving at
rankings for the alternatives. Unlike models based on
welfare economics or information-processing theory, it does
not make any explicit assumptions about maximizing or
satisfying behavior. Multiple regression and analysis of

variance are two of the mathematical techniques that can be used to infer the weights. Linear regression provides results that are easiest to interpret although it assumes simple relationships without interaction effects among attributes. In a regression model, the multiple correlation coefficient, R^2, calculated across the judgments of one individual, indicates the consistency of that individual's preferences. Also, the change in R^2 going from an individual's regression equation to the aggregated one for a group measures the homogeneity of preferences within the group.

After the weights have been inferred, factor analysis can be used to classify the sets of preferences by judgment types. Judgment types are groups of people who place similar value weights on a set of attributes (Hammond *et al*. 1975). Classification of preferences by judgment types may be useful in conflict resolution because it makes the differences among groups explicit. It also may help in building a constituency around a potential action because it points out who agrees.

Social judgment theory resembles the hedonic price approach in economics (section 4.4.1) in two ways. Both theories decompose preferences for an outcome into its associated attributes and use mathematical techniques to find the implied value weights on the attributes from a set of decisions. However, the social judgment approach analyzes people's actual decisions after they have been made, while the hedonic approach looks at hypothetical decisions.

For example, suppose five alternative sites for a power plant are under consideration and the potential effects on human health, aesthetics, water quality, commercial and sport fishing, game and nongame wildlife, and socioeconomic conditions are known and vary according to the site, with no site being best in all respects. Since people find it hard to make pairwise comparisons on the relative importance of each type of effect, it is better to present them with a list of the likely effects associated with each site (as determined by scientists), and then ask the respondents to decide which site is best overall. If this process is repeated using a large number of hypothetical sets of sites with different effects, it is possible to make statistical inferences about the relative weights that the participants place on each effect. On the basis of systematic differences in preferences, one could divide the group into such categories of people as the health conscious, recreationists, conservationists, and the economic development oriented.

Social judgment theory has three main implications for environmental assessment. First, respondents find techniques for direct rating or ranking of their preferences too difficult. Second, indirect techniques can be used successfully to elicit environmental preferences and values. Third, there is enough consistency in environmental values to categorize people into judgment types.

Techniques based on social judgment theory are relatively free of the scaling problems associated with other psychological techniques of measuring values. However, they do have the drawback of relying on classifications of attributes that are determined by the investigator and which must be uniform for all subjects. All in all, the approach "seems to hold great promise" in the study of scenic beauty (Propst 1979).

5.3 THEORIES OF AESTHETIC PREFERENCES

Aesthetics, the study of beauty, is derived from a Greek word meaning "things apprehended by the senses." Aesthetic values are specifically mentioned in NEPA's statement of congressional intent to "use all practicable means...[to] assure for all Americans safe, healthful, productive, and aesthetically and culturally pleasing surroundings" (Section 4331). Although aesthetics is a vital component of environmental quality, it is difficult to evaluate. There are opposing viewpoints on whether aesthetic preferences are (1) highly individualistic and idiosyncratic, (2) best evaluated by experts, or (3) systematic and consistent across individuals.

The first viewpoint is held by many members of the public and certain philosophers:

> These aestheticians think their subject is some
> kind of peppermint bonbon they're entitled to
> smack their fat lips on; something to be
> devoured; something to be intellectually knifed,
> and forked, and spooned bit by bit with
> appropriate delicate remarks . . . something they
> long ago killed (Pirsig 1974).

According to this view, experts have no business judging people's aesthetic preferences and an environmental assessment should tap the preferences of the general public. Since these preferences vary, a majority or plurality rule should be followed in making decisions that affect aesthetic quality. This view is consistent with social judgment theory.

The second viewpoint is advocated by many in the arts and the design professions:

> Aesthetic criteria are not whimsical nor are they
> spur-of-the-moment ideas. They are not determined
> by popularity contests. They represent a body of
> knowledge and need to be applied by those who are
> competent in their application (Litton et al.
> 1971).

Landscape architects have formalized the study of scenic quality by adopting principles from the arts. Litton (1972) identified three elements of aesthetic quality: (1) unity, (2) vividness, (3) variety. Unity refers to the way in which different parts of an environment fit together in a balanced or coherent whole. Vivid environments have a sense of identity and distinctiveness. Variety includes such factors as diversity, transitions, organization, and contrast.

Litton (1972) also classified environmental attributes into primary and secondary recognition factors. Primary recognition factors exist outside of an observer's ability to change them. These include form, space, time variability, texture, sound, olfactory sensations, and movement. Secondary recognition factors such as sense of security, emotional response, observer position, visual experience, and cultural interface come from within the observer. Secondary recognition factors should be analyzed separately from primary factors, but they are a vital part of how people perceive environments. Shafer, Hamilton, and Schmidt (1969) and Litton (1973) incorporated aesthetic criteria into the prediction of visual impacts. The U.S. Forest Service (1974) system of assessing aesthetic impacts built on the terminology of Litton (1972). It identified and mapped landscape classes through objective criteria only, and highlighted the sensitivity of aesthetic quality to modifications.

The third viewpoint is exemplified by Rachel and Stephen Kaplan who offer a theory of aesthetic preferences. This theory builds on information-processing theory and functionalism. Functionalism is the idea associated with William James that behaviors may be understood in terms of their functions. The premise of the Kaplans' theory is that humans are influenced by their evolutionary history in the way that they process information and in the types of environments and activities they prefer (Kaplan and Kaplan 1978).

Since humans are not the fastest or strongest animals, their survival has depended on the ability to process information rapidly, evaluate and anticipate situations, and use tools to modify environmental conditions. In this way, the species has been able to take greater advantage of its territory to identify the location of food, water, predators, and safe refuges (Kaplan and Kaplan 1978). Advocates of this theory believe that people still tend to prefer those environments in which humans could operate best in the past. Although some of these preferences are subconscious, cultural socialization and education can override them.

This theory implies that the preferred environments of humans resemble the savannas that favored the survival of early man. A savanna consists of broad expanses of land with periodic clumps of trees, some rolling hills, and scattered water bodies. Large forests were dangerous because of predators and flat, open land left no places for hiding and observation. The environments generally preferred by people have two major characteristics: coherence and involvement. Coherent environments are easy to understand, view, and interpret in three dimensions. Because their parts fit together and make sense, these environments provide safety and tranquility. Involving environments exhibit mystery, distinctiveness of place, and some complexity. An environment is more mysterious when the scene contains features that are implied, but outside of view. Involving environments, such as wilderness and mountains, offer challenge and adventure. By contrast, open, undifferentiated environments provide neither security nor interest (S. Kaplan 1978a; Kaplan and Kaplan 1978; S. Kaplan 1978a; S. Kaplan 1979).

In fact, modern humans need two types of environments: undisturbed wilderness which helps maintain contact with biological origins and other living things, and surroundings that meet the needs of today's patterns of social and economic organization (Dubos 1976). Cultural factors also play an important role in the formation of environmental preferences.

A number of studies have tried to identify the general characteristics of preferred environments by correlating the preferences expressed by people with key features of various environments as seen in person or shown in pictures (Craik 1972; Brown 1974; Laurie 1975). In this way, people are not forced to specify in words the characteristics that they prefer in a site. This indirect approach is important because what people are most aware of in a scene might not be what they discuss most freely, and stereotypes based on names of sites (e.g., swamps, parks, and wilderness) govern many responses to environments.

These studies have found considerable consistency in the types of features that relate most closely to aesthetic preferences for natural environments. Table 5-1 lists some of these preferred characteristics. Of course, not all of these features appear in any one landscape and their relative importance varies. Nor does the absence of a particular characteristic necessarily detract from the overall quality of a scene. An ideal scene cannot be created by grouping all of these features together without any thought to the interrelationships among them. Aesthetic preferences are not a function of scarcity; indeed, some common and familiar environments may be valued the most.

There are no simple formulas for predicting aesthetic preferences because a handful of environmental attributes cannot represent the varied and unique characteristics of natural environments, and an overall impression might not be the same as the sum of its parts. Consequently, Gussow (1979) warned against basing preservation decisions on "objective" numerical rankings that assign points to preferred features, such as the computerized "Viewit" system (Elsner 1971). Felleman (1982) compared the results of different computer methods for mapping the views from a site. Predictive models of visual impacts have been

TABLE 5-1
General features of preferred natural environments

1. Presence of water unless grossly polluted

2. Dominance of undisturbed land forms and contrast

3. Uniformity of scale and character between near, intermediate, and distant zones

4. Distinct area of forest cover

5. Framing elements or composed or panoramic quality

6. Diversity of land use

7. Integration of buildings and other man-made elements

8. Absence of incongruities or distracting elements

9. Presence of flowers

10. Varied or rolling topography

11. Clean air and high visibility

developed for the effects of urbanization (Brush and Palmer 1979) and the effects of forest management practices (Daniel and Schroeder 1979). Experience shows that the assessment of aesthetic quality must involve the participation of publics.

5.4 TECHNIQUES FOR DETERMINING PUBLIC ATTITUDES, TASTES, AND PREFERENCES

The early studies of landscape quality were based on criteria assessing the suitability of landscape features for particular land uses or on expert judgments. They were not concerned with visual impacts on users or the general public (Palmer 1983). Other techniques, known as perceived environmental quality indicators (PEQIs), can be useful in eliciting social values on the relationship between the natural environment and quality of life.

5.4.1 Types of Perceived Environmental Quality Indicators

In a PEQI study, people are asked to describe, rank, or rate attributes of the environment. This information usually is analyzed in some way for the purposes of data reduction and interpretability, but it is not necessarily combined into a single measure of environmental quality (figure 5-1). Generally, PEQIs rely on data from surveys or interviews.

PEQIs are especially important in the evaluation of extramarket goods and services because there is no systematic economic mechanism to reveal individual preferences for these goods. However, PEQI techniques avoid placing economic values on attitudes, tastes, or preferences. Instead, information from PEQIs can be translated into weighted societal goals through the political or administrative system.

Resource managers generally are unable to predict user's attitudes toward wilderness correctly (Hendee and Harris 1970) but are better able to predict users' motivations for traditional park sites than for wilderness or beaches (Wellman, Dawson, and Roggenbuck 1982). A study of beach users and management staff found that although both groups actually shared similar perceptions of the recreational attributes of the beach, the managers could not predict the perceptions of the users (Buerger 1983). These findings indicate the need for public participation in planning and evaluating recreational sites so that the preferences of users can be taken into account.

Often, a random sample of the general public is taken for a PEQI. However, in some cases, it may be more useful to target specific geographic or interest groups, users of a resource, or key decision makers at various levels of government. The information generated by PEQIs may be presented as statistics (mean, median, mode, standard deviation, percentiles, or ranges) or left in disaggregated form as frequency tables. Averages can be very helpful, but they do not guide decision makers in coping with the conflicting values of diverse groups and are not meaningful unless there is a substantial amount of consensus. Decisions on natural resource development or the use of environmental amenities may be too bland if significant differences in values are not respected. Decision makers can weigh dissenting values best when PEQIs are stratified by interest groups. For this reason, the SAGE method (discussed in chapter 8) displays an array of values by judgment types.

PEQI's can be based on field or nonfield tests. Field tests rely on direct experience of an environment by subjects who look at, drive or walk through, or live at a place. Thus, field tests allow subjects to perceive a scene in their own way. However, they are expensive and time consuming both for researchers and respondents.

Nonfield tests provide indirect visual experience of a site through photographs, slides, paintings, drawings, videotapes, or films. Sometimes, written descriptions or tape recordings are used exclusively or in combination with visual images. The Berkeley Environmental Simulation Laboratory has presented simulations of remotely guided, eye-level television camera tours through a scale model (Appleyard *et al.* 1973). In a nonfield test, it is easier to control key variables for sequential investigation and

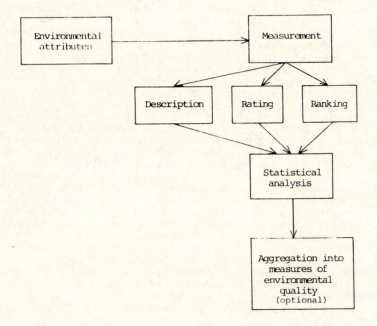

Figure 5-1 Design of a perceived environmental
quality indicator

results are more transferable because reactions to specific
components can be identified. Consequently, nonfield tests
make it easier to identify variables that can be altered to
improve perceived environmental quality. Simulated views
of the environment seem to provide sufficiently valid
representations for ratings or rankings (Shuttlesworth
1980).

Formats for PEQIs that rely on survey or interview
techniques may be open-ended or closed-ended. Since an
open-ended format does not contain a preselected list of
responses, it gives respondents a chance to express
themselves in their own words. The advantage of this
format is that responses may be more natural and
spontaneous. There are three major disadvantages of an
open-ended format. First, respondents often forget to
mention things that are not brought to their attention,
especially if they are unaccustomed to participating in
surveys. Second, because it is harder to interpret data in
this form, the analyst still has to categorize the
responses so that they can be tabulated in a useful way.
Third, the responses are strongly affected by differences
in characteristics of the respondents, such as personality,
education, and socioeconomic status. It is more difficult
to isolate the effects of these individual differences by
cross-tabulating responses by the characteristics of the
respondents when open formats are used.

In a closed-ended format, the questions are followed
by a list of possible choices so that respondents just have
to answer "yes" or "no," or select one or more responses
from a list. A big advantage of a closed-ended format is
its greater simplicity for respondents. However, the
designer of the questionnaire must anticipate the full
range of responses in advance and refine this list through
pretesting. Otherwise, the answers might not reflect the
true opinions, values, or conditions of the respondents.
Still, no closed-ended checklist can completely cover
interrelationships or subtleties in responses, assessments,
or judgments.

Closed-ended formats are more useful than open-ended
formats in an environmental assessment. When respondents
feel that the preselected responses are inadequate, they
should be encouraged to specify others. Some of the most
interesting information frequently comes from
supplementary, verbal explanations. Because the phrasing
of survey questions can restrict the ability of respondents
to express their opinions and preferences, a compromise
between open-ended and closed-ended formats may be
desirable. In the first stage, interviewers identify
public problems and interests by asking a small number of
respondents a series of open-ended questions. These
questions can be answered by a simple "yes" or "no"
response. Subsequent questions can then provide a
follow-up using the respondents' own words. The second
stage consists of a quantitative assessment of preferences
through more structured interviews of a larger sample of

respondents using the set of questions developed in the
first stage.
   There are four basic types of PEQI techniques: (1)
descriptive assessments, (2) evaluative appraisals, (3)
preferential judgments, and (4) indirect judgment tasks.

   Descriptive Assessments. Descriptive assessments ask
respondents to express what they are aware of, feel, or
experience in a particular environment or a nonfield
representation of a site. For example, such questions
might ask "What do you find noteworthy about this scene?"
or "What is there about this picture that makes you feel
peaceful?" Types of descriptive assessments include (1)
free descriptions, (2) adjective checklists, (3) semantic
differential scales, and (4) landscape ratings.
   Some PEQIs ask respondents to describe an environment
using their own words (Michelson 1966; Stankey 1972). The
respondent usually is allowed to view the environment while
constructing a free description, but some researchers
prefer to analyze what people remember. Free descriptions
have the advantages and disadvantages of open-ended
formats. Content analysis may be used to interpret the
responses. Because free descriptions do not deal with
tradeoffs, priorities, or values, they are of limited use
in environmental assessment.
   Adjective checklists are the closed-ended equivalent
of free descriptions (Gough and Heilbrun 1965). With this
technique, respondents select the relevant descriptors for
an environment from a standard list. Sometimes factor
analysis is used to simplify a long set of descriptors.
Adjective checklists provide little information that can
contribute to decisions regarding the preservation or
development of natural environments.
   The semantic differential scale is a method for
combining associations and scaling their meanings verbally
(Osgood, Suri, and Tannenbaum 1957). This instrument
consists of sets of bipolar adjective scales that indicate
both the direction and the intensity of associations. For
example, a scale might consist of the words "pretty" and
"ugly" at each end and a continuum of responses in between
these two opposites. A seven-point scale commonly is used
because respondents may become confused if the scale has
too many points. There have been a number of applications
of semantic differential scales in studies of environmental
perception (Dearinger *et al*. 1973; Moeller, MacLachlan, and
Morrison 1974; Golant and Burton 1976; Gollub 1976).
However, semantic differential scales are imprecise and
provide limited guidance for decision making.
   The U.S. Bureau of Land Management (BLM 1978; 1980a)
produced a system for rating the quality of various
landscape features (landforms, vegetation, water, cultural
modifications, adjacent scenery, and scarcity). The
evaluation elements in the system are form, color, line,
and texture, and the relative weights for each element may
be equal or variable. Visual resource contrast ratings for

each element of a site are elicited on a scale of 0 to 3 and are then multiplied by the corresponding weights. The visual impacts of potential modifications of the site can be projected by comparing the change in ratings expected to result from the modifications. This method implies the need for simulations of the visual impacts of alternative proposed actions. Unfortunately, BLM offered little guidance on how to implement this subjective system of visual inventory and impact evaluation. In particular, it does not show how tradeoffs are to be made between visual impacts and other objectives. An associated manual discusses simulation techniques (U.S. Bureau of Land Management 1980b).

Smardon (1979) expanded on the BLM system by adding two more elements of quality (scale and spatial character) and by discussing the subelements and the effects of such variables as distance, atmospheric conditions, and lighting. He suggested a generalized ranking of weights. In decreasing order of importance, they are scale dominance, color contrast, form contrast, spatial dominance, scale contrast, line contrast, and textural contrast. Four elements of landscape compatibility are each assigned up to 3 points, while up to 12 points are assigned to both scale contrast and spatial dominance. He recommended converting the difference between the weighted sum of the quantitative ratings with and without the proposed modification into summary judgments of visual impacts: severe, strong, moderate, weak, or negligible.

The U.S. Army Corps of Engineers has a Visual Assessment Procedure (Smardon et al. 1984). This procedure has several different levels of detail, depending on the scale and type of project under consideration. The basic procedure has ten steps:

1. Selection of viewpoints to represent typical viewer location, viewer activities and expectations, and potential project visibility;
2. Selection of the analysts;
3. Collection of data;
4. Inventory of water (resources, movement, and scale), landform type, vegetation (cover, diversity, and seasonal change), land and water uses (intensity and type, access type, user activity (degree and frequency), amount of pollution and litter, similarity of adjacent scenery, sounds (presence and type), smells (presence and type), and visibility (amount and position);
5. Forecast of without plan conditions;
6. Forecast of with plan conditions;
7. Identification of effects;
8. Professional assessment of the magnitude and significance of impacts;

9. Public assessment of the magnitude and
    significance of impacts; and
10. Reconciliation of the professional and
    public assessment to appraise the net
    impacts

The Corps of Engineers procedure includes sample
formats for the inventory and forecasting steps, which are
largely descriptive. The format for the professional
assessment is based on qualitative ratings. The main
characteristics of the site (water resources, landform,
vegetation, land use, user activity, special
considerations, and landscape composition) are rated on a
three-point scale ranging from minimal or inconspicuous to
distinctive or prominent for both the with and without plan
cases. Then, the difference between the two cases is found
by subtracting the two ratings for each characteristic.
The professional assessment also includes ratings of the
compatibility, scale, contrast, and spatial dominance of
the site as well as space for general comments and answers
to specific questions.

Evaluative Appraisals. Evaluative appraisals ask
people to rank alternatives based on their wants or
feelings about a particular scene or object relative to an
explicit standard of comparison. A sample question would
be, "Which is more beautiful, the Grand Canyon or
Yellowstone Park?" The rules for manipulating ordinal data
should be followed in analyzing evaluative appraisals (see
section 2.2.3). Three examples of evaluative appraisals
are landscape rankings, card-sorting, and opinion polls.
Landscape rankings are based on pairwise comparisons
of a series of scenes (Sonnenfeld 1966; Hart and Graham
1967; Litton *et al.* 1971; Pitt and Anderson 1975). When n
items are ranked through pairwise comparisons $[n(n-1)/2]$,
judgments must be made.
A card-sorting process known as a "Q-sort" is a
variant of landscape assessment rankings. Respondents
often find it easier to make pairwise rankings by shuffling
cards rather than considering a list of items on a
questionnaire because this allows them to modify their
choices more easily. These cards may contain statements
describing a site, hypothetical levels of quality for a set
of environmental attributes, or photographs of a scene.
The deck should consist of no more than 100 cards or the
task becomes too complex. Respondents are instructed to
sort the cards in order of their preferences, either into a
certain number of stacks or as many stacks as they want.
Card-sorting assumes that people can judge equal distances
between stacks and have a common frame of reference. Pitt
and Zube (1979) found that most respondents understood and
enjoyed a Q-sort process. The Q-sort has also been used
for visual quality inventories in coastal wetlands plans
(Palmer 1982). The SAGE method (discussed in chapter 8)

employs a card-sorting technique to elicit values in an environmental assessment.

Opinion polls have become an important institution in politics. Polls ask respondents to state their approval or disapproval of particular government actions, rank the seriousness of various problems or the feasibility of policies to solve them, or rank priorities for public spending by allocating a hypothetical budget.

The sample may consist of the general public, experts, or decision makers. Usually, the results are tabulated by percent frequency, but they may be analyzed through more sophisticated statistical clustering or scaling techniques. For example, Dornbusch (1975) developed an index of perceived water quality from relative importance weights. Clary (1978) computed a "grand index" from the coefficient of variation of policy priorities across respondents. A serious problem with these grand indices is that they do not show whether a high total score results from a few very high factor scores or a large number of moderate scores.

A major problem with opinion polls is that people might not express their real opinions publicly, particularly if they conflict with social norms or the values of the interviewer. Words are cheap; it is easy for respondents to say they want improved environmental quality when they do not have to back up their statements with expenditures, contributions of time, or changes in their lifestyles. This is especially true for general issues, but is less of a problem when questions deal with specific priorities and tradeoffs.

Preferential Judgments. Preferential judgment techniques attempt to capture subjective attitudes and preferences on a numerical scale. They are commonly used for landscapes, water scenes, noise, and odors. A large number of landscape rating studies have been conducted (Coughlin and Goldstein 1970; Shafer and Mietz 1970; Appleyard et al. 1973; Leff, Gordon, and Ferguson 1974). Many of these studies have contributed to the general understanding of human aesthetic preferences and some have been useful in planning particular environments.

Noise is often neglected in environmental assessments. However, prolonged noise can cause serious physical and mental health problems and can result in sizeable reductions in property values. Noise is easier to quantify than visual quality because it can be measured objectively on a meaningful scale by instruments. The logarithmic decibel scale is weighted so that it reflects the relationship between volume, pitch, and perceived discomfort (Bugliarello et al. 1976; Rau and Wooten 1980). The effects of noise can be evaluated in a PEQI by asking respondents to rate tape-recorded sounds.

Odor is one of the most frequent public complaints about water pollution and solid waste disposal. Although scentometers can measure strong, constant odors that pervade a large area, it is difficult to measure odors

objectively because they can result from chemical
concentrations as low as one part per billion. Regardless
of scentometer measurements, odors do not pose a problem
unless people perceive them or the odors are associated
with hazardous substances. That is why odors usually are
measured by organoleptic methods that involve people's
ratings of odor strength. Even though individual odor
perception abilities frequently differ by an order of
magnitude, the human nose remains more accurate than other
measuring instruments, particularly when several different
compounds interact (Agrafiotis 1978).

A common odor judgment scale ranges from zero to five:

0	-	no odor
1	-	threshold odor
2	-	slight odor
3	-	moderate odor
4	-	strong odor
5	-	very strong odor

The threshold odor is defined as the lowest concentration
that can be detected by 5 to 10 percent of the population.
Slight odors can be detected by 20 to 25 percent of the
sample, moderate odors by 40 percent, and strong odors by
nearly all observers (Jain, Urban, and Stacey 1979). The
disamenity value of an odor is often a nonlinear function
of concentration.

Odor ratings are subject to several complications:
(1) the loss of the ability to distinguish an odor after
people have adapted to its presence, (2) the presence of
chemicals that block odor receptors, and (3) the presence
of chemicals that react with an odorant or simultaneously
reach odor receptors, making it less offensive. At high
concentrations of odorants, these three phenomena do not
cause significant testing problems, but they can be
important at low odor levels.

Results also may differ depending on whether subjects
are taken to a site and asked to judge ambient odor
concentrations or are given samples to inhale. It may be
difficult to control for other perceptual factors in a
field test. Common sampling methods include (1) opening a
container and sniffing, (2) injecting an odorous mixture
into the nostrils with a syringe, (3) using a nosepiece or
facepiece to bring in an odorant, or (4) having subjects
breathe the odor under a hood or in a chamber. With an
open container, it is impossible to control the amount of
dilution that takes place after the container is opened. A
syringe allows control of intake velocity and quantity, but
it may disturb normal breathing as does pressure from a
nosepiece or facepiece. Although a chamber allows normal
breathing, odors may rest on the hood or the chamber walls
and on the subject's clothing. With a chamber, it is
difficult to change odor levels except in the direction of
increasing odor content. Odor judgment tests should be

double-blind experiments in which neither the technician
nor the subject is aware of the concentrations and types of
odors presented.

Indirect Judgment Tasks. Some psychologists distrust
direct, verbal expressions of values. Instead, they infer
preferences through observations of natural or controlled
behavior. Natural behavior can be measured on the
macrolevel through a person's choice of activities in an
environment (Craik 1975). At a microlevel, physiological
behavior can be measured through galvanic skin responses,
electroencephalograms, electrocardiograms, or viewing time
and eye-motion studies (Wenger and Videbeck 1969; Gollub
1976).
     Four major types of controlled behavior tests have
been suggested for determining environmental preferences:
(1) thematic potential analysis, (2) emphatic
interpretations, (3) symbolic equivalents, and (4) social
stereotype cues (Craik 1968). Thematic potential analysis
requires residents to create a story that could be set in a
particular environment. It provides some indication of
people's expectations for the kinds of activities that can
take place at a site. Emphatic interpretations or role
playing is a way of drawing out individual reactions to an
environment. Symbolic equivalents consist of
representations of an environment prepared by people such
as sketches, maps, models, music, or colors. In the social
stereotype cues approach, subjects judge how they would
feel about living, working, or spending leisure time in a
particular environment for a certain period of time.
     Indirect judgment tasks are not very useful in an
environmental assessment because they are too difficult to
interpret and muddle information about the characteristics
of the environment and the respondents. The results are
highly subjective and variable across respondents.

5.4.2.   The Validity, Reliability, and Bias of PEQIs

     Section 2.4 defines validity, reliability, and bias.
This section discusses the problems that perceived
environmental quality indicators face in this regard. The
selection of response formats has a large effect on the
validity, reliability, bias, and generalizability of PEQIs
(Palmer 1983).

     Validity. PEQIs are subject to three main shortcomings
with respect to validity: (1) incorrect knowledge or
assumptions about the future underlying expressions of
preference, (2) poor ability to communicate preferences,
and (3) failure of preference statements to match actual
behavior. To judge the validity of PEQIs, it is important
to know how much people really know about the attributes of
environmental quality. Can individuals recognize different
levels of pollution when trained observers or chemical

tests reveal its presence? If people do perceive pollution, are they observing real phenomena related to objective characteristics of the environment? Most studies show that the public has a limited awareness of what constitutes water pollution. Generally, people only identify easily sensed characteristics such as algae, mud, odor, foam, garbage and debris, weeds, dead animals, unusual color, and oil as pollutants. Few people mention radioactive contaminants, hazardous and toxic chemicals, or biological pathogens as causes of polluted water (Barker 1971; David 1971). Therefore, high perceived water quality ratings might be assigned to a transparent, colorless river that is biologically dead from acid rain.

Water quality perceptions of people living near a water body generally do not match the judgments of experts (Dornbusch 1975). In a study of twelve streams, perceived water pollution had a strong negative correlation with scientific measurements of overall water pollution, but was positively correlated with levels of fecal streptococci, total phosphates, orthophosphate, nitrogen dioxide, chlorides, chemical oxygen demand, nitrates, total dissolved solids, temperature, and dissolved oxygen (Scherer and Coughlin 1971). In fact, high levels of dissolved oxygen and organic solids can be a sign of a healthy, productive stream. Ironically, high fecal coliform turned out to be the largest correlate of the descriptor "pleasant stream," perhaps because the streams with the highest coliform counts were in rural areas and had waste runoff from agriculture and livestock.

The ability to perceive water pollution also varies with the type of user. One study found that beach users tend to be better judges of water pollution than cottage residents, but both types of users erroneously believed that areas that they do not use regularly are more polluted than their usual sites (Barker 1971).

Second, people tend to express too much satisfaction with the status quo over a large range of water quality because of a general tendency toward expressing satisfaction even when their true feelings are less positive (Campbell, Converse, and Rodgers 1976). This validity problem can be reduced by asking specific questions that require relative comparisons of components of water quality. Oddly enough, although respondents tend to be more satisfied with future government policies toward water quality than current policies, they are less satisfied with future water quality (Sproule-Jones 1978).

Since the ability of people to communicate their preferences depends on the complexity of the task, questions should be kept simple. Item response rates decline as the complexity of the question increases and this reduces the effective sample size for particular questions. Since humans are visual animals, they assimilate pictures more readily than written information (R. Kaplan 1979). Thus, a PEQI should rely on either field visits or pictures of sites.

Most people have a greater ability to express preferences than to describe an environment in words because descriptive skills are more cognitive and depend on training and practice. Errors or stereotyped responses occur more frequently when verbal expressions are required; for example, people sometimes describe a summer scene as "green" when they really mean that it is "natural" or "rural" (R. Kaplan 1978). As a rule, evaluative appraisals are likely to be more valid than either descriptive assessments or preferential judgments. Similarly, economic techniques of hypothetical valuation are less valid than simple expressions of preference because hypothetical valuation forces respondents to take an additional cognitive step in translating preferences into dollars.

Sometimes, people's expressed preferences toward the sites that they are familiar with are at odds with the preferences of people from outside the area. Out of habit, people may become accustomed to an unpleasant environment such as a strip-mined valley, or indifferent to a beautiful coastal resort. This raises the question of whether validity should be defined in objective or subjective terms. If something is perceived as real, it becomes real in its consequences for human satisfaction. Yet, incongruous expressions of preference can stem from errors in perception and might best be ignored in an environmental assessment.

Third, even if people can recognize the quality of a site, this might not affect their activities very much. Perceived characteristics of the landscape affect a site's attractiveness to users more than perceived water quality because activities other than swimming and fishing (e.g., hiking, picnicking, and relaxation) are not affected by water quality. There might not be any relationship between water quality and the respondent's desire to return to an area or substitute another site (Scherer and Coughlin 1971). Site suitability ratings for various activities are not good proxies for environmental quality except where there is gross pollution (Pitt and Zube 1979). Nevertheless, a less individual-oriented question may be a more valid indicator of objective conditions. For example, when respondents are asked whether a site should be converted into a park, affirmative answers correlate positively with water quality (Scherer and Coughlin 1971).

Expressions of the seriousness of a problem and priorities also may poorly match actual behavior. Constantini and Hanf (1972) used an "environmental action scale" to test the relationship between stated levels of environmental concern and willingness for action to be taken. Surprisingly, a significant number of the people who expressed some concern for the environment did not transfer their concern into any action commitment because of conflicts with other more basic personal beliefs. Similarly, some people who expressed little environmental concern were more action oriented out of a general sense of liberalism.

The generalizability of the findings of PEQIs for evaluating aesthetic quality needs to be considered carefully, and the conditions under which the estimated values and relationships hold should be specified. For example, the representations of the before and after project conditions should control for such variables as observer position, lighting, time of day, and season of the views (Feimer, Smardon, and Craik 1981).

Reliability. Two types of reliability are most applicable to PEQIs: intraobserver reliability and interobserver reliability. Intraobserver reliability refers to the consistency of results across the same set of respondents, either over time or when slightly different techniques are used. Intraobserver reliability requires that individuals understand the questions and express attitudes, tastes, and preferences systematically. This means that responses are not erratic, but it does not imply that respondents do not change their minds over time. An observer's values at any time depend on state of mind, current perceptions, past experiences, and future expectations, and all of these factors vary over time. Individuals take on a number of different roles that affect their responses and some of these roles may conflict with others.

Other factors such as learning effects, primacy effects, and recency effects can cause problems in intraobserver reliability. Learning effects result from improvements in a respondent's understanding of the task in the course of a PEQI test. Primacy effects occur when respondents remember items that were shown first best because they left a stable impression (Luchins 1957). Recency effects exist when the items that were perceived last interfere with the recall of earlier information (Insko and Schopler 1972). A common way of testing for these effects is to administer the same PEQI instrument twice to a subset of the sample at a 1-month interval. The degree of reliability can be measured statistically through correlation coefficients. A correlation coefficient of more than 0.7 is considered high for a PEQI, while a level below 0.3 is low (Feimer *et al.* 1979).

The effects of lack of familiarity with test procedures on initial responses or of fatigue on later responses usually are minor. Although the order of presentation of slides explains a significant amount of the variance among respondents, it does not change the mean responses significantly (Coughlin and Goldstein 1970). Inconsistencies in PEQIs caused by learning effects can be minimized by excluding responses to preliminary sample questions from the analysis, and fatigue can be reduced by shortening the test.

Intraobserver reliability also requires consistency in descriptions, rankings, or ratings of a scene under field and nonfield conditions. Pitt and Anderson (1975) found high correlation coefficients (0.76 to 0.99) between field and nonfield results for three techniques: (1) semantic differential scales, (2) landscape ratings, and (3) Q-sorts. Brush and Shafer (1975) confirmed the consistency of results between site observations and photographs. However, in both of these studies the high correlation could be due to respondent's memories of their initial impressions of the sites. Even if mean ratings are the same for field and nonfield experiments, the variance may differ. The type of representation may influence the reliability of nonfield tests. Feimer *et al.* (1979) noted higher reliability with photos than with verbal descriptions or artist's sketches. For most individuals, the best mode is the one most closely approximating reality (Pitt and Anderson 1975). Differences in the quality of the pictures can influence people's perceptions of the environmental quality at a site.

The effect of question length on intraobserver reliability is unclear. Giving respondents lengthier instructions for the same basic question sometimes does not change mean ratings much (Coughlin and Goldstein 1970). However, moderately longer questions can elicit more accurate information because they give respondents more time to think about answers (Spindler 1975).

A PEQI exhibits high interobserver reliability when the results are consistent across different random samples of respondents. Interobserver reliability varies with the soundness of the sampling procedure. Shafer and Tooby (1973) and Wellman and Buhyoff (1980) tested whether familiarity with a type of landscape influences the preferences of different observers. Neither found significant differences in responses between people who are familiar with a site and those who are not. Although nonusers and users have different values, nonusers often claim strong preferences for preservation of a site (Shafer and Burke 1965; Peterson and Newman 1969; Coughlin *et al.* 1972). The preferences of wilderness users differ significantly from those of the general population (Hendee *et al.* 1968). Another study found that the reliability of direct ratings of pre-impact or post-impact views across respondents were as low as 0.21-0.26, while 0.70 would be considered acceptable. The reliability was even lower for contrast ratings comparing before and after changes in land use, 0.12, because of their greater cognitive complexity. As a result, the authors recommended using averages or panels of respondents so that some of the variation across observers would net out, and to keep the rating tasks as simple as possible (Feimer, Smardon, and Craik 1981).

The environmental awareness and values of individuals are affected by such factors as occupation, income, education, age, sex, ethnic background and culture, political affiliation and ideology, union membership, geographic location and mobility, preferences toward leisure activities, and personality (Sonnenfeld 1966; Gramlich 1970; Constantini and Hanf 1972; Coughlin *et al.* 1972; Tognacci *et al.* 1972; Althoff and Grieg 1974; Zube

1974; Berry 1975). The socioeconomic and demographic characteristics of a sample can be modeled without much difficulty through stratified sampling, but it is much harder to control for personality.

Personality appears to be the key variable in explaining people's responses to environments (Berry 1975). Arbuthnot (1977) employed factor analysis to explain most of the variation in individual responses to a PEQI in terms of seven personality characteristics: (1) general conservatism, (2) self-esteem, (3) preservationist attitudes, (4) social isolation, (5) cynicism, (6) lack of personal control, and (7) acceptance of responsibility. For example, cynicism may explain the finding that an individual's willingness to pay for cleaning up the water in the Charles River is negatively correlated with length of residence in the Boston area (Gramlich 1970).

Personality also affects the intensity of an individual's values and the ability to express them. The same words or scenes can have a different cognitive and affective content to various individuals. People have different abilities to perceive beauty or hazards, convey associations, or use the vocabulary of aesthetics (Golant and Burton 1975). Temporary moods can also affect an individual's responses, but the prevalence of good and bad moods should net out in a random sample unless some traumatic public event has just occurred. Personality variables may have a different effect in personal interviews than in written questionnaires filled out in private. Landscape assessment surveys could be combined with personality inventories, but such inventories are long and redundant to ensure their validity. Many respondents will refuse to complete a personality inventory or may become bored or impatient in the middle of one. Furthermore, these tests are expensive and time consuming and the results are subject to misuse.

As long as the sampling procedure is random and unbiased, interobserver reliability should not be a serious problem. Coughlin and Goldstein (1970) found good correlations between ratings of the same scene by different respondents, but noted that different judges agree more on the attractiveness of natural environments than on built environments. In general, the types of PEQI techniques that have relatively high validity exhibit better intraobserver and interobserver reliability as well. Composite rankings of environmental quality can be obtained with greater reliability than descriptions or ratings, and simple preferences are more reliable than use suitability ratings.

Systematic Bias. Figure 5-2 identifies the sources of systematic bias in each stage of the development and use of a perceived environmental quality indicator. Instrumental bias is probably the largest source of bias in a PEQI. In its most obvious form, instrumental bias results from leading questions or vague questions subject to multiple interpretations. Field tests that allow direct experience

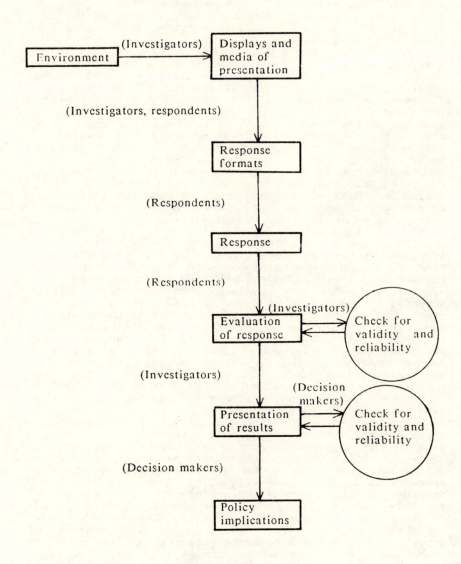

Figure 5-2 Sources of bias in PEQIs[a] (Source: Hyman 1981, p. 98). Copyright (c) 1981 by D. Reidel Publishing Co., Dordrecht, Holland. Reprinted by permission.

[a]The groups within parentheses may introduce bias between the indicated steps.

of a site remove some of the instrumental bias of a nonfield test because respondents have an opportunity to see a scene in their own way, rather than how someone else chooses to illustrate or photograph it.

Explanatory information accompanying questions can have a large influence on the results. For example, the American Falls International Board (1974) arranged to have several periodicals carry different articles about three alternatives for enhancing the aesthetic quality of Niagara Falls and to include a questionnaire to find out the opinions of the readers. Each article was written to favor a different alternative. Not surprisingly, the responses to the questionnaire reflected the slant of the accompanying article.

A more subtle source of instrumental bias stems from the relationship between the interviewer and the respondent. Many respondents try to please the interviewers by giving the responses they think the interviewer wants to hear. Less commonly, respondents may want to contradict the interviewer because of a personality conflict. Although the effects of the interviewer-respondent relationship are strongest in personal interviews, they also result from the tone of voice used by telephone interviewers or the format and wording of written questionnaires. When the name of a sponsoring organization such as Sierra Club, Mobil Oil Company, or the League of Women Voters is listed on a questionnaire, it provides strong cues about the desired findings. The type of questions can also indicate the responses desired by the interviewers. For example, respondents might evaluate the visual quality of a site more favorably when they are asked to give ratings than when asked to suggest ways in which a site could be improved because the respondents expect that the interviewer wants to build a case for modification of the site (Leff and Ferguson 1974).

Strategic behavior should be a smaller problem for perceived environmental quality indicators than for economic techniques of hypothetical valuation because self-interest is less at stake. Yet, people do respond differently as consumers than as citizens stating their concerns about environmental quality (Koenig 1975). Sensitive questions about socioeconomic status or controversial issues should be put at the end of a questionnaire to reduce strategic bias. Because of uncertainty and external factors, hypothetical bias can be a problem when surveys focus on future activities or intention to make a return visit to a site. Hypothetical bias should be lower when people are asked to evaluate specific places that they are already familiar with.

Information bias increases with the complexity of the PEQI task. Verbal descriptions or numerical valuations on an interval or ratio scale are more demanding than intuitive rankings of preferences toward actual scenes or pictures. In addition, respondents might not understand

environmental issues that require some scientific
background or consideration of uncertain, long-run effects.

5.5 CONCLUSIONS

Theories from psychology explain how humans perceive
and react to environments and shed some light on basic
principles of aesthetics. These theories have important
implications for the justification and understanding of
techniques based on public preferences or perceptions. A
wide variety of perceived environmental quality indicators
(PEQIs) exist: descriptive assessments, evaluative
appraisals, preferential judgments, and indirect judgment
tasks. Evaluative appraisals and preferential judgments
are the most relevant of these techniques for environmental
assessment.

PEQIs can help governments avoid losing sight of the
overall public interest due to the tunnel vision of
experts. Governments can be made more accountable without
mobilizing client or taxpayer interests. They can also
broaden alternatives and bring up new ideas or help build
consensus among opposing camps. Information on public
preferences reveals the different and changing responses of
groups, bringing conflicts out into the open so that they
can be discussed in the early stages of planning. PEQIs
reflect a broad set of values because preferences are
weighted by a head count rather than by income or
participation in elections. Of course, this assumes that
under-represented groups (1) can be identified, (2) will
cooperate with surveys, and (3) are able to communicate
their preferences effectively. If the view that government
should educate people to adopt more "rational" or broader
values is accepted, PEQIs can be used to learn about gaps
in public knowledge and the prevalence of "irrational" or
narrow values.

Nevertheless, the data from PEQIs must be collected
and interpreted with care. Results may differ significantly
depending on the particular techniques used; the selected
sample; and problems with validity, reliability, and bias.
The Panel on Aesthetic Attributes (1982) made the following
recommendations regarding the use of PEQIs in environmental
assessment:

1. Assessment should focus on the levels of
    enjoyment experienced by people.
2. Indicators should recognize that people evaluate
    environments in their totality.
3. Maps and visual representations are better tools
    than lists of environmental attributes.
4. Samples should be drawn from the general public
    rather than just experts.
5. The appropriate role of environmental
    professionals is to prepare representations and
    analyze the evaluations of the publics.

    6.   Simulation is more difficult for noise and odor effects than for visual effects and these different types of effects may interact.

Additional refinements in the conceptual framework of PEQIs are required before the techniques can be applied more widely. The SAGE method (chapter 8) recognizes the importance of public input in the determination of environmental values as well as the limitations of this type of information in measuring physical, chemical, and biological impacts.

6
Energy Analysis:
An Alternative Approach?

6.1 INTRODUCTION

The recent concern over depletion of nonrenewable fuels revived interest in energy analysis as a means of evaluating the physical effects of human activities. Much of this concern arose out of the work of ecologists and energy systems analysts who were seeking an alternative source of values for assessing the natural resource base. Some proponents also argue that impacts on ecosystems can be expressed in energy terms. This chapter begins by discussing the stated rationale for energy analysis and its development and forms. It then covers the conceptual and practical problems in the application of these techniques, and their possible relevance in environmental assessments.

6.2 HISTORICAL ROOTS OF ENERGY ANALYSIS

Neither the neoclassical economists nor the Marxists perceived the scarcity of energy as a constraint to economic growth because of their faith in technological change and the ability to locate new discoveries. This view is a product of historical experience. For example, despite a shortage of fuelwood which caused serious deforestation in some countries in Europe during the Middle Ages, increases in international trade and the substitution of coal alleviated the problem. The discovery of uncharted continents instilled an optimism that the earth's bounties were unlimited.

In the face of the worldwide Great Depression, some energy scarcity alarms were sounded in the United Kingdom by Sir Frederick Soddy and in America by the Technocratic Alliance. Soddy (1933) saw the simultaneous unemployment of

labor and underdevelopment of natural resources as a
contradiction and concluded that this stagnation was
caused by an inadequate financial system based on monetary
returns rather than thermodynamic and resource constraints.

The Technocratic Alliance believed that economic
theory was incapable of handling technological change and
that resource prices moved in sudden jumps rather than in
gradual steps as depletion occurred (Scott 1933; Elsner
1967). Consequently, the Technocrats wanted to replace the
monetary system with energy units on the grounds that
energy would provide an "objective" basis for efficient and
equitable resource allocation. They rejected the validity
of subjective public attitudes, preferences, and tastes as
a basis for decision making. To keep production and
consumption balanced, the Technocrats recommended placing a
time limit on the legal tender status of energy units.

In the 1950s and 1960s, future resource availability
came into question again as a result of the historically
unprecedented increase in consumption. In fact, although
coal mining began 800 years ago, half of the total amount
ever mined was extracted in the past 30 years
(Georgescu-Roegen 1976). Just as labor was the predominant
concern of the nineteenth century, energy became the vital
issue of the 1970s. The short-term and long-term
availabilities of petroleum, coal, and uranium became a
major public policy issue. During the 1970s, some
ecologists began to advocate the use of energy analysis in
measuring or evaluating the effects of private and public
sector activities (Odum 1971). Soon, engineers and some
economists were looking at the full use of energy in human
activities such as automobile use (Berry and Fels 1973),
agriculture (Slesser and Leach 1973), production of a wide
variety of goods and services (Development Sciences 1977)
and extraction and conversion of fossil fuels, nuclear
fuels, and alternative energy sources such as gasohol and
solar power stations (Price 1974; Chapman and Mortimer
1974; Herendeen 1978; Williamson 1978).

Energy consumption became less of an immediate concern
in the United States during the early 1980s because of the
worldwide slowdown in economic activities, price-induced
conservation, and the strong performance of the U.S. dollar
in foreign exchange markets which reduced the burden of
imports. Uranium availability was no longer seen as a
serious problem because of the decreased expected future
reliance on nuclear power. Fossil fuel consumption received
renewed attention for its environmental consequences,
particularly acid rain. In many other industrial countries
and in most less developed countries, petroleum import
costs remained a serious difficulty. At least temporarily,
however, energy analysis fell out of vogue, although it may
regain prominence as long-run energy availability questions
arise again.

6.3 TYPES OF ENERGY ANALYSIS

Energy analysis may take place at the micro- or macro-level. Micro-level energy analysis examines energy flows in a particular production process, while a macrolevel analysis examines energy flows in a whole region or nation. There are three major types of energy analysis: (1) energetics, (2) energy accounting, and (3) thermodynamic analysis (table 6-1). Energetics deals with the full consequences of all fuel and nonfuel energy inputs, including land, labor, and renewable resources. Energy accounting measures the direct and indirect requirements for major fuels in the production and distribution of goods and services. Thermodynamic analysis looks at the efficiency limits of certain processes.

All of these types of analysis assume that energy is important because it cannot be recycled and the potential for substituting other inputs for energy is restricted. They also share two common features. The first is the assessment of the full energy costs for goods and activities, including "embodied" or indirect energy "subsidies". The second is a reliance on physical modeling of energy flows or transformation processes between inputs and outputs instead of monetary values. The various types of energy analysis differ in purpose, methods, and their degree of divergence from economic analysis. Energy accounting and thermodynamic analyses are based on a more limited view of the purpose of energy analysis.

6.3.1 Energetics

Energetics, the most extreme version of energy analysis, is a resurrection of the energy theory of value. Its most active proponent, H.T. Odum, recommends maximization of thermodynamic potential instead of gross national product as a social goal. According to Odum, energy is the most crucial limiting factor in economic production or maintenance of environmental quality. Odum believes that long-run social survival favors efficient users of energy. Odum attributes the limitation of economic markets to imperfect linkages between money and the work done or the resulting environmental stresses.

Thus, Hannon (1973) and Odum and Odum (1976) have advocated the use of energy units as a measure of value. These units would be based on the flows of potential energy and would be independent of money prices. This imputes the total value of a product to energy, including the marginal value product of other inputs that require energy for their transformation. Odum and Odum used a crude energy measure value based on the ratio of the total energy consumption in an economy to GNP. For example, if 10^{16} kilocalories are used in an economy with a GNP of $\$10^{12}$, then 10^4 kilocalories are presumed to be worth $\$1$.

TABLE 6-1
Types of energy analysis

Types of Analysis	Major Purposes	Principal Methods	Measure of Energy Content	System Boundary
Energetics	Resource allocation systems analysis	Energy pricing	Enthalpy	All economic activities labor and environmental
Energy accounting	Assessment of resource requirements and conservation potential	Process analysis input-output analysis	Enthalpy	Primary fuels
Thermodynamic analysis	Definition of the efficiency limits for a particular process	Comparisons of actual and theoretical efficiencies	Work	Primary fuels

[a]Enthalpy measures heat of combustion. Work is a measure of available energy.

Proponents claim that energetics eliminates evaluation problems caused by hidden subsidies, regulated prices, taxes, or the exclusion of money flows associated with most environmental services. It is alleged that energy units, unlike monetary prices, reflect payments to nature for land taken out of biological production or for the formation of fossil fuels (Gilliland 1975). Odum and Odum asserted that energetics accounts "for the contribution of nature . . . the work of the rain, soil, wind, and sun" (1976, p. 50).

In an energetics analysis, the value of a manufactured good would consist of the energy content of the raw materials, a prorated share of the energy it took to make the machines and feed the workers, and the energy consumed in the manufacturing process. The energy cost of land would be measured by the change in biomass produced by plants. Environmental effects such as decreased water quality would be valued in terms of the resulting reduction in photosynthesis by aquatic plants.

To maximize net energy, the relative prices of all goods and services must be determined solely by the ratios of their energy content. In practice, central planning would be required to implement an allocation system based on net energy analysis. Planners would need net energy assessments to guide them in making each decision. Slesser advocated a modified approach, a joint-energy-labor theory of value (1978). He excluded capital on the grounds that it is a product of labor (information), materials, and energy, but explicitly separated the "prior energy" used in making inputs from "direct energy" used in production."

6.3.2 Energy Accounting

Energy accounting documents the flows of energy for various uses in physical units without specifying what society's tradeoffs should be for energy consumption. Energy accounting tabulates the net energy costs of converting resources into usable forms of energy. Net energy is defined as "the amount of energy that remains for consumer use after the costs of finding, producing, upgrading and delivering the energy have been paid" (Gilliland 1975, p. 1051). Process analysis and input-output analysis are two techniques for energy accounting.

Process Analysis. Process analysis is based on the flow of materials and energy required to yield a specific product. The procedure involves five steps:

1. Choice of system boundary
2. Identification of all inputs
3. Assignment of energy value to all inputs in terms of enthalpy or work
4. Listing all outputs
5. Determination of net energy for energy outputs or embodied energy for goods and services

Figure 6-1 shows a process analysis. Process analysis can yield accurate data for a particular process, but the data might not be representative of an entire industry. Furthermore, the technique is expensive and time consuming. Examples of process analyses include Berry and Fels (1973) for automobiles, Berry and Makino (1974) for packaging, Lenchek (1976) for solar heaters, and Chapman, Leach, and Slesser (1977) for the costs of fuels.

Energy Input-Output Analysis. The purpose of energy input-output analysis is to predict the direct and indirect requirements for each type of fuel needed to meet a change in the demand for a particular good or service. The method is similar to the input-output matrix used in modeling economic production except that the coefficients represent units of energy input per dollar value of output in each sector, rather than value added. It is most applicable in planning at the regional or national level.

The major advantage of energy input-output analysis is that this general equilibrium technique can handle a large number of goods and services. In other words, it shows how the whole system is affected by a change in one of its parts. The most serious drawback of the technique is its static nature. As technology and economic costs change over time, the "snapshot" energy coefficients will no longer be applicable. Input-output analysis only measures energy flows in terms of enthalpy. In addition, the definitions of the sectors may be too highly aggregated over a wide range of activities. Another major problem is that the data frequently are obsolete or unavailable. Furthermore, the primary sectors must be defined carefully to avoid double counting.

Table 6-2 illustrates a portion of an input-output analysis. This table shows that producing another dollar's worth of new residential construction would take 14,635 BTU of coal from the various sectors of the economy. Bullard, Penner, and Pilati (1976) have prepared a handbook on energy input-output analysis. Development Sciences (1976) and Pilati (1977) have combined a process analysis with an energy input-output matrix for a detailed evaluation of a particular product or process.

6.3.3 Thermodynamic Analysis

The first law of thermodynamics states that "energy or enthalpy is neither created nor destroyed," excluding nuclear reactions. The second law states that the entropy or randomness of a closed system increases continuously, but it does not specify the rate of energy degradation over time. These laws have been humorously described as (1) "you can't win"; and (2) "you can't break even either." The purpose of thermodynamic analysis is to define the limits on energy efficiency for a particular process according to the laws of thermodynamics. By focusing on the availability of energy to perform useful work, it provides a basis for

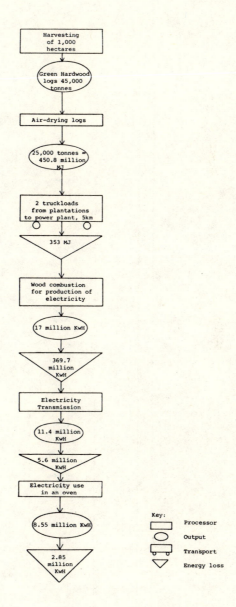

Figure 6-1   A process analysis for use of electricity
produced from hardwood logs

144

TABLE 6-2
Some energy input-output coefficients[a]

Sector Number	Industry	Coal	Crude Oil	Refined Oil	Electricity	Natural Gas	Primary Fuels
500	Iron ore mining	35,461	83,501	21,445	14,185	59,317	127,700
1101	Coal mining	1.0025	0.0041	0.0023	0.0004	0.0016	1.0060
1101	New residential construction	14,635	38,317	18,843	3,468	10,369	55,043
1301	Guided missiles	9,760	18,040	8,491	3,460	9,028	29,933
1403	Cheese production	15,136	54,713	29,567	4,313	23,603	72,509

Source: Herendeen and Bullard (1974).

[a]Btus per unit of final output. Avoid comparisons across sectors due to variations in the units.

measuring current and potential efficiencies. Thermodynamic
analysis recognizes that an increase in energy consumption
does not necessarily imply an increase in the capacity to
do work.

Measures of efficiency derived from the first law of
thermodynamics represent energy performance indices
(American Physical Society 1975). A first law measure of
efficiency, E_1, may be defined as

$$E_1 = \frac{\text{Energy transfer achieved by a device}}{\text{Energy input to the device}}$$

Examples of E_1 measures of efficiency include ratings of
automobile fuel efficiency in miles per gallon and the
ratio of heat removed to electricity consumed by an air
conditioning unit. Since an E_1 measure is based on the
assumption of energy constancy over time, it cannot
recognize changes in the quality of energy--the potential
to do the work. A second law measure of efficiency, E_2, is

$$E_2 = \frac{\text{Minimum amount of available energy required to perform a given task}}{\text{Maximum available energy that could be extracted from the consumer fuel}}$$

An E_2 measure is based on the amount of useful work that
can be obtained from the total energy content of a given
system. For example, an E_2 measure compares the energy
effectiveness of electricity versus fuel oil combustion for
home heating.

Thermodynamic analysis differs from other types of
energy analysis in that it usually excludes the indirect
energy inputs to a particular process, although, in theory,
they could be included as well. Figure 6-2 illustrates a
thermodynamic analysis curve for the production of ammonia
as it approaches its limit of second law efficiency.
Movement along a thermodynamic curve can occur when the
quantity or quality of other production inputs is varied.
An outward shift of a limit is possible as new technology
becomes available over time.

Thermodynamic analysis calls attention to the energy
conservation potential within a consumption or production
process or alternative processes. Energy analysis and
economic analysis can lead to different prescriptions. A
low thermodynamic efficiency may be economically optimal
considering the prices of all inputs, particularly if the
relative prices of fuels are low (Berndt 1978).
Consequently, the information contained in a thermodynamic
index is insufficient to determine the optimal level of
energy efficiency or the appropriate allocation of
resources for energy research and development.

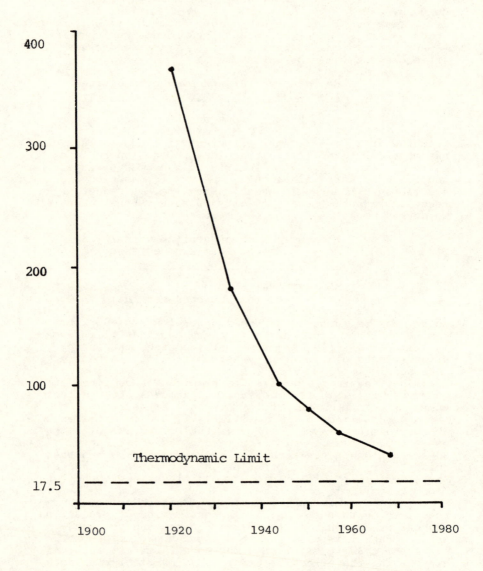

Figure 6-2   Trend in energy required for the production
of ammonia (Source: International Federation of
Institutes for Advanced Study 1976b.)

6.4 PROBLEMS WITH ENERGY ANALYSIS

There are some serious problems with the use of the various forms of energy analysis in an environmental assessment. This is particularly true for energetics, which is based on a limited conception of facts and values. Nevertheless, energy accounting and thermodynamic analysis do have some validity as one part of an environmental assessment. The main problems with energy analysis are the (1) reliance on a single-factor theory of value, (2) treatment of the time dimension, (3) aggregation of different qualities of energy into a single unit, (4) ambiguous delineation of system boundaries, (5) allocation of energy costs in the joint production of multiple outputs, and (6) inability to reflect impacts on natural systems.

6.4.1 A Single-Factor Theory of Economic Value

Some light can be shed on the value judgments in energetics by examining its analogue, the labor theory of value. Adam Smith distinguished between two types of value--"value in use" and "value in exchange." Value in use refers to the marginal utility of a good and value in exchange is its market price. Adam Smith used this distinction to explain the apparent paradox that diamonds have a higher value than water even though water is much more essential. Adam Smith used labor as the real measure of value in exchange, but he did not view labor as the source of value in use.

David Ricardo (1911) proposed a real cost theory of the natural price of a good. Ricardo saw labor as the most important factor of production and viewed capital as embodied labor, but he also emphasized the importance of the availability and quality of land for agriculture. Marx considered labor the sole source of all value and ignored energy and natural resources as "a gift from nature." Advocates of energetics attribute value to another physical property of goods, energy content rather than labor. Sir William Petty, a predecessor of Marx, described labor as the father and nature as the mother of wealth.

Neoclassical economic theory provides a more complete explanation of the sources of value. Marshall (1922) taught that value has two sources: (1) consumer demand, which is based on the subjective utility of consumers, and (2) supply--the incremental cost of all the inputs in the production including land, labor, capital, energy, resources, technology, and expertise. Although energy may be one limiting factor in production, these other inputs are also scarce. Using the same logic as energetics, water could be attributed all of the value of production inputs because it too is often an indispensable input. Georgescu-Roegen recognized the multiple sources of value:

We need both matter and energy to obtain either matter or energy. And since matter and energy cannot be brought to a common denominator; there is no way to reduce our economic balance sheet to a single coordinate--even if we were to ignore the other important factor, the disutility of labor. There is...no such thing as net energy (1976, p. xvii).

The pricing of goods according to their energy content leads to absurd results. When the supply or demand for a good changes, the value of the good also should change; yet energy based prices would not change under those circumstances because the energy content of the good remains constant. Obviously, the difference in value between a Rembrandt painting and a child's painting cannot be accounted for by the energy content of the paint. Does the amount of wood that can release 5,000 kilocalories of heat when burned have the same value as soybeans containing the equivalent heat value in food content or a lump of metallurgical coal?
If an energy-to-GNP conversion ratio of 10^4 kilocalories per dollar and a 5 percent discount rate are accepted, the perpetual value of hay land in Virginia would be $6,950 per acre. Yet, measured by willingness to pay, hay is not worth that much to human users. This can be seen by comparing this energy value with the average prices of farmland in Virginia at that time ($556 per acre, including buildings), and hay is a relatively low-valued crop (Shabman and Batie 1979). Clearly, value depends on the uses of energy. The contribution of energy to GNP needs to be weighed against the cost of producing or replacing that energy.
An environmental assessment must handle both facts and values. Yet, energy analysis only yields scientific information on physical quantities and qualities of energy; it does not say anything about human values. We are really interested in maximizing social welfare, which is composed of multiple objectives. Net energy, by itself, does not satisfy human wants.

6.4.2 The Time Dimension

All three types of energy analysis have conceptual difficulties in the treatment of time. Again, energetics is the weakest in this regard. Even if one were to accept the proposition that energy is the only valuable factor of production, various production processes take different amounts of time. If investors require a positive interest rate on their investments of energy, two processes that consume an equal amount of energy will not have the same value if the time lags in production are greater for one good (Alessio 1981). Thus, it could be argued that energy values at different points in time should be discounted like monetary values (see section 4.2.4). Also, deciding what time horizon to adopt in an energy analysis can be a problem. As Georgescu-Roegen notes, "The time horizon at which the limits become important may be measured in centuries or millenia . . . well beyond the period considered in environmental assessment and public policy formulation (1979, p. 101)."

All types of energy analysis are sensitive to changes in the effective energy resource base over time because of (1) new discoveries and changes in technology, (2) the potential for substitution and recycling, (3) changes in consumer preferences or the composition of goods, (4) speculative holdings, and (5) institutional factors. The total energy-to-GNP conversion ratio, changes over time and differs from country to country. In kilocalories per dollar, the average ratio of total energy to real GNP in the U.S. was 21,200 in 1963; 17,300 in 1970; and 15,800 in 1972. The ratio also varies across sectors of an economy. For example, it was 28,665 for the primary metals sectors and 22,050 in the mining sector in 1963 (Gilliland 1975, p. 1053).

6.4.3 The Quality of Energy

Just as Marx and Petty ignored differences in the quality of labor, all types of energy analysis are fuzzy on the relative values of different types of energy. Consequently, it becomes difficult to aggregate different forms of energy into a single index. Gilliland (1975) attempted to solve the quality problem by multiplying the energy content of a particular form of energy by a factor reflecting its concentration relative to solar energy: 7,000 for electricity, 2,000 for petroleum, 100 for photosynthetic sugar, and 50 for wind.

However, concentration is only one aspect of energy quality. Obviously, 500 BTU of petroleum, electricity, and firewood do not all have the same value. Energy quality also depends on how easy it is to harness the form of energy into useful work as well as its storability, versatility, cleanliness, and ease of transport. For example, wind is harder to harness than petroleum. Electricity is versatile, but difficult to store. The combustion of bituminous coal without expensive abatement devices pollutes the air. Fuelwood is expensive to transport since wood has a low heat content relative to its bulk. Many crop residuals burn poorly with a lot of smoke and are expensive to convert to secondary liquid or gas fuels. The production of secondary fuels such as gasoline or electricity involves large energy losses. For instance, electric power plants yield only about one-third of the energy content of the fossil fuel inputs, but electricity is more valuable than the primary fuel used in generating it. Similarly, pumped storage consumes four units of electricity for every three units produced, yet it is more

economical in meeting peak power demands than small gas
turbines.

When energy analysts have recognized differences in
energy quality, their assumptions have varied a great deal.
As Chapman notes, "Where by chance, the same product has
been analyzed by different methods, the results often vary
widely" (1977. p. 1). Discrepancies often arise in the

1. Way in which different types of energy are added
    together
2. Inclusion or exclusion of solar energy
3. Treatment of secondary energy sources
4. Assumptions about efficiencies and losses
5. Assumed kilocalorie values of the primary fuels
6. Exclusion of certain inputs

The International Federation of Institutes for Advanced
Study (1976a) brought together some of the principal
practitioners of energy analysis to standardize the
definitions and guidelines for energy analysis, but the
attempt was not wholly successful.

6.4.4   The Delineation of System Boundaries

The boundary is an abstract element that defines what
activities and geographic areas are included in the system.
Although energy analysis suggests the need to go beyond the
traditional boundaries of engineering and economic analysis
to incorporate resource losses and hidden energy
"subsidies," limits have to be set on what indirect effects
to count or else the analysis becomes too complex. For
example, in analyzing nuclear power production, should the
energy consumed in uranium mining and milling be included?
Should an energy analysis of automobile transportation
consider the extra energy consumption associated with the
sprawling land use pattern induced by auto traffic?

The system boundary depends on how one defines the
tasks energy performs. For example:

> Rather than asking what is the most second law
> efficient system for heating a house, one might
> ask what is the most efficient system for
> providing all the energy needs of a house (hot
> water, space heat, electricity). While the answer
> to the first might be a heat pump, the answer to
> the second might well be cogeneration steam and
> electricity in decentralized power plants
> (Gilliland 1978, p. 100).

Another boundary question is whether to assign energy
values to the sun and human labor. Odum, Gilliland, and the
International Federation of Institute of Advanced Study all
did so; however, Huettner (1976) treated the sun as a free
good and excluded labor.

6.4.5 Joint Production

Often, energy is consumed in the joint production of
two goods, and it is difficult to separately attribute
energy flows to each product. For example, uranium and
phosphate are mined together and gasoline and
petrochemicals can be produced from the same petroleum
feedstock. Energy use in joint products can be allocated
in one of the following ways, to

1.   The principal product (this implies a judgment of
      purpose or usefulness in the production process
      and may yield inconsistent results when the same
      product is the principal output elsewhere)
2.   All products so that each has the energy cost per
      dollar of final value (this mixes up the
      conflicting concepts of energy pricing and market
      pricing)
3.   All products so that each has the same energy
      cost per unit weight (this alternative leads to
      illogical conclusions since energy cost could be
      decreased without changing energy consumption)
4.   All products so that each has the same energy
      cost per kilocalorie (this method ignores
      differences in the quality of energy)

6.4.6 Inability to Reflect Impacts on Natural Systems

Odum asserted that natural systems have an energy
budget that developed purposively through evolution and not
for the enjoyment of humans. Consequently, Odum and some of
his followers have suggested the use of energy analysis in
placing values on the public service functions that nature
provides for free. Yet, can energy analysis account for the
value of natural systems and will it safeguard the
interests of future generations in maintaining
environmental quality?
    Although the services provided by nature may
contribute to value in use, some have no value in exchange
because the quantity supplied is greater than the quantity
demanded at a zero price. Nor does energy analysis solve
the problem of irreversible impacts. Sometimes an
environmental amenity can be restored at high money and
entropy costs. For instance, it might be possible to revive
a dead lake through oxygenation and restocking of plants
and animals. Unfortunately, many environmental amenities
cannot be replaced once destroyed.
    When an environmental assessment is based on energy
budgets, absurd conclusions are likely. For example, energy
analysis implies that if a whooping crane and a Canada
goose contain the same amount of biomass, they have the
same value despite the difference in relative scarcity.
Another example is the erroneous use of energy analysis in

valuing a Louisiana salt marsh. Gosselink, Odum, and Pope (1974) applied the conversion factor of $\$1 = 10^4$ kilocalories to the gross primary production of salt marsh cordgrass and concluded that a marsh had an annual energy value of $4,070 per acre. This approach says nothing about how useful that energy is to people.

There is also no reason to believe that energy flows capture the true worth of valuable ecosystem functions such as photosynthesis, atmospheric circulation, operation of the hydrological cycle and nutrient cycles, waste assimilation, provision of habitat, or amenity values. The energy content of wood production does not correspond to the natural services of forests in reducing erosion and runoff, moderating microclimate, or providing opportunities for recreation and observation of scenic beauty. Although eutrophic lakes may be a larger net energy producer than oligotrophic lakes, that does not imply that water pollution is beneficial. Floods and strong winds are high in energy, yet these natural phenomena are not necessarily of value and often are very destructive to human societies and natural ecosystems.

Energy flows are not good indicators of ecosystem stability. Not all species are equally important with respect to ecosystem stability and there is no simple relationship between stability and the numbers, biomass, or lifespan of a species. Some of the simplest natural ecosystems are highly stable while more complex ones often are the most prone to human disturbance because of their high degree of specialization. In fact, stability is a myth of ecology because living things have always adapted to their environments or become extinct (Holling 1978). Moreover, energy analysis may suggest the desirability of environmental modification because land use conversions such as intensive plantations of crops or trees produce more net energy per unit area than unmodified habitat.

6.5 USES OF ENERGY ANALYSIS

The most appropriate role for energy analysis in environmental assessment is to increase the awareness of physical and thermodynamic constraints in production and consumption decisions. Clearly, energy analysis is not the only information needed for planning the allocation of resources within or across generations because it focuses on just a single resource. Most important, an environmental assessment based solely on an energy analysis would be incomplete because it does not reflect human values or ecosystem maintenance. Whether natural resources or environmental quality have been underpriced in conventional environmental assessments is another matter. The techniques for determining human values discussed in chapters 4 and 5 have greater validity than energy analysis, despite their limitations.

Energy accounting and thermodynamic analysis can be useful as one component of an environmental assessment by providing objective information on (1) the prospects of technological change, (2) energy production alternatives to achieve national security goals, (3) possible market failures in price adjustment mechanisms, and (4) the potential for energy conservation. This information can then be used as one input in determining the values society places on the present and future availability of particular energy resources or in predicting the environmental impacts associated with production and consumption of energy.

Energy accounting can also provide detailed data in a common format on the patterns of energy consumption: who uses energy; what forms are being used, and when, where, or how they are used. This information can aid in forecasting macrolevel energy consumption for demand management and in assessing the consequences of technological trends and effects of acute or chronic fuel shortages.

One of the most important reasons for energy accounting is to highlight the substantial embodied or hidden energy consumption in various processes and activities (Hannon 1975). For example, one-third of the energy requirements of automobiles can be attributed to construction, maintenance, and replacement of vehicles and roads (Berry and Fels 1973).

Net energy analysis has been proposed for determining a mix of final products that minimizes energy consumption. Pimentel *et al.* (1975) tried to do this for agricultural crop selection. Since minimizing energy use is not the sole measure of production efficiency, it is wrong to conclude that a certain product or process is x times better than another if it consumes x times less energy than another. In the case of crops, differences in nutritional content, taste, adaptability to climatic conditions, soil types, and water, and management practices, including requirements for labor, machines, and chemical inputs, matter as well.

Energy accounting has been recommended for analyzing the net energy gain from various energy production programs. This use is important in (1) determining whether the energy required to extract and process a diffuse energy source such as tar sands is prohibitive, (2) deciding on the cutoff grade for mining fossil fuels, (3) comparing alternative energy supply systems, and (4) comparing the net gains from energy production versus those from energy conservation. One lesson of energy analysis for environmental assessment is that the market system may not always respond correctly. Prices often move in discontinuous jumps rather than gradual adjustments over time in response to increased scarcity. Moreover, people's behavior may be slow to change after prices adjust. Although he disapproves of an energy theory of value, Georgescu-Roegen recognizes that monetary prices can be manipulated to reflect social concerns about natural resource policies:

All this calls for a radical change of the values
everywhere. Only economists still put the cart
before the horse by claiming that the growing
turmoil of mankind can be eliminated if prices
are right. The truth is that only if our values
are right will prices also be so. We had to
introduce progressive taxation, social security,
and strict rules for forest exploitation and now
we struggle with antipollution laws precisely
because the market mechanism by itself can never
heal a wrong (1976, p. xix).

Georgescu-Roegen's policy prescription is similar to
that of the theories of environmental economics discussed
in chapter 4. However, Georgescu-Roegen goes a step further
than that in reconciling economics and energy analysis by
describing the economic process as an "entropic,
unidirectional transformation" rather than a "mechanical
analogue" (1976, p. xiv). His entropy law states that
matter and energy gradually degrade to forms that are no
longer economically useful. Although entropy is a
consequence of natural phenomena, it is accelerated by
human activity.
    Because of entropy, complete reversibility of economic
processes is impossible. Georgescu-Roegen noted that the
myth of continued technological progress can lead to
solutions that violate physical laws, "Natural resources
are the very sap of the economic process. They are not just
like any other production factor . . . no agent can create
the material on which it works" (1979, p. 98). Similarly,
Smith emphasized the need to incorporate mass and energy
balance constraints in economic analysis, "Implied
substitutions in a production function can be deceiving.
They . . . do not necessarily imply that substitution can
continue indefinitely as the abstract generalization
suggests" (1979, p. 30). For example, in converting to a
more efficient process for making steel, some capital can
be substituted for iron, but only up to a point because it
can never take less than 1 ton of iron to produce 1 ton of
steel.
    In conclusion, although energy analysis is an
incomplete tool, some of these techniques do have uses in
environmental assessment. Energy analysis points out the
importance of recognizing physical constraints in
production and consumption. It also offers a reminder that
human values should take a long-run perspective in order to
evolve into a more sustainable, harmonious relationship
with nature.

7
A Review and Analysis of Fourteen Environmental Assessment Methods

7.1 INTRODUCTION

The preceding chapters deal with specific techniques and indicators for environmental assessment derived from a variety of disciplines. In addition to those developments, a large number of more comprehensive procedures and formats for environmental assessment have been produced. Most of the efforts that resulted in broader methods took place in the 1970s following implementation of NEPA and the adoption of Principles and Standards by the U.S. Water Resources Council (see chapter 1). This chapter describes and evaluates fourteen of these methods.

Each of the major types of methods is represented in this review: land suitability analysis; checklists, matrices, and networks; multiple-objective decision analysis; as well as simulation modeling and resource management approaches (table 7-1). These methods do not share a common theoretical base since they arose within different contexts such as water resources development, land use planning and landscape architecture, natural systems management, and environmental standard-setting.

7.2 SEVEN EVALUATION CRITERIA

Seven criteria are used in evaluating the environmental assessment methods discussed here. The first three criteria reflect the complex attributes of natural systems and their responses to modification by human actions. The remaining four criteria involve desirable characteristics of planning and decision-making processes. These criteria take into account the pitfalls of analysis discussed in chapter 2 as well as key points raised in chapters 3 through 6.

TABLE 7-1
Fourteen representative environmental assessment methods

1. Land-suitability map overlays (McHarg 1969)

2. METLAND--the metropolitan landscape planning model
    (Fabos, Greene, and Joyner 1978)

3. The Leopold matrix (Leopold *et al.* 1971)

4. The environmental evaluation system (Dee *et al.* 1972)

5. The environmental quality assessment method (Duke *et al.* 1977)

6. The water resources assessment method (Solomon *et al.* 1977)

7. The wetland evaluation system (Galloway 1978)

8. The Sorenson network (Sorenson 1971)

9. The Kane simulation model (Kane, Vertinsky, and Thompson 1973)

10. The goals-achievement matrix (Hill 1968)

11. The surrogate-worth tradeoff approach (Haimes and Hall 1974)

12. Applied decision analysis (Keeney and Raiffa 1976)

13. The habitat evaluation procedures (U.S. Fish and Wildlife Service 1980)

14. Adaptive environmental assessment and management (Holling 1978)

The different criteria do not apply equally to each of the methods. The relative importance of a criterion depends on the purpose of the analysis and the stage in decision making at which a particular environmental assessment is conducted. Table 7-2 lists the criteria in a continuum in which the right-hand side represents greater realism and complexity and is preferable, all other things being equal. These criteria may be satisfied wholly, in part, or not at all by a particular assessment method. In practice, some criteria may conflict with others, especially the efficiency criterion. Some of these criteria are not applicable for methods that only attempt to be a partial system for environment assessment.

The reasons for these criteria are discussed briefly below. First, assessment methods should explicitly recognize uncertainty and handle risk systematically so that it assists, but does not confuse, decision makers. Causal relationships in natural systems are probabilistic since they are affected by random factors and conditional links between human activities and states of nature.

Second, cumulative and indirect effects are important although there are limits on the extent to which they can be considered in an environmental assessment. Natural systems are highly interrelated and a series of minor actions may have a significant cumulative impact. Indirect effects may be cyclical because of positive or negative feedbacks.

Third, a good method should reflect dynamic environmental relationships by distinguishing between short-term and long-term effects. When impacts vary over time in direction, magnitude, or rates of change, a dynamic model can show how a system moves from initial to final levels. Furthermore, decision makers have time horizons of varying lengths.

Fourth, multiple objectives should be taken into account when evaluating impacts. Although it may be desirable to combine objectives in a small number of incommensurable scales, a single measure of net benefits cannot fully reflect social welfare.

Fifth, environmental assessment involves weighing both facts and values. Factual data must be obtained in a valid, reliable, and bias-free way. Then, values are used to decide which impacts should be examined, whether they are good or bad, and how important they are relative to other impacts. As much as possible, assessment methods should separate facts and values. When facts and values are mixed, value judgments should be clearly identified so that the analysis itself does not become a source of conflict. A well-documented assessment allows decision makers to measure the sensitivity of the conclusions to alternative value judgments.

Sixth, it is important to consider whose values enter the analysis. Assessment techniques should encourage a participatory approach not only in reviewing outputs, but also in scoping the problem and evaluating impacts. In

TABLE 7-2
Criteria for evaluating environmental assessment methods

_____

A.   Attributes of Natural Systems

        1.   Treats impacts as deterministic/Explicitly
              recognizes risk probabilities

        2.   Examines direct effects only/Examines
              indirect and feedback effects in addition to
              direct effects

        3.   Assumes relationships are static/Considers
              dynamic aspects or changes in relationships
              over time

B.   Characteristics of Planning and Decision-Making
      Attributes

        1.   Emphasizes a single objective/Adopts a
              multiple-objective approach

        2.   Blurs facts and values/Clearly separates
              facts from value judgments

        3.   Relies on expert judgments only/Encourages
              public participation

        4.   Uses money, time, and resources
              inefficiently/Uses money, time, and
              resources efficiently

_____

addition to decision makers such as government officials
and private sector managers, various publics should have a
say in what is to be decided and how it is to be
implemented. Lack of participation by key actors will
reduce the usefulness of the assessment results in an
environmental dispute.
    Seventh, all other things being the same, the best
decision process is efficient in its requirements for time,
money, and skilled labor. Increased complexity is justified
only when there is a sufficient increase in the validity of
the findings and their consequences for decision making.

7.3 DESCRIPTIONS, APPLICATIONS, AND EVALUATIONS OF THE METHODS

This section describes fourteen assessment methods in terms of how they (1) select and measure environmental attributes, (2) rank the attributes on personal or social preference scales, (3) display the results, and (4) are related to other methods. Where the method has been applied, the applications are discussed. In addition, each method is evaluated in the abstract using the seven criteria outlined.

7.3.1 McHarg's Map Overlay Method -- land-suitability analysis

Description. McHarg was among the first to develop a systematic ecological planning process to aid in screening sites or routes for development projects (Wallace-McHarg Associates 1964; McHarg 1969). This method examines four basic concerns: (1) inherent aesthetic quality; (2) productivity of land for agriculture, forestry, or recreation; (3) maintenance of ecological balance and services such as water purification or storage; and (4) potential hazards from the improper use of land.

The first step in the process is to select the environmental attributes that are relevant in a particular case. Data on these attributes are gathered or produced through additional studies. For each attribute, the analyst constructs a map to indicate the site's quality or suitability for development and its size. The map uses an ordinal scale based on shades of gray, with the darkest areas representing more severe environmental constraints or higher social costs of development. Then, each map is drawn on transparent sheets and superimposed on the others. The resulting set of overlays combines the values for all of the attributes, giving equal weight to each. This display is accompanied with maps or charts showing the rankings of individual attributes. In this way, the overall suitability of specific sites for particular land uses such as agriculture, industry, recreation, or residences is shown.

Applications. McHarg (1969) presented six applications of the map overlay method in development planning at the urban, metropolitan, and river basin levels. In one example, he handled route selection for an interstate highway by mapping six physiographic features (slope, surface drainage, soil drainage, bedrock foundation, soil foundation, and susceptibility to erosion) as well as ten "social values" (land prices, tidal inundation, historical features, scenic features, recreation potential, water sources and quality, forests and swamps, wildlife habitat, residential property, and institutions). Each physiographic feature and social value was ranked on an ordinal scale of one to three, while accompanying charts described the attributes corresponding to each value rating (table 7-3).

TABLE 7-3
Attributes used in a map overlay analysis
of alternative highway routes

SOCIAL VALUES

Land Values
ZONE 1 $3.50 a square foot and over
ZONE 2 $2.50-$3.50 a square foot
ZONE 3   Less than $2.50 a square foot

Tidal Inundation
ZONE 1   Inundation during last major hurricane
ZONE 2   Area of hurricane surge
ZONE 3   Areas above flood line

Historical Values
ZONE 1   Richmondtown historical area
ZONE 2   Historical landmarks
ZONE 3   Absence of historic sites

Scenic Values
ZONE 1   Scenic elements
ZONE 2   Open areas of high scenic value
ZONE 3   Urbanized areas with low scenic value

Recreation Values
ZONE 1   Public open space and institutions
ZONE 2   Non-urbanized areas with high potential
ZONE 3   Area with low recreation potential

Water Values
ZONE 1   Lakes, ponds, streams and marshes
ZONE 2   Major aquifer and watersheds of important
           streams
ZONE 3   Secondary aquifers and urbanized streams

Forest Values
ZONE 1   Forests and marshes of high quality
ZONE 2   All other existing forests and marshes
ZONE 3   Unforested lands

Wildlife Values
ZONE 1   Best quality habitats
ZONE 2   Second quality habitats
ZONE 3   Poor habitat areas

(Continued)

TABLE 7-3 Continued.

Residential Values
    ZONE 1   Market value over $50,000
    ZONE 2   Market value $25,000-$50,000
    ZONE 3   Market value less than $25,000

Institutional Values
    ZONE 1   Highest value
    ZONE 2   Intermediate value
    ZONE 3   Least value

PHYSIOGRAPHIC FEATURES

Slope
    ZONE 1   Areas with slopes in excess of 10 percent
    ZONE 2   Areas with slopes less than 10 percent but
                in excess of 2.5 percent
    ZONE 3   Areas with slopes less than 2.5 percent

Surface Drainage
    ZONE 1   Surface water features--streams, lakes, and
                ponds
    ZONE 2   Natural drainage of channels and areas of
                constricted drainage
    ZONE 3   Absence of surface water or pronounced
                drainage channels

Soil Drainage
    ZONE 1   Salt marshes, brackish marshes, swamps, and
                other low-lying areas with poor drainage
    ZONE 2   Areas with high water table
    ZONE 3   Areas with good internal drainage

Bedrock Foundation
    ZONE 1   Areas identified as marshlands are the most
                obstructive to the highway; they have an
                extremely low compressive strength
    ZONE 2   Cretaceous sediments: sand, clay, gravel;
                and shale
    ZONE 3   The most suitable foundation conditions are
                available on crystalline rocks: serpentine
                and diabase

(Continued)

TABLE 7-3 <u>Continued</u>.

Soil Foundation
    ZONE 1   Silts and clays are a major obstruction to
                        the highway; they have poor stability and
                        low compressive strength
    ZONE 2   Sandy loams and gravelly sandy to fine sandy
                        loams
    ZONE 3   Gravelly sand or silt loams and gravelly to
                        stony sandy loams

Susceptibility to Erosion
    ZONE 1   All slopes in excess of 10 percent and
                        gravelly sandy to fine sandy loam soils
    ZONE 2   Gravelly sand or silt loam soils and areas
                        with slopes in excess of 2.5 percent
    ZONE 3   On gravelly to stony sandy loams and flat
                        topography

Source: McHarg (1969, pp. 37-38). Reprinted by permission.

Numerous versions of the method are in common use by public agencies and corporations. For instance, the Metropolitan Washington Council of Governments has used overlays in its open space planning program to designate "areas of maximum environmental quality". Duke Power Company has found the method helpful in siting nuclear power plants.

<u>Evaluation</u>. McHarg's method treats natural system relationships as deterministic outcomes of the features of the land. Thus, it does not attempt to project the probability of a particular impact. The map overlay method does not separate direct from indirect effects and only a limited number of effects can be considered. Causal relationships are not clearly specified in this method because each natural attribute is treated as a constraint of equal importance. Although the maps may contain assumptions about long-term trends, alternatives are evaluated at a single point in time for a projected land use. Thus, an overlay is a static tool that does not allow for changes over time.

Even though McHarg's method considers a variety of physical and social attributes, it is not really a multiple-objective approach because it is mainly concerned with classifying land. The method exaggerates the role of physical factors as determinants of development and underemphasizes economic, social, and political factors. The embedded assumption that all factors are equally important is questionable. The suitability rankings lump factual data together with values in a way that makes it impossible to separate them for

further scrutiny. The method lends itself most to execution
by experts and does not facilitate input from public
values. Nor does it provide any standards to guide the
suitability rankings. The key advantages of McHarg's method
are its flexibility and efficiency. It can be carried out
at varying levels of detail, depending on data
availability. The basic principles are simple and easily
understandable, but thorough preparation of accurate,
detailed maps may be costly.

7.3.2 The Metropolitan Landscape Planning Model (METLAND) -- land-suitability analysis

Description. The metropolitan landscape planning model
(METLAND) presents spatial information on the comparability
of land use developments and environmental quality (Fabos
and Caswell 1977; Fabos, Greene, and Joyner 1978; Fabos
1979). It extends McHarg's map overlay method in three
ways. First, METLAND relies extensively on computers to
manipulate and display data and to generate alternative
plans. As a result, a large number of variables and
combinations of variables can be included. Second, METLAND
evaluates plans in terms of efficiency benefits and costs
as well as effectiveness (goals attainment). The
efficiency evaluation may be based on either economic units
(dollars) or energy units. Third, METLAND is intended
primarily for comprehensive or regional planning rather
than project formulation and site selection.
METLAND consists of three phases: (1) composite
assessment, (2) alternative plan formulation, and (3)
evaluation. The initial phase includes three separate
analyses called "value profiles": (1) a landscape
assessment, (2) an ecological compatibility assessment, and
(3) a public service assessment. METLAND provides indicator
variables as well as measurement and evaluation procedures
for each value profile (table 7-4).
The landscape profile consists of special-value resources
(renewables, nonrenewables, and aesthetics), environmental
hazards, and development suitability. Each of these
components is valued in either economic or energy units per
hectare and the values aggregated since they are expressed
on a common scale.
The ecological compatibility profile consists of an
ordinal scale ranging from -3 to +3 to indicate the
relative compatibility of a land use with ecological
functions. The public service profile ranks the indirect
impacts on both the quantity and quality of various public
services on an ordinal scale. Each public service is mapped
separately and then combined by using overlays that
implicitly assign equal weights to each. Alternatively,
public opinion surveys can be used to provide relative
importance weights for each public service.

TABLE 7-4
Attributes used in METLAND composite assessment phase

LANDSCAPE ASSESSMENT

Assessment of Special-Value Resources
    Renewable
        Agricultural productivity
        Forest productivity
        Wildlife productivity
        Groundwater
    Nonrenewable
        Sand and gravel
    Aesthetic
        Visual amenities

Assessment of Hazards
        Flood hazard
        Air pollution
        Noise

Assessment of Development Suitability
        Physical development suitability
        Topoclimatic development suitability
        Visual development suitability

ECOLOGICAL COMPATIBILITY ASSESSMENT

Ecological Land Use Classification[a]
        Protective--assimilate wastes, prevent erosion
        Productive--agricultural
        Productive--natural
        Non-vital--urban, industrial areas
        Compromise--low-density residential, commercial

Substrate (Land) Assessment
        Biological potential--soil productivity, solar
        energy
        Denudation (erosion) Potential--soil type, slope

(Continued)

TABLE 7-4 <u>Continued.</u>

PUBLIC SERVICE ASSESSMENT

Resource Assessment
        Sanitary sewerage: current and potential area
        Water supply
        Outdoor recreation
        Police protection
        Fire protection
        Schools
  Emergency medical transportation

Adapted from: Fabos, Greene, and Joyner (1978). Reprinted by permission.

[a]From Odum (1969, p.269).

Phase two of METLAND produces alternative land use maps under three value sets: (1) an emphasis on community values which places a high priority on environmental preservation, (2) an emphasis on community preferences, which places an intermediate value on environmental protection and (3) an emphasis on the status quo, which allows all development consistent with existing zoning.

In the third phase of METLAND, the effects of alternative plans are evaluated over each of the attributes by using the original measurement scales for the value profiles. Then, the results are displayed on computer maps or grid photographs along with tables showing the actual values and their percent changes.

<u>Applications</u>. METLAND has been applied to an area of approximately 80 square miles, comprising three small towns in Franklin County, Massachusetts: Bernardston, Greenfield, and Deerfield (Fabos, Greene, and Joyner 1978). Figure 7-1 shows a sample composite map for the first value profile. Table 7-5 contains an evaluation of two alternative plans with respect to special-value resources, hazards, and development suitability. Plan 1 emphasizes environmental preservation and allows the development of 5,000 acres compared with 13,000 acres under Plan 2, which follows existing zoning policies. Table 7-6 compares the two plans using the ecological compatibility value profile. In the application, since no single area was superior with respect to all of the value profiles, the authors dropped the public service objective. The analysis shows that Plan 1 is far better than Plan 2 on both the composite assessment and ecological compatibility value profiles. The case study would have been more challenging if each plan had scored higher on at least one of the value profiles.

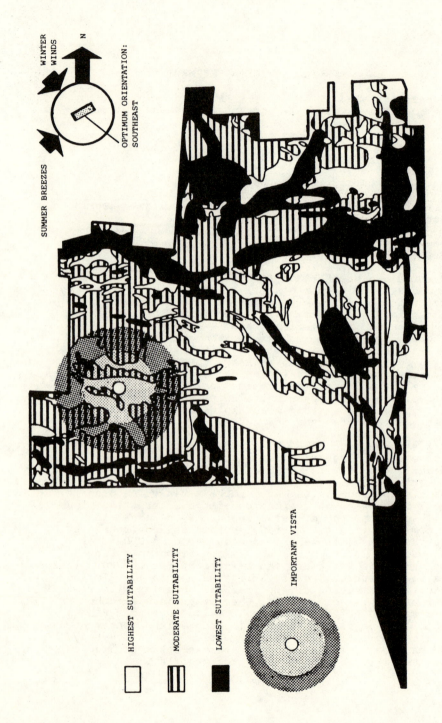

HIGHEST SUITABILITY

MODERATE SUITABILITY

LOWEST SUITABILITY

IMPORTANT VISTA

WINTER WINDS

SUMMER BREEZES

N

OPTIMUM ORIENTATION: SOUTHEAST

Figure 7-1 A composite map of development suitability produced by METLAND (Source: Fabos 1979, p. 129) Reprinted by permission.

Evaluation. METLAND does not consider risk in
measuring or valuing environmental attributes since all of
its numbers are expressed as point estimates. Furthermore,
it is difficult to incorporate information on probabilities
in a visual presentation. METLAND's structure is not
conducive to analyzing indirect or feedback effects even
though it can handle a large number of direct effects.
Since evaluation of environmental effects is static,
METLAND does not account for changes in the economic value
of environmental attributes over time. As a comprehensive
process for analyzing land suitability rather than impacts,
METLAND's primary function is to suggest a pattern of
development, not to model development processes.

METLAND only partially addresses multiple objectives
because it ignores human health and safety, and social
equity. For example, it would consider effects of air
pollution on property values, but not on the incidence of
lung disease. The method is mostly concerned with those
attributes of the natural environment that increase the
direct social costs of development. The requirement that
composite assessment values be expressed as dollars makes
judgments more accountable and allows for the use of data
from revealed preference or hypothetical valuation studies
(see chapter 4). For the assessment of ecological effects
and public service compatibility, METLAND only requires
that the relative values be correct. The rating criteria
for these ordinal-level data should be made explicit to
enable subsequent review.

METLAND depends on technical experts; participation by
decision makers or publics is limited to an after-the-fact
review. Conceivably, the roles of publics and decision
makers could be expanded through surveys to find the
relative importance weights. Also, one can argue that
public values for market goods are reflected in prices if
the existing distribution of income is accepted. METLAND is
a highly technical, time-consuming, and costly procedure.
Yet, because of the difficulty of determining dollar values
or ordinal ratings for extramarket effects, the validity of
much of the information can be questioned. The method's
complexity and comprehensiveness does not necessarily
generate additional decision-making utility.

7.3.3 The Leopold Matrix -- simple, scaled matrix

Description. One of the earliest attempts at creating
a systematic format for environmental assessment was
developed at the U.S. Geological Survey by Leopold *et al.*
(1971). The Leopold matrix is important as a precursor of
later methods and because it may be useful as a first-cut
analysis.

The procedure centers around a large matrix containing
8,800 cells. The horizontal axis has 100 columns for
activities that may cause environmental impacts. The
vertical axis consists of 88 rows of environmental quality

TABLE 7-5
Comparison of two plans under METLAND composite assessment

Composite Landscape Evaluation Components	Plan	Bernardston	Greenfield	Deerfield	Aggregate Value (millions of dollars) Total
Special value resources	Plan 2	101.58	328.92	378.60	809.10
	Plan 1	272.71	535.52	650.29	1458.52
	Difference	171.13	206.60	271.69	649.42
	Difference P2 over P1	63%	38%	42%	44%
Hazard potential	Plan 2	N/A	-1.98	-7.84	-9.82
	Plan 1	N/A	-1.58	-0.31	-1.89
	Difference	N/A	0.40	7.53	7.93
	Difference P2 over P1	N/A	25%	2,429%	419%
Development suitability	Plan 2	+3.81	-12.99	-19.06	-28.24
	Plan 1	+3.10	-7.83	-4.19	-8.91
	Difference	0.71	5.16	14.87	19.33
	Difference P2 over P1	23%	66%	354%	216%

Composite Landscape Evaluation Components	Plan	Aggregate Value (millions of dollars)			
		Bernardston	Greenfield	Deerfield	Total
Composite	Plan 2	105.39	313.95	351.70	771.64
	Plan 1	275.81	526.11	645.79	1447.71
	Difference	170.42	-212.16	-294.09	676.67
	Difference P2 over P1	62%	40%	45%	47%

Source: Fabos, Greene, and Joyner (1978, p. 197). Reprinted by permission.

TABLE 7-6
Comparison of two plans using METLAND's ecological
compatibility scale

	Bernardston	Greenfield	Deerfield	Total
Plan 2	+700	−8,603	−2,548	−10,441
Plan 1	+10,400	+2,512	+16,244	+29,656
Difference	−9,690	−11,115	−19,292	−40,097
Difference between Plan 2 and Plan 1	92%	−442%	−115%	−135%

Source: Fabos, Greene and Joyner (1978, p. 197).
Reprinted by permission.

variables grouped under four categories: (1) physical and chemical, (2) biological, (3) cultural, and (4) ecological. Only a limited number of cells may be relevant for any one proposal.

To use the matrix, the analyst first marks those activities that are likely to be associated with the project. Then, the analyst examines the entire row of environmental factors and enters a slash in cells where impacts are possible for each activity marked. Next, the identified impacts are evaluated according to both their magnitude and importance on a scale of 1 to 10 (where 10 indicates the largest effect), and the results are entered in the relevant cells. The magnitude is defined as the degree, extensiveness, or scale of the impact. Significance refers to the importance of the impact. Thus, the matrix serves as a checklist as well as a summary of the impact assessment (figure 7-2). An accompanying text should justify the ratings for cells containing high magnitude or importance scores.

Although the Leopold matrix organizes an analysis, it does not prescribe measurement strategies for the projected impacts or procedures for weighing diverse magnitude and importance scores. A summation of the values in each column or a simple tally of the number of rows and columns can only offer limited insight into the overall impact of the project.

Applications. There have been many applications of the Leopold matrix. For example, the Federal Aviation Administration (1973) used it for airport siting and expansion. The California State Water Resource Control Board (1972) also adopted the method. Modified versions that included fewer levels of magnitude and importance and

Key: Magnitude / Importance (diagonal split box)

Figure 7-2 Portion of a hypothetical Leopold matrix

Proposed Actions

Existing Characteristics and Conditions of the Environment	A. Modification of Regime					B. Land Transport and Construction				
	Modification of Habitat	Alteration of Drainage	Alteration of River Flows	Alteration of Groundwater Flows	Irrigation	Urbanization	Channel Dredging	Dams and Impoundments	Blasting and Drilling	Cut and Fill
I. Physical and Chemical Characteristics										
Mineral resources									6/7	6/7
Construction materials	4/4	5/4	3/4		6/4		3/4	3/4	6/7	6/7
Soils	6/7	3/5	3/4		5/5	6/5	3/5	5/5	8/7	8/7
Land form	9/7	5/6	9/7	3/4	8/5	9/7	9/7	9/7		
Surface water	3/4	9/7	6/5	9/8	8/5	8/6	8/6	8/6		
Groundwater	8/7	7/5	8/8	8/8		8/8	8/8	8/8		
Water quality	7/4	2/3	4/3			7/4	7/4	7/4		
Water temperature										
Air quality	4/4	1/4	3/4			4/4	4/4	6/4	2/4	2/4
Microclimate	5/8	6/8	6/8		4/8	6/8	6/8	4/6	8/8	8/8
Floods	6/7	6/7	5/5		4/6	4/5	4/5	3/4	8/8	8/8
Erosion	6/7	6/7	5/5		4/6	4/5	4/5	3/4	8/8	8/8
Deposition	5/7	5/7	5/5	2/4	2/4	4/5	4/5	3/4	8/8	8/8
Soil stability										

shorter lists of environmental attributes and proposed actions have been applied by a number of state and local governments (Canter 1977).

Evaluation. The Leopold matrix does not recognize the probabilistic nature of impacts directly, although risk evaluations may be buried within the ratings. As a result, the analyst cannot systematically distinguish between a low-impact event of high probability and a catastrophic event of low probability. The Leopold matrix takes a static view of human-environment relations. It offers no means of capturing indirect or feedback effects and does not address the time horizon of impacts.

The original matrix concentrates only on the environmental quality objective. Conceptually, it could be expanded to suit multiple-objective decision making, but the matrix becomes cumbersome as the number of variables increases. The method relies heavily on the subjective evaluation of experts. Since the listed environmental variables are too general for measurement unless broken down further, much is left to judgment. The method does not facilitate public involvement in the rating process because it relies on an interdisciplinary team of experts. Since no criteria for making the magnitude and importance ratings are provided, the assumptions embedded in the ratings are not open to public scrutiny.

Because the matrix is easy to construct, it can serve as a focal point for discussion and information gathering during the initial phase of an environmental assessment. Beyond this, the matrix does not facilitate comparisons of alternative plans. Despite the low resource requirements, the method may not be effective for a large-scale, complex analysis.

7.3.4 The Environmental Evaluation System -- weighted and scaled checklist

Description. Dee et al. (1972) developed the environmental evaluation system (EES) at Battelle-Columbus Laboratories to increase the consistency and comprehensiveness of environmental impact statements prepared by the U.S. Bureau of Reclamation. This method is based on a quantitative, aggregated index of 78 environmental attributes falling under 18 subcategories and 4 broad categories: (1) ecology, (2) environmental pollution, (3) aesthetics, and (4) human interest. At least one measurement technique is given for each attribute.

The EES expresses all beneficial and adverse impacts in common units by transforming physical, chemical, and biological measurements into environmental quality values on a 0 to 1 scale through the use of value functions developed by field staff (figure 7-3). The value functions have various shapes depending on the hypothesized relationship between the attribute and environmental

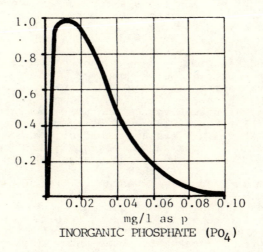

mg/l as p

INORGANIC PHOSPHATE (PO_4)

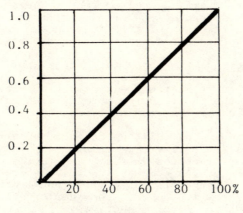

NATURAL VEGETATION

Figure 7-3 Two sample value functions for the EES
(Source: Dee *et al*. 1972)

quality. The value functions may be linear or curved, continuous or discrete, upward sloping or downward sloping, and of constant or variable slope.

Dee *et al.* partitioned a set of 1,000 parameter importance units (PIUs) across the 18 subcategories. Figure 7-4 lists the environmental attributes and the suggested set of PIU weights for them. Alternatively, the authors suggest having a team of experts use a Delphi technique to distribute the PIU weights across the attributes included in each subcategory. The same set of PIU weights would be used for each project being compared.

The evaluation and weighting steps are combined to obtain commensurable environmental impact units (EIUs) by multiplying the scaled values and the associated PIU weights. All of the EIU values are summed separately for each alternative to yield a measure of total environmental quality and then compared to indicate impacts of alternative projects and the no-project case.

Dee *et al.* also attached a special warning system of major and minor red flags when any EIU value becomes significantly worse. The threshold for assignment of a red flag depends on the percent decrease in value and the environmental category in which it occurs. However, once triggered, all red flags are treated with equal importance. The EIU scores for each attribute under the with and without project cases are compared. The net impact is the difference between the corresponding EIU scores (table 7-7). The results may be aggregated at the subcategory and category levels (table 7-8). The final index number represents the net sum of all EIU changes and serves as a measure of the project's composite environmental impact.

Applications. The only full-scale application of the method is the Bear River Basin test case (Dee *et al.* 1972). The U.S. Bureau of Reclamation has not directly incorporated the EES into its more general guidelines for the preparation of environmental impact statements.

Evaluation. The EES does not deal with risk probabilities since it relies on single point estimates. Perhaps yellow flags could be used to indicate areas of high uncertainty. The EES may incorporate some indirect effects in its large list of environmental attributes. In general, however, it does not consider secondary effects or interrelationships among objectives.

The temporal aspect of the EES is limited. It groups temporary construction impacts with long-term impacts in a single figure and predicted future with and without project conditions are made with reference to some unspecified time horizon. Also, the importance weights are not likely to be constant over time.

The four categories of the EES do establish a limited framework for multiple-objective analysis, but they are weak on environmental effects with economic consequences. The EES requires a large number of value judgments by the

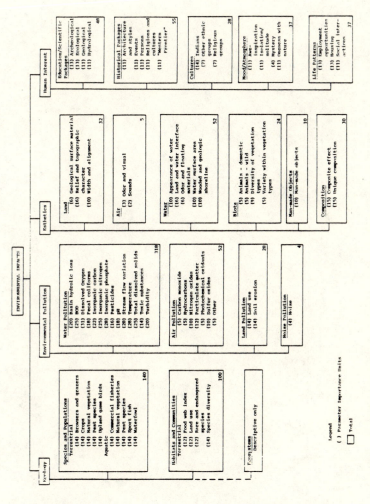

Figure 7-4 Environmental attributes and parameter importance units for the EES (Source: Dee et al. 1972, Figure 3).

TABLE 7-7
Sample EES evaluation of the ecology category

Species and Populations	Parameter Importance Units	Score With the Project	Score Without the Project	Net Project Impact
Terrestrial				
Browsers and grazers	14	14.00	14.00	0.00
Crops	14	9.24	8.12	+1.12
Natural vegetation	14	5.88	5.88	0.00
Pest species	14	ND	ND	(0)[a]
Upland game birds	14	ND	ND	ND
Aquatic				
Commercial fisheries	14	0.00	0.00	0.00
Natural vegetation	14	11.48	11.62	-0.14
Pest species	14	ND	ND	(-1.4)[a]
Sport fish	14	5.74	4.90	+0.84
Waterfowl	14	12.04	12.04	0.00

Habitats and Communities	Parameter Importance Units	Score Score With the Project	Without the Project	Net Project Impact
Terrestrial				
Food web index	12	6.00	6.00	0.00
Land Use	12	10.08	10.20	-0.12
Rare/endangered species	12	3.60	3.60	0.00
Species diversity	14	ND	ND	ND
Aquatic				
Food web index	12	ND	ND	ND
Rare/endangered species	12	10.80	10.80	0.00
River characteristics	12	6.72	8.52	-1.80
Species diversity	14	ND	ND	ND
Total[b]		95.58	95.68	-0.10

ND = No data.
[a]Estimated change since no quantitative information available.
[b]Total does not include estimated changes.

Source: Dee *et al.* (1972, p. 146).

TABLE 7-8
Summary EES evaluation

VALUE OF IMPACT IN EIUs

Category	Quantitative			Estimated Qualitative Change	Net Change
	With Project	Without Project	Differences		
Ecology	96	96	0	-1	-1
Environmental pollution	195	201	-6	0	-6
Aesthetics	56	60	-4	0	-4
Human interests	49	66	-17	0	-17
Total	396	423	-27	-1	-28

NUMBER OF RED FLAGS: PROBLEM AREAS AND NEEDS

Category	Component	Problem Areas		Data Needs
		Minor	Major	
Ecology	Species and populations	0	1	3
	Habitats and communities	0	1	3

| | | Problem Areas | | |
Category	Component	Minor	Major	Data Needs
Environmental pollution	Water pollution	2	2	1
	Air pollution	0	0	3
	Land pollution	0	0	0
	Noise pollution	0	0	1
Aesthetics	Land	1	0	0
	Air	1	0	0
	Water	0	0	0
	Biota	0	0	0
	Manmade objects	0	0	0
	Composition	0	1	0
Human interest	Education/scientific packages	0	0	1
	Historical packages	0	0	0
	Cultures	1	3	0
	Mood/atmosphere	0	1	0
	Life patterns	2	2	0
Total		7	9	6

Source: Dee et al. (1972, p. 161).

analysis team. Many assumptions regarding the choice of indicators, value functions, and relative weights are embedded in the method. A great deal of information on facts and values is lost when the scaled impact scores are multiplied by the corresponding PIU weights.

The EES is intended for use by a team of experts. Although there is room for participation by decision makers and publics in the development or modification of value functions, Dee *et al.* do not consider this practical or desirable. Despite the apparent straightforwardness of the procedure, it has numerous value judgments that may be debatable. The method will be efficient only when all parties agree on the indicators, value functions, and weights.

7.3.5 The Environmental Quality Assessment Method -- checklist with descriptive scale

Duke *et al.* (1977) developed the environmental quality assessment method (EQA) for the U.S. Bureau of Reclamation as a modification of the EES. Like the EES, the EQA method adopts a checklist of environmental variables divided into four levels: (1) components, (2) categories, (3) factors, and (4) measurements (table 7-9). The factor is the key level for the data collection. However, the EQA deemphasizes numerical weighting and index formation (Dee *et al.* 1972). Instead, it emphasizes physical measures and qualitative descriptions of impacts limited to just those aspects of environmental quality contained in the EQ account of the U.S. Water Resources Council (1973).

The EQA begins with the creation of an interdisciplinary team that identifies the relevant environmental factors and delineates the spatial and temporal boundaries applicable to each. Factor selection is completed using a matrix similar to the one developed by Leopold *et al.* (1971). Baseline data and projections of future conditions with and without the project are tabulated in physical units (table 7-10). The environmental effect is defined as the difference between the with and without project effects.

The significance of impacts is assessed according to evaluation guidelines developed by the analysis team for each environmental factor. An evaluation guideline is defined as the smallest significant change in the highest existing quality level for each factor in the region. For example, if the best existing dissolved oxygen content of rivers in the region is 8 milligrams per liter, the smallest significant decrease at that level of water quality might be 1.5 milligrams per liter. The guidelines are developed with assistance from local planning agencies and interested members of the public. The analysis team then compares the anticipated impacts with the evaluation guidelines and flags especially significant effects. The output is displayed as a series of tables that include the

TABLE 7-9
Components, categories, and factors for the EQA method

Ecological Component

Biological Resources Category

       Aquatic flora
       Trees
       Grasses and shrubs
       Aquatic animals
       Terrestrial animals
       Endangered and threatened
         species
       Unique biota
       Educational and scientific
         value
       Legal and administrative
         protection

Ecological Systems Category

       Ecosystem type
       Ecosystem quality
       Uniqueness
       Educational and scientific
         value
       Legal and administrative
         protection

Estuarine and Wetland Areas
Category

       Estuarine areas
       Wetland areas
       Water Quality
       Productivity
       Uniqueness
       Educational and scientific
         value
       Legal and administrative
         protection
       Institutional mitigation

Visual Quality Category

       Scale
       Variety
       Naturalness
       Human use

(Continued)

TABLE 7-9 <u>Continued</u>.

    <u>Land</u> <u>Quality</u> <u>Category</u>

        Land use
        Land degradation
        Land use regulations

<u>Geological</u> <u>Resources</u> <u>Category</u>

        Processes and formulations
        Fossil beds
        Uniqueness
        Educational and scientific
          value
        Legal and administrative
          protection

    Cultural Component

<u>Historical</u> <u>and</u> <u>Archeological</u>
    <u>Resources</u> <u>Category</u>

        Sites
        Level of investigation
        Educational value
        Symbolic land features
        Extent used by public
        Protection of significant
          sites

    Recreational Component

<u>Streams</u> <u>and</u> <u>Stream</u> <u>Systems</u>
    <u>Category</u>

        Amount of significant
          land/water features

Source: Duke *et al.* (1977)

physical measurements or estimates for each factor with and
without the project, along with a summary of the
evaluation results: (1) beneficial effect, (2) significant
beneficial effect, (3) no significant effect, (4)
significant adverse effect, or (5) adverse effect.

Applications. The Bureau of Reclamation distributed
documentation on the EQA method to its regional offices.
During the Carter administration, the Bureau required use
of the method in environmental impact studies.

Evaluation. The EQA method fails to address risk
explicitly. Probability considerations may be implicit in
selecting the factors for the matrix. The EQA method is
weak in its recognition of indirect effects unless the
checklist becomes so extensive that it is unwieldy.
Temporal considerations are limited to an implicit
weighting of short-term and long-term effects. Evaluation
guidelines based on the highest existing quality might not
be applicable to future conditions. The EQA method is only
designed to assess the components of the environmental
quality account--ecological, physical, cultural, and
recreational values. Thus, it does not constitute a
multiple-objective analysis.
    The EQA method carefully separates facts from value
judgments in the tabulation of effects. It uses explicit
criteria to evaluate the data and does not rely on
intermediate indices or subjective scaling and weighting
procedures. The analysis team is urged to document all
decisions with a clear audit trail. Of course, there are
implicit value judgments in the selection of environmental
factors in any checklist. More important, however, the
method provides no guidance to decision makers on how to
combine and weight the diverse effects. Although there is
some opportunity for participation in drafting the
evaluation guidelines and examining the display tables, the
EQA method is geared to expert judgment of facts, leaving
decision makers' judgments of values undocumented.
    The EQA procedure appears efficient because time is
not spent in developing indices or explicit scaling or
weighting functions, and it is not overly complex. Yet, the
method fails to synthesize a large number of environmental
variables into smaller, more workable issues.

7.3.6 Water Resources Assessment Methodology --
weighted and scaled checklist

Description. The water resource assessment methodology
(WRAM) was developed by the U.S. Army Corps of Engineers
(Solomon et al. 1977) to conform to the four accounts of
the U.S. Water Resources Council. The approach resembles
that of the EES (Dee et al. 1972), where diverse
measurements are made commensurable through scaling and
weighting factors. WRAM begins with the selection of an

TABLE 7-10
Sample EQA evaluation of the ecological systems category

Factor and Measurements	Present Conditions	Without Project	Future Conditions	
			Alternative A	Alternative B
Ecosystem Types				
Grassland (acres)	10,069	10,044	7,086	6,869
Stream (miles)	7	7	2	2
Lake (acres)	57	71	3,057	3,257
Ecosystem Quality				
Climax				
Grasslands (acres)	77	70	70	67
Wetlands (acres)	73	66	60	55
Stream (miles)	2	2	0	0
Subclimax				
Grasslands (acres)	51	55	50	48
Wetlands (acres)	44	62	45	28
Stream (miles)	5	5	2	2
Lake (acres)	18	18	3,018	3,257

Factor and Measurements	Present Conditions	Without Project	Future Conditions	
			Alternative A	Alternative B
Disclimax				
Grassland (acres)	9,945	9,419	6,965	6,781
Lake (acres)	39	53	39	39
Uniqueness				
Area (acres)	23	23	23	23
Educational and Scientific Value				
Area (acres)	120	120	120	120
Legal and Administrative Protection				
Area protected (acres)	50	80	4,500	5,000

Source: Duke et al. (1977, p. B-3)

interdisciplinary team of professionals and local
representatives familiar with the area under study. WRAM
provides categories and critical variables for each of the
four accounts (table 7-11). The team may develop its own
list of evaluation variables in lieu of the tentative list
supplied with the method.

Each impact is multiplied by a scaling factor to
produce alternative choice coefficients (ACCs) that express
the diverse impacts of alternative plans in common
measurement units. These scaling factors can be found in
one of two ways. The first approach is to rely on
functional curves similar to those in the EES to establish
scales with a range of 0.0 to 1.0 (figure 7-3). Canter and
Hill (1979) have developed a set of value function graphs
for 62 environmental attributes specifically for WRAM. The
second approach employs a subjective pairwise ranking
technique for effects that can only be expressed
qualitatively (Dean and Nishry 1965). Guseman and Dietrich
(1978) have elaborated on the measurement of the social
well-being account for WRAM.

The weighting assigns relative importance coefficients
(RICs) to each scaled impact score. The sum of all of the
RICs must equal unity. WRAM relies on a pairwise
comparison technique to generate the RICs (Dean and Nishry
1965). Each variable is compared with all of the other
variables one at a time. A variable is assigned 1.0 point
if it is more important than the other variable, 0.0 points
if it is less important, and 0.5 points if both are equally
important. The relative importance coefficients then are
calculated by dividing the sum of the points assigned to a
variable by the total number of points for all N variables,
which equals $[N(N-1)/2]$.

The last step involves multiplying the alternative
choice coefficients by the relative importance coefficients
for each of the critical variables under all of the
alternatives. The results are displayed in a final
coefficients matrix (table 7-12). Unlike the EES, the
composite scores are not aggregated across different
accounts. In the example shown, alternative A is the most
beneficial with respect to the single objective.

Applications. The U.S. Army Corps of Engineers applied
WRAM in the Tensas River Basin in eastern Louisiana
(Richardson et al. 1978). This field test analyzed the
effects of five flood control alternatives and a no-project
alternative. Table 7-13 lists the critical variables that
were selected and the relative importance coefficient
assigned to each. Although the study team ultimately did
not choose the alternative with the highest score, it was
felt that WRAM helped reveal the strengths and weaknesses
of each alternative in making tradeoffs. Participants also
stated that the method facilitated interdisciplinary
interaction, highlighted the relationships among the four
accounts, and was useful in screening critical variables
for more detailed analysis.

TABLE 7-11
Critical variables in WRAM

THE ENVIRONMENTAL QUALITY ACCOUNT

Terrestrial

        Habitat and land use quantity and quality
        a.   Habitat type (example: upland forest)
                1. Habitat subtype (Example: pine forest)
                2. Habitat subtype
        b.   Habitat type
        Land quality and soil erosion
        Critical community relationships
        Threatened and/or endangered species
        Pests

Aquatic

        Habitat quantity and quality
                a.   Habitat type A
                1. Habitat subtype A1
                2. Habitat subtype A2
        b.   Habitat type B
        Water quality
                a.   Physical
                b.   Chemical
                c.   Bacteriological
        Water quantity
        Critical community relationship
        Threatened and/or endangered species
        Pests

Air

        Quality
                a.   Gases
                b.   Particulates
        Climatology
        Human Interface

                Aesthetic
                Historical
                Archeological

                                      (Continued)

TABLE 7-11 Continued.

THE NATIONAL ECONOMIC DEVELOPMENT ACCOUNT

Beneficial

    Increased output
        a.   Flood control
        b.   Water supply (municipal and industrial)
        c.   Irrigation
        d.   Recreation
        e.   Navigation
        f.   Water quality
        g.   Power
        h.   Fisheries production
        i.   Other
    External economies
    Value of output from unemployed or underemployed resources

Adverse

    Value of construction and operation and maintenance
    External diseconomies

THE SOCIAL WELL-BEING ACCOUNT

Real Income Distribution
    Income generated
    Contributions

Life, Health, and Safety
    Risk
    Pathogens
    Noxious effects

Educational, Cultural, and Recreational Opportunities
    Amenities
    Opportunities

    Emergency Preparedness
    Resources
    Spatial distribution

Demographic characteristics
    Population
    Vital rates (migration)

(Continued)

TABLE 7-11 Continued.

Community Organization
        Cohesion
        Employment mix
        Displacement

Noise

Aesthetic Values

THE REGIONAL DEVELOPMENT ACCOUNT

Income Effects
        Value of outputs
        Value of underemployed or unemployed resources
        User payments
        Increase from induced or stemming activities
        Increase from construction and operation and
        maintenance activities
        Losses from displaced regional activities
        Losses of assistance and welfare
        Indirect increases in public expenditures

Employment
        Long-term
        Short-term

Economic Base and Stability

Environmental Effects of Regional Concern

Regional Effects on Education, Cultural, and Recreational
Opportunities

Source: Solomon *et al.* (1977, pp. 30-32).

TABLE 7-12
Calculating final coefficients matrix for a single
account under WRAM

Variable	Relative Importance Coefficients (RIC)	Alternative Choice Coefficients (ACC)			
		A	B	C	D
V1	.20	.25	.25	.40	.10
V2	.40	.33	.00	.17	.50
V3	.10	.30	.30	.20	.20
V4	.20	.30	.30	.30	.10
V5	.10	.50	.17	.33	.00

Variable	Final Coefficients Matrix (RIC x ACC)			
	A	B	C	D
V1	.05	.05	.08	.02
V2	.13	.00	.07	.20
V3	.03	.03	.02	.02
V4	.06	.06	.06	.02
V5	.05	.02	.03	.00
Total	.32	.16	.26	.26

Source: Solomon *et al.* (1977, p. 25).

TABLE 7-13
Relative importance coefficients assigned to
critical variables in a field test of WRAM

Critical Variable	RIC

TERRESTRIAL

Habitat
     Forested wetlands   .0804
     Cleared land   .0396

Land quality
     Flood frequency   .0130
     Toxic materials   .0208
     Soil nutrients
     Short term   .0034
     Long term   .0402
  Soil texture   .0078

Critical community relationships
  Species diversity
     Short term   .0198
     Long term   .0402
  Species number
     Short term   .0198
     Long term   .0402
  Threatened species   .0800
  Pests   .0280

HUMAN INTERFACE

Aesthetic   .1260

Historical   .0480

Archeological   .1260

AQUATIC

Habitat
  Short term   .0158
  Long term   .0322

Water quality
  Physical
     Temperature   .0095
     Turbidity   .0095

(Continued)

TABLE 7-13 Continued.

Critical Variable	RIC
Chemical	
pH	.0038
Dissolved oxygen (DO)	.0038
Nitrates	.0038
Biochemical oxygen demand (BOD)	.0038
Pesticides	.0038
Water quantity	.0200
Critical community relationships	
Species diversity	
Short term	.0191
Long term	.0389
Threatened species	
Short term	.0192
Long term	.0188
Pests	.0080
AIR	
Quality	
Gases	.0221
Particulates	.0449
Climatology	.0330

Source: Richardson *et al.* (1978, p. 30).

The lack of acceptable functional curves and the cost of developing new ones proved to be a serious limitation of the preferred scaling technique.

The future of WRAM within the Army Corps of Engineers is uncertain. Currently, no additional applications are planned and some staff members feel that the method is too complex for district-level use and that its highly quantitative nature obscures the importance of engineering and political judgment. However, some aspects of WRAM have influenced the habitat evaluation procedures of the U.S. Fish and Wildlife Service (1980).

Evaluation. WRAM does not suggest a means for dealing with risk in factual information, scaling, or weighting. Some subjectively recognized risk may be buried within the process so that it is no longer identifiable in the resulting ACCs and RICs. The method does not address indirect or cumulative impacts because it assumes that an action causes a specific, direct effect. Short-term and

long-term effects are not separated in this static
analysis.
    Standard value function graphs (e.g. Canter and Hill
1979) should be used with caution since the environmental
quality consequences of a given change in the level of an
attribute can vary substantially in different regions and
across sites in the same region. At best, these value
functions should be viewed only as rules of thumb, which
local experts can compare with their own scaling factors
for a site.
    WRAM is designed to be a multiple-objective decision
tool. Its shortcomings in this regard arise from the
restricted definition of the environmental quality and the
small amount of attention paid to social well-being in the
Principles and Standards accounts. The choice of the
weights across objectives is left open for decision makers.
WRAM has some of the same difficulties of fact and value
separation that appear in the EES. The attempt to attain
commensurability among all evaluation factors necessitates
numerous value judgments which become embedded in several
mathematical operations. WRAM does allow flexibility in
weighting because the relative importance coefficients are
not fixed as they are in the EES (Dee et al. 1972). In
spite of WRAM's emphasis on documenting each step of the
process, decision makers may have difficulty separating
factual information from the value judgments made by the
assessment team.
    The method is intended for use by an interdisciplinary
team of experts. Members of the general public and local
decision makers probably would not be directly involved in
an application of WRAM. WRAM is a complex assessment
procedure requiring extensive data although its costs can
be kept down by screening potential variables and focusing
on the most critical issues.

7.3.7 Wetland Evaluation System -- checklist with the
spatial characteristics of land-suitability analysis

    Description. Galloway (1978) developed the wetland
evaluation system (WES) to assist the U.S. Army Corps of
Engineers in assessing the environmental impacts of
dredging and filling wetlands prior to issuing permits
under Section 404 of the Federal Water Pollution Control
Act. The WES begins with the formation of an
interdisciplinary team consisting of local experts who
divide the area into biologically homogeneous sub-areas.
The method includes 9 aggregate evaluation factors composed
of lower-level indicators such as (1) endangered species
habitat, (2) the quantity and quality of aquatic
ecosystems, (3) terrestrial ecosystems, (4) waterfowl, (5)
uniqueness, (6) appearance, (7) natural protection against
floods and storm waves, (8) life-cycle support through
waste assimilation and oxygenation or hydrological
maintenance, and (9) historical and cultural factors. To

provide greater focus, the evaluation team determines which six factors are the most important in each of the areas.

There are three stages in the WES evaluation process. First, experts assign baseline quality values on a 1 to 10 scale for the six selected factors in each sub-area. Thus, if there are five sub-areas in a wetland, thirty baseline quality assignments must be made. Second, a group of local officials concurrently assigns relative importance weights to each factor on a decreasing scale from 0 to 10. The quality ratings and the corresponding weights are then multiplied to yield environmental quality points which are summed for each area. Third, experts estimate the percentage change in each factor's quality level due to direct and indirect impacts of the project as well as other non-project conditions. The experts also assign an explicit probability of occurrence to each of these potential impacts. The expected value of environmental quality points is used to incorporate the likelihood of impacts.

> The impact V = WCPIA, where
> W is the relative weight;
> C is the change in wetland value;
> P is the probability of the event causing the
> change;
> I is the indicator's base value, and
> A is the area of wetland affected.

The output of WES consists of computer printouts and maps of the spatial distribution of value changes (figure 7-5). The evaluation team reviews these maps to assess any cumulative impacts that may occur due to the contiguity of affected areas or changing effects over time.

Applications. The WES has not been adopted directly in the environmental assessment procedures of the Army Corps of Engineers. Trial applications have been conducted in the Yazoo River basin in Mississippi and the Neuse River Estuary of North Carolina (Galloway 1978).

Evaluation. The WES explicitly considers the probabilities of occurrence of the impacts, but does not allow for risk aversion. Although the method accounts for indirect effects, it does not describe the specific pathways mediating those effects nor the interactions that result in feedback effects. It handles dynamic effects through a series of maps showing progressive changes in factor values at various points in time, including the accretion effects that have occurred up to that point.

The evaluation factors in the WES serve as a partial framework for multiple-objective analysis; however, much depends on the interpretations by the analysis team. More needs to be done to clarify or expand the variables to address economic and public health consequences.

The WES has a serious deficiency in that the expert-based evaluation merges facts and values. The nature

195

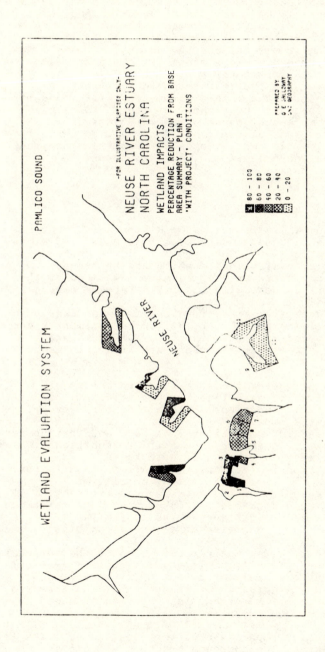

Figure 7-5 Sample output of WES (Source: Galloway 1978, p. 59).
Reprinted by permission.

of the evaluation factors makes it difficult to define each
factor by consensus. The large number of value judgments
and the map format discourage documentation of how each
rating is made. Facts and values also are merged in the
nondimensional environmental quality points.

The method recognizes the necessity of local
participation in environmental policy. Since
representatives of the public form an integral part of the
evaluation procedure, the method gains credibility and may
be better understood by those who will use it to make a
decision. The comprehensiveness of the WES demands a
significant investment of time and resources. Fortunately,
the method is flexible and attempts to zero in on the most
important issues and organize a large amount of
environmental information.

7.3.8 The Sorenson Network -- network analysis

Description. The Sorenson network's primary focus is
on the environmental costs of coastal land uses (Travelers
Research Corporation 1969; Sorenson 1971). The method
leaves the task of evaluating benefits to the project
proponents. This network or stepped matrix was one of the
earliest attempts to deal with the links between direct and
indirect impacts.

Sorenson identifies fifty-five coastal zone uses on
the basis of their potential for environmental impacts and
their generality for regional planning. For each land use
type (the rows in the matrix), there are five columns to
complete:

1. Causal factors -- specific alterations or
    activities associated with particular land uses
2. Initial conditions -- resulting first-order,
    adverse impacts
3. Consequent conditions -- second and third-order
    impacts induced by the initial conditions
4. Ultimate environmental effects
5. Constructive actions (mitigation measures for
    physical impacts), control mechanisms
    (regulatory instruments such as licenses,
    zoning ordinances and easements), and reference
    indices (specific examples of similar
    use-cause-condition-effect relationships)

This method requires the determination of the temporal
and spatial boundaries of each impact. It combines a matrix
format with a network diagram to show what interactions
occur and how they are produced (figure 7-6). The Sorenson
network is most useful in organizing information and
deciding on mitigation measures.

Applications. Preparation of the detailed networks is
a major undertaking. The approach has been applied to

197

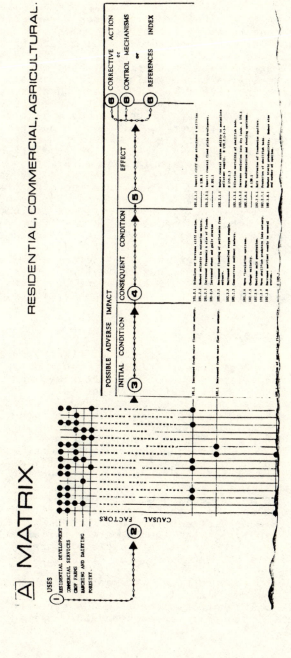

Figure 7-6 Portion of Sorenson's network (Source: Sorenson 1971, p. 15). Reprinted by permission.

proposed commercial, residential, and transportation developments in the California coastal zone (Sorenson 1971).

Evaluation. Although the Sorenson network recognizes the probabilistic nature of environmental impacts, it does not assign probabilities to each impact. The major strength of network analysis is its ability to trace the pathways of occurrence for direct and indirect effects; however, it is less suited for cumulative effects. This method could be adapted to separate short-term from long-term changes by giving the networks a temporal dimension although Sorenson did not do so. All possible effects on various objectives can be illustrated in the networks, but they do not provide a framework for making tradeoffs across multiple objectives, and the network only considers adverse effects. The Sorenson network displays factual information effectively; however, it fails to suggest a means for going beyond physical, chemical, and biological effects to place values or importance ratings on these effects. The network is primarily a tool for identifying impacts, not evaluating them. It is not well-equipped to handle inputs from individuals or interest groups although it can be used to highlight particular resource conflicts. If indirect effects are not investigated extensively, Sorenson's network can be used quickly and inexpensively. Since a network does not constitute a full assessment procedure, the total cost of completing the task is indeterminate.

7.3.9 The Kane Simulation Model -- simulation approach

Description. The Kane simulation model (KSIM) is a computer algorithm for systems analysis in resource management and impact assessment (Kane, Vertinsky, and Thompson 1973). KSIM uses ordinal and structural information about relationships to create a model of the connections among variables, direction of system forces, and threshold (minimum) and saturation (maximum) levels of variables. Its main purpose is to clarify system interrelationships for planners and decision makers.

The first step in the procedure is to identify a set of nine or fewer significant variables to describe the system with reasonable accuracy. One of the nine variables is reserved for the proposed project alternative, while the remaining variables should capture measurable, well-defined system elements. Since this step is crucial, the interdisciplinary analysis team should select variables carefully before determining initial levels or threshold and saturation levels for each variable. All levels are scaled between 0 and 100 percent.

Next, the group constructs an interaction matrix in which both the rows and columns contain the list of selected variables. The participants rate the strength and direction of the relationship for each possible paired interaction through a Delphi process. These estimates are made on a numerical scale ranging from -3 to +3, but the program can include mathematical functions.

The simulation program uses information from two matrices. The first matrix rates the long-term impact of X on Y, and the second matrix represents the short-term impact of that change. The computer then produces a graph of interactions among variables, assuming a nonlinear growth curve. Alternatives may be introduced either by restructuring the matrix values or changing a variable.

Applications. KSIM has been used in several applications. Table 7-14 shows the long-term and short-term impact matrices used by Kruzic (1974) in water resource management. Guter, Westermeier, and Ryan (1976) used KSIM in preparing an EIS for an area-wide wastewater collection, treatment, and disposal system in California.

Figure 7-7 shows that increases in population, resource consumption, and urban service levels must be accommodated by expanded wastewater system capacity. Employment dispersal and residential desirability levels are expected to decline over the period. Guter, Westermeier, and Ryan found KSIM a useful tool in opening up discussions at work sessions or public hearings although the process was time-consuming. They state that, "It is particularly well suited for projects requiring master planning techniques [or] a decision about implications of future growth" (1976, p. 428).

Bonnicksen and Becker (1983) extended the cross-impact simulation procedure in an application on the impacts of increased commercial navigation on recreation in the Upper Mississippi River. They asked panels to assign importance ratings to the twenty most critical variables. These ratings were used in determining a set of weights for the impacts. The results were shown in a matrix indicating the importance and direction of relationships among variables in the system. The matrix also helped in the construction of a mathematical model.

Evaluation. KSIM produces a deterministic model of interactions on the basis of subjective judgments that may contain some implicit information on probabilities. KSIM can incorporate indirect and feedback effects within the constraints of the spatial and temporal resolution adopted, but only a small number of variables can be handled. Cumulative effects can be computed iteratively.

Since KSIM is a dynamic method, it can depict interactions that change over time. This can be done by changing the impact matrices, functional relationships as threshold or saturation levels are approached interactions, or the list of included variables. Although it can address multiple facets of a problem, KSIM is not designed to resolve problems of choice under conflicting, multiple objectives. Because KSIM does not rank preferences for

TABLE 7-14
Long-term and short-term impact matrices for an application of KSIM

Long-Term Impact Matrix[a]

$\underline{A}$

$\underline{B}$	UD(.27)	ED(.4)	FOC(.5)	RD(.3)	H_2O(.6)	SAT(.7)	$(.2)
Urban Services (US)	1.25	.75	1.40	-1.90	0	-1.00	1.60
Employment Dispersal (ED)	1.63	2.50	.87	-1.60	.12	0	0
Flexibility of Choice (FOC)	1.50	1.40	1.25	-.25	0	0	0
Residential Density (RD)	-2.00	-1.00	-.50	-.75	0	0	0
Water Demand (H_2O)	2.00	2.00	1.87	-1.40	-.50	0	0
Satisfaction (SAT)	.75	A	1.00	-.25	-1.12	B	-1.30
Costs ($)	1.00	1.50	1.00	-.75	1.60	-1.00	1.00

Short-Term Impact Matrix[a]

$\underline{A}$

$\underline{B}$	UD(.27)	ED(.4)	FOC(.5)	RD(.3)	H_2O(.6)	SAT(.7)	$(.2)
Urban Services (US)	25	-.75	.25	-.70	-.12	0	1.00
Employment Dispersal (ED)	.13	.60	0	0	0	0	0
Flexibility of Choice (FOC)	.75	.25	.25	-.25	0	0	0

Short-Term Impact Matrix[a]

A

B	UD(.27)	ED(.4)	FOC(.5)	RD(.3)	H₂0(.6)	SAT(.7)	$(.2)
Residential Density (RD)	0	.25	0	0	0	0	0
Water Demand (H_2O)	.50	.50	.25	0	0	0	0
Satisfaction (SAT)	.13	-1.00	1.75	-.75	-1.50	1.90	-2.00
Costs ($)	1.40	.50	.25	-.38	.25	0	-3.00

Source: Kruzic (1974, p. 12).

[a]Entries represent the impact of the column variable A on the row variable B. Zero indicates no impact. Letters indicate functional entries. The initial values are shown in parenthesis.

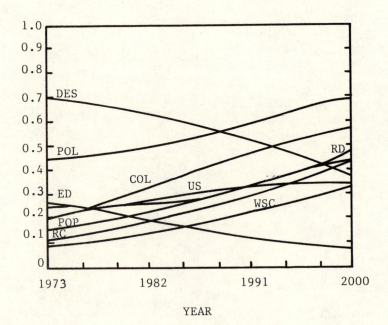

COL -- cost of living
DES -- residential desirability
POL -- employment dispersal
ED -- pollution levels relative to
        regulatory standard
POP -- population
RC -- resource consumption
US -- urban services
WSC -- wastewater systems capacity
RD -- residential density

Figure 7-7 Results of a KSIM application for planning
        area-wide wastewater facilities (Source: Guter,
        Westermeier and Ryan 1976, p. 426).

alternatives, it does not incorporate value judgments. The
inputs are objective to the extent that system variables
are measurable.

Participation in KSIM is limited to the number of
persons that can interact comfortably in a group process.
However, any number of small groups might use KSIM as an
educational tool as long as someone is present who is
thoroughly familiar with the procedure and the system in
question. KSIM requires access to a computer and a support
staff with programming skills. The method's data
requirements are relatively small and can be adapted to the
problem and resources at hand; however, this may be at the
expense of validity. KSIM does not attempt to be a full
assessment procedure.

7.3.10 The Goals-Achievement Matrix -- multiple-objective analysis

The goals-achievement matrix (Hill 1968) is an
extension of Lichfield's (1960) planning balance sheet.
Both methods account for the incidence of benefits and
costs across various groups in project evaluation. The
goals-achievement matrix is oriented toward a set of
multiple community objectives.

The first step in producing a goals-achievement matrix
is to define the important objectives in quantitative
(monetary or nonmonetary), or qualitative terms.
Subsequently, weights may be attached to each objective by
planners, public representatives, and constituency groups.

The next step is to project the anticipated impacts of
various actions, including the no-project action, on each
objective. To account for risk and uncertainty, objective
or subjective probability statements about impacts may be
made or values can be expressed as a range rather than
single-point estimate. These consequences are then
disaggregated to indicate the incidence of benefits and
costs within the population across income or occupational
groups, locations, or sectors. Finally, weights may be
applied to reflect the relative importance of each goal and
a desirable distribution of benefits and costs. Figure 7-8
contains a sample goals-achievement matrix.

Alternatives may be ranked in one of three ways: (1)
the entire matrix can be turned over to the decision maker
without making benefits and costs commensurable, thus
forcing the decision maker to make the tradeoffs; (2) the
analyst can combine the weights on the objectives and their
incidence to produce a weighted sum of goals achievement on
an ordinal scale; or (3) the analyst can rely on
transformation functions to measure all of the weighted
outcomes on a monetary scale.

Applications. A simplified version of the
goals-achievement matrix has been applied in evaluating
alternative sites for power plants (Hill and Alterman

204

Goal	G1			G2			G3			G4		
Relative Weight	2			3			5			4		
Incidence	Benefits a	Costs a	Distributional	Benefits a	Costs a	Distributional	Benefits a	Costs a	Distributional	Benefits a	Costs a	Distributional
Group a	B_1	C_1	1	—	C_4	5	B_7	—	1	B_9	C_7	1
Group b	—	C_2	3	B_4	—	4	—	—	2	B_{10}	C_8	2
Group c	B_2	C_3	1	B	—	3	—	C_6	3	B_{11}	C_9	1
Group d	—	—	2	—	—	2	—	—	4	—	—	2
Group e	B_3	—	1	B_6	C_5	1	B_8	—	5	—	—	1

Figure 7-8 A goals achievement matrix (Source: Adapted from Hill (1968, p. 23)). Reprinted by permission.

a Indicates that costs and benefits in a particular column are commensurable.

1974). A more extensive application was conducted for two transportation plans for Cambridge, England (Hill 1973). Miller (1980) applied it to project location analysis.

In the transportation example, Hill identified thirteen objectives common to both of the plans and seven categories of land uses contiguous to proposed transportation improvements. The effects of the two plans were assessed on an ordinal scale (negative, insignificant, or beneficial) for each land use at specific locations. The resulting set of ninety-one possible factors was reduced to about fifty after eliminating duplicate or irrelevant items.

Rather than deriving weights for the goals and land uses by interviewing decision makers or publics, Hill assumed that all weights were equal. Under that assumption, Plan A was preferable to Plan B by 50 percent. In a sensitivity test, Hill investigated what changes would be necessary in the relative weights to reverse the outcome of the analysis. When the weights assigned to only four of the factors were tripled, Plan B became superior.

Evaluation. The goals-achievement matrix recognizes the problem of risk in both the assessment of impacts and the determination of their incidence. Hill suggests accompanying estimates with probability statements and varying them in a sensitivity analysis. Nevertheless, he does not discuss how to allow for adequate margins of safety in the value judgments.

Since the goals-achievement matrix assumes that all consequences can be predicted successfully, the validity of the analysis depends on the quality of the particular predictive techniques used in conjunction with it. Although the matrix may provide some directions for data collection, its format is not conducive to the incorporation of indirect and dynamic effects. This method is clearly multiple objective and allows for flexibility in defining objectives and actions.

The selection of objectives and the measurement of consequences of actions are crucial. Once these steps have been completed, the method distinguishes clearly between facts and values as long as the disaggregated matrix is presented to the decision makers. If the decision-making process is open, the method can encourage active participation in the formulation of objectives, analysis, and evaluation. Nevertheless, the structuring of these tasks to fit specific situations can be difficult. The time and resources required for this analysis depend on the complexity of the problem and the time allocated for public discussion.

7.3.11 The Surrogate-Worth Tradeoff Method -- multiple-objective analysis

Description. The surrogate-worth tradeoff (SWT) method (Haimes and Hall 1974; Haimes, Hall and Freedman

1975) is derived from welfare economics and extends the approach pioneered in the Harvard Water Program (Maass *et al.* 1962). The theory assumes that people are rational creatures who make choices to maximize net utility, and that the social welfare function is the sum of the utility of each individual. Although many of the attributes of social welfare are not commensurable and prices do not exist for many environmental goods, a surrogate-worth function can be developed through successive comparisons of alternative sets of attributes that differ only marginally.

In the SWT method, iterative interviews are conducted to ask people to compare their relative utilities for sets of attributes on an ordinal scale ranging from -10 to +10. A positive (negative) score indicates a superior (inferior) set while a zero implies indifference. The intensity of the preference is proportional to the absolute value of the rating. For example, the interviewer may suggest an initial combination of flood control benefits and a river quality level and then ask whether the respondents prefer the initial combination or a new one with X more units of flood control at the expense of Y fewer units of water quality. The questioning continues in this direction until the sign of the function's value changes; in other words, when the respondent is no longer willing to give up water purity for flood control.

Applications. Haimes *et al.* (1977) applied the surrogate-worth tradeoff method in basin-wide planning for the Maumee River in Ohio. In this case study, participants were drawn from a Citizens' Advisory Committee composed of representatives from public interest organizations in three states. Although the application was judged a success by the authors, it was a limited test of the method because it only addressed the delineation of objectives, leaving aside the more difficult problems of making choices among specific alternative projects.

Evaluation. The surrogate-worth tradeoff method does not explicitly account for risk. As a result, it is impossible to tell whether respondents are ignoring risk or are assuming some probability of risk. Haimes *et al.* (1977) have suggested setting up probable and ideal scenarios, but that is a limited solution.

The SWT method is incomplete as an environmental assessment method because it assumes that baseline conditions and project impacts already have been predicted. Conceivably, indirect effects could be incorporated if the information is known. Dynamic effects would be difficult to incorporate in this method.

Haimes and Hall designed the method to be compatible with the limited multiple-objective accounts of the U.S. Water Resources Council. Additional objectives could be brought into the analysis, but the method might become too complicated for the respondents when it is expanded.

The SWT method may be prone to the unwarranted confidence sometimes placed in complicated solution techniques that produce a single number. Indeed, the method is subjective and blurs facts and values. To counteract divergent interpretations, all directions should be unambiguous, specific, and exactly the same for all participants.

The validity of the SWT method depends on the selected participants and the weighting scheme for expert versus uninformed opinions. Some theoretical evidence suggests that direct elicitation of values in this manner produces less valid results than an indirect process. The lengthy interview process and complexity of tradeoff questions may limit use of the method to interviews of experts and key actors. Despite a potential for more active involvement by decision makers in the analysis, broad public participation in the method would probably be limited to minor modifications after completion of the assessment.

The SWT method does not handle many of the key problems in environmental assessment because it assumes adequate factual information. Its emphasis on values is useful, but the expense of direct interviews might not be matched by corresponding gains in the validity and reliability of results.

7.3.12 Applied Decision Analysis -- multiple-objective analysis

Description. Decision analysis, also known as utility analysis, is a sophisticated quantitative approach designed largely for use by experts (Keeney and Raiffa 1976). It makes many of the same assumptions as the surrogate-worth tradeoff method, although it places more emphasis on systems modeling and evaluation under risk and uncertainty.

A decision analysis has four steps. The first step is a formal structuring of the problem through the identification of objectives and definition of measurements called "attributes" for each objective. This step includes analysis of the incidence of impacts across groups or sectors, and location of the key decision points in the implementation process. Flexibility is encouraged to allow implementors to take advantage of additional information learned during experience.

In the second step, a team of experts predicts the probability of future values of the attributes for each alternative plan using frequency distributions or a fractile method (Raiffa 1968). The third step requires respondents to express their preferences for each attribute on a decreasing scale of 0 to 1. The range of attribute values considered is obtained from the probability assessment. The shape of the utility function will vary with risk attitudes. The fourth step is for the analyst to use optimization procedures to determine multi-attribute

utility functions for the individuals and the group. After
that, the alternative that maximizes expected utility can
be chosen.

   Applications. Keeney and Raiffa (1976) presented eight
applications of decision analysis, including such problem
settings as air pollution control in New York City, the
development of water quality indices, and airport expansion
in Mexico City. Table 7-15 lists the objectives and
measurement attributes for the airport siting example.
   Keeney and Robilliard (1977) presented an extensive
application of decision analysis for nuclear power plant
siting. After a preliminary screening, they identified nine
sites for detailed analysis under five major objectives:
(1) maximization of public health and safety, (2)
minimization of adverse socioeconomic effects, (3)
maximization of the quality of services, (4) minimization
of system cost, and (5) minimization of adverse ecological
effects. However, the decision analysis concentrated mainly
on the ecological objective, especially on the effects on
salmonids and biologically important areas.
   In analyzing effects on the fish population, three
variables were considered: X--the percentage of adult
salmonids lost per year, Y--the number of salmonids in the
stream, and Z--the total number of salmonids lost in the
lower reaches of the river. These variables were needed
because the impact of the loss of 1,000 fish in a stream
containing 1,500 of that species is much greater than the
same loss in a stream with 50,000 of them. Experts
constructed single-attribute utility functions for X, Y, Z
and estimated the probability distribution of salmonid
losses to calculate expected utilities for each of the nine
sites (figure 7-9).
   Keeney and Robilliard developed a subjective index
for impacts on biologically important areas on a decreasing
scale ranging from 0 to 8. The levels of the scale
reflected the degree and type of biological impact. For
example, level 7 represented loss of 1 square mile of
mature second-growth forest community, 90 percent loss of
local productive wetlands and local endangered species
habitat. By definition, utility values of 1.00 and 0.00
were assigned to impact levels 0 and 8, respectively. The
experts assigned utility values to the intermediate points
by estimating the indifference levels for impact
probabilities. For instance, they were asked to give a
probability such that the consequences of impact level 4
were indifferent to a chance of (p) at impact level 0 and
(1-p) at impact level 8. The indifference probability
turned out to be 0.6 in this case. Figure 7-10 shows the
resulting utility function.
   The next step was to predict the impacts at each site
through field visits, comparisons with similar existing
facilities and sites, and consultations. Keeney and
Robilliard assessed the probability of impacts in each
range at each site through field visits, comparisons with

TABLE 7-15
Objectives and measurement attributes in a decision
analysis of airport siting

Objectives	Attributes
1. Minimize total construction and maintenance <u>costs</u>	X_1 = Total cost in millions of pesos with "suitability" discounting
2. Provide adequate <u>capacity</u> to meet the air traffic demands	X_2 = Practical capacity in terms of the number of aircraft operations per hour
3. Minimize the <u>access time</u> to the airport	$X3$ = Access time to and from the airport in minutes weighted by the number of travelers from each zone in Mexico City
4. Maximize the <u>safety</u> of the system	X_4 = Number of people (including non-passengers) seriously injured or killed per aircraft accident
5. Minimize the <u>social disruption</u> caused by the provision of new airport facilities	X_5 = Number of people displaced by airport development
6. Minimize the effects of <u>noise</u> pollution due to air traffic	X_6 = Number of people subjected to a high noise level

Source: Keeney and Raiffa (1976, p.443). Reprinted by
permission.

210

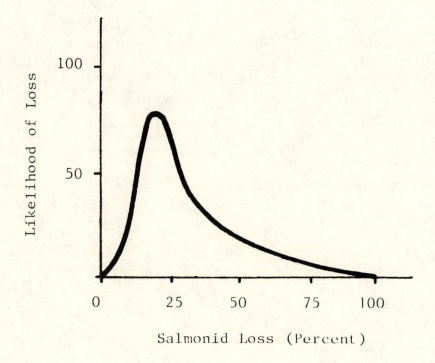

Figure 7-9 Decision analysis of salmonid loss
resulting from a nuclear power plant
(Source: Keeney and Robillard 1976, p. 160).
Reprinted by permission.

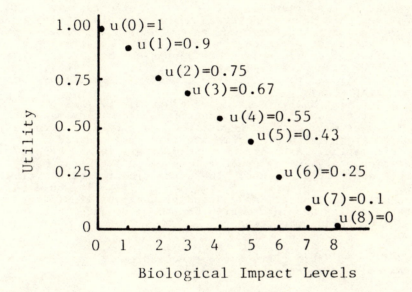

Figure 7-10 Sample utility function for impacts
on biologically important areas
(Source: Keeney and Robillard 1977, p. 163).
Reprinted by permission.

similar existing facilities and sites, and consultations.
They then calculated the expected utility of all sites by
multiplying the probability of an impact within each range
by the corresponding level, and summing these products over
all of the ranges.

Evaluation. Decision analysis treats risk clearly and
comprehensively, and allows for risk preference or risk
aversion. In some cases, it may be difficult to assign
probabilities to possible outcomes. The method is most
useful where weighted objectives are additive; utility
functions are independent, and rankings are based on
expected values. It does not deal with the question of
what effects are considered and their time pattern.
Instead, it assumes that all important effects have been
included in a prior analysis. Decision analysis clearly is
designed for multiple-objective evaluation. This version
is flexible but demanding in that it does not provide a
checklist of objectives. When a problem involves a large
number of objectives and separate utility functions, it may
prove difficult to isolate the effects of specific values
in a simple way.
Decision analysis is designed primarily for
applications with a single identifiable decision maker.
Utility estimates could be derived for public preferences,
but the complexity of the method discourages broad
participation. As a direct method of eliciting values,
decision analysis may produce less valid results than
would an indirect method. The sophistication of decision
analysis requires a lot of time and effort. It would be
expensive to generate models and projections of system
states and gather information on the value judgments of a
large number of participants.

7.3.13 The Habitat Evaluation Procedures -- resource
management/simulation approach

Description. The habitat evaluation procedures (HEP)
assess the effects of development on a single aspect of the
environment -- fish and wildlife habitat (U.S. Fish and
Wildlife Service 1980). The HEP can support
recommendations for selecting project alternatives or for
designing mitigation and compensation measures. The method
is based on the assumption that changes in habitat
quantity or quality can serve as a shortcut for estimating
impacts on wildlife populations. It includes both a
nonmonetary and a monetary procedure. The method is
carried out by a team of experts.
The first step in the HEP is to identify the habitat
types in the project area by examining plant associations
and land cover types through aerial photos or field work.
Each habitat type is treated separately throughout the
analysis. The second step is to select an unspecified
number of indicator species based on their (1) economic or

social importance, (2) sensitivity to proposed actions, (3) role in the community's nutrient cycling and energy flows, and (4) representativeness in various ecological niches.

The third step is to estimate the change in "habitat units" associated with the proposed alternatives. Habitat units (HUs) are the product of the area of habitat and the "habitat suitability index" (HSI). The HU value is calculated separately for each indicator species and site. It may be annualized over the life of the project or expressed as percent changes from baseline conditions at various target dates in the future. The impact of the project is defined as the difference between the number of habitat units for each species with and without the project. The weighting and aggregation of habitat units across species is optional in the HEP.

The method relies on habitat value functions to estimate the suitability of a habitat for various species rather than the use of vegetative cover types as an indicator. These value functions range on a scale of 0.0 to 1.0. They are obtained through the use of models based on measurable variables and are similar to the broader-purpose graphs used in the EES and WRAM. Schamberger, Farmer, and Terrell (1982) have discussed habitat suitability models for the HEP. The process of documenting assumptions in model-building may increase the repeatability of HSI estimates (Ellis 1979).

Since a proposed action may result in gains in habitat for some species and losses for others, a systematic means of weighting these tradeoffs is needed. The HEP accomplishes this weighting through an optional process of determining "relative value indices" (RVIs) for each species in a pairwise ranking system similar to the one used in WRAM. The criteria for the rankings include the abundance, vulnerability, replaceability, and aesthetic value of the species as well as the efforts by the public and private sectors to manage the species. Figure 7-11 and Tables 7-16 to 7-18 provide examples of how the method is used.

An optional step places a monetary value on the estimated fish and wildlife populations corresponding to different HU levels. Consider the following example. The estimated future deer population in an area (44) is derived by multiplying the baseline population (88) by the ratio of the future HU levels to the baseline levels (0.5). The team then estimates the harvest or use rates associated with the change in the deer population. In this case, it is a loss of 102 sustainable user-days of hunting and a decrease of 14 in the annual deer catch. If each user-day of hunting time is worth $25 to hunters, the recreational value of the site would decrease by $2,550. In addition, if each harvested deer is worth $200, hunters would also lose annual benefits of $2,800 for the catch. For water resources projects covered under Principles and Standards, the economic evaluation under the HEP follows the procedures of the U.S. Water Resources Council (1979).

214

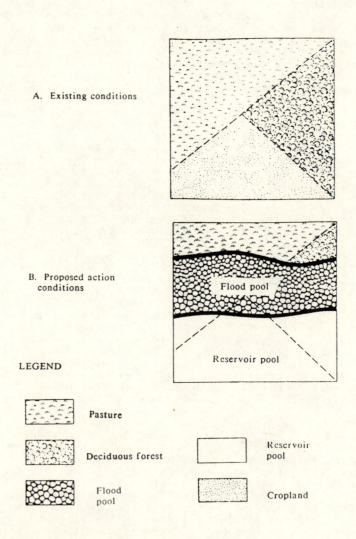

A. Existing conditions

B. Proposed action
conditions

Flood pool

Reservoir pool

LEGEND

Pasture

Deciduous forest

Reservoir pool

Flood pool

Cropland

Figure 7-11 Determining changes in the quantity of
habitat under the HEP (Source: U.S. Fish and
Wildlife Service, Figure 5-1).

TABLE 7-16
Calculating annualized habitat unit values for a single
species under one plan in the HEP

Evaluation Species	Change in Annual Average Habitat Units	Relative Value Index	Adjusted Value (HUxRVI)
White-tailed deer	-722	0.60	-433
Ruffled grouse	-400	0.78	-312
Red squirrel	-300	0.10	-30
Red fox	-120	0.35	-42
Yellow-rumped warbler	-550	1.00	-550
Total			-1,367

Source: U.S. Fish and Wildlife Service (1980, Table 6-2).

TABLE 7-17
Determining the relative value index for different species in the HEP.

Evaluation species	Criteria and Weights			Relative Value	Relative Value Index
	Scarcity (0.33)	Vulnerability (0.50)	Replaceability (0.17)		
White-tailed deer	0.50	0.80	0.20		
Product[a]	0.17	0.40	0.03	0.60	0.60
Ruffed grouse	0.80	0.90	0.40		
Product[a]	0.26	0.45	0.07	0.78	0.78
Red squirrel	0.10	0.10	0.10		
Product[a]	0.03	0.05	0.02	0.10	0.10
Red fox	0.60	0.20	0.30		
Product[a]	0.20	0.10	0.05	0.35	0.35
Yellow-rumped warbler	1.00	1.00	1.00		
Product[a]	0.33	0.50	0.17	1.00	1.00

Source: U.S. Fish and Wildlife Service (1980, Figure 6-3).

[a]Criteria weight multiplied by the species rating

TABLE 7-18
Calculating tradeoffs between two habitats for different
species in the HEP

Evaluation Species	Change in Annual Average Habitat Units	Relative Value Index	Adjusted Value (HUxRVI)
White-tailed deer	−722	0.60	−433
Ruffled grouse	−400	0.78	−312
Red squirrel	−300	0.10	−30
Red fox	−120	0.35	−42
Yellow-rumped warbler	−550	1.00	−550
Total			−1,367

Source: U.S. Fish and Wildlife Service (1980, Table 6-2).

Unit-day values based on expert judgments of the public's
willingness to pay are used for other projects.

   Applications. The U.S. Fish and Wildlife Service has
applied the HEP extensively in preparing reports required
by the Fish and Wildlife Coordination Act for all federal
water resource projects. Schamberger (1982) discussed an
application in siting facilities for a surface mine and in
planning reclamation activities.

   Evaluation. The HEP do not incorporate probabilities
of impacts into the analysis, but the evaluation team could
estimate confidence levels for HU values. Since the method
makes no attempt to model ecosystem interactions
explicitly, the degree to which indirect effects on fish
and wildlife are considered depends on the study team. The
method is based on static relationships although it does
estimate impacts at a series of points in time. A more
careful analysis of wildlife populations requires dynamic
models (Adams 1980; Boyce 1982).
   This single-objective method is not concerned with
impacts on other aspects of the environment besides fish
and wildlife. The basic procedures do not deal with
utilitarian, aesthetic, or scientific values of flora and
fauna. The optional monetary evaluation is oriented
mainly to the value of person-days of hunting or fishing
and the catch of pelts or fish.

Facts and values are merged in the HEP because only the acreage and index values are displayed. Furthermore, the multiplicative factors make the HU index very sensitive to small errors. The method depends heavily on the subjective judgment of experts. The ability to coordinate this team and reach a consensus is critical. Although the evaluation team can include representatives from state or local agencies as well as the federal government, the procedure does not facilitate public participation.

The method is relatively straightforward, but a major application can require a lot of resources. The U.S. Fish and Wildlife Service estimates that a computer-assisted application for a major water resources project with 3 proposed actions, 20 evaluation species, and 5 cover types over 20,000 acres would require 49-98 person-days of work.

7.3.14 Adaptive Environmental Assessment and Management -- resource management/simulation

Description. The adaptive environmental assessment process (AEA) is designed to be responsive to changes in both the decision-making and environmental domains (Holling et al. 1978). It is not a cookbook approach. The heart of the AEA process is personal contact and communication in a series of workshops centered around the creation and solution of a systems model. The process begins with the selection of a project manager who coordinates a team of interdisciplinary experts. A core group from the study team runs the workshops, develops models, and analyzes alternatives. Other specialists are called in as needed.

The AEA process emphasizes the importance of holding a workshop in the early stages of planning to bring decision makers and resource managers together for a short, intensive session to define the problem and identify information needs. The initial workshop helps the key actors understand the problem, share a common sense of identity and purpose, and feel that the subsequent analysis will meet their needs. The initial stages aim at building momentum and transferring information smoothly rather than producing a consensus on the details. By the end of the first workshop, a first-cut model of the problem should be ready for further refinement. This model does not have to be computerized or a mathematical representation, but it should reflect the important attributes and values of the system. Subsequently, the core group develops the model further to assist in analyzing the impacts of alternative policies.

During a second workshop, the full team and decision makers review each specialist's plans for detailed data collection and testing of options. Following field research, the model is simplified and tested for invalidity. After more in-depth investigation, a longer, third workshop convenes to make final revisions in the model, incorporate new data, and evaluate the resource management alternatives. The AEA process emphasizes the use of sensitivity analysis to explore the implications of varying the model's time and space boundaries and basic assumptions, and to explore the range of uncertainty.

The final step produces information packages for decision makers and publics that summarize the outcomes of the simulation runs. The authors recommend the use of pictures and graphs to increase the comprehensibility and usefulness of the results.

Applications. Holling *et al.* (1978) have presented five case studies of adaptive environmental assessment and management. One of the most cited cases concerns spruce budworm infestations in the forests of New Brunswick, Canada. This study included the participation of scientists as well as local and national government officials. The study team based the model of the budworm - forest interaction on four key variables: the host tree, foliage condition, budworm population, and weather. It identified indicators of immediate and long-run concern.

The goal of the exercise was the creative design of management policies rather than the ranking of alternatives. Figure 7-12 illustrates some of the graphs produced by the model. It was claimed that the analysis led to significant changes in the way the management agency collected and analyzed information. The process and the results have been extended to other areas of the North American boreal forest. AEA has also been applied to over fifty resource management problems in North America and Europe, and for the Nam Pong River basin in Thailand (Mekong Secretariat 1981).

Evaluation. The AEA process promotes a useful set of general principles on ecosystem flux, risk and uncertainty, and the role of information in decision making. It preserves flexibility by predisposing participants to respond to new information, preliminary failures, and unexpected conditions as opportunities to refine the model and design alternative policies. The AEA process can handle important indirect effects, cumulative effects, and feedback cycles because of its emphasis on systems modeling. As a reaction to static assessment methods, the AEA process strives for a dynamic analysis of natural systems through graphs of simulation runs showing the behavior of key indicators over time and space.

Although AEA is based on ecological modeling, the authors tried to cover multiple objectives by including representatives of various disciplinary backgrounds in the study team. Since the process does not specify a systematic way of dealing with multiple objectives, the results are very sensitive to the composition of the study team.

The separation of facts and values becomes difficult once a model has been developed. Users of a model may place too much reliance on numerical solutions without scrutinizing the model's basic assumptions and limitations;

220

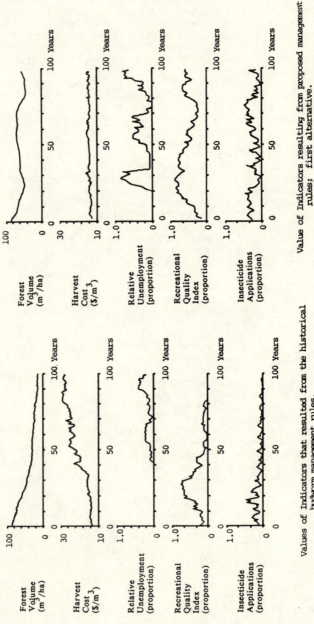

Figure 7-12 Calculating a habitat suitability index for a single species and habitat
type in the HEP (Adapted from: U.S. Fish and Wildlife Service 1980, Figure C-1).

however, this problem can be overcome through sensitivity analysis to uncover the effects of the assumptions. The AEA process depends heavily on expert opinion and assumes a high degree of consensus among different experts and across disciplines. Although decision makers are an integral part of the assessment and the results are packaged to facilitate communication, the public remains largely outside the process.

An adaptive procedure is time consuming, but resource allotments can be varied to suit the needs of the problem and meet constraints. Managing the logistics of the workshops can be complex. The process recognizes that more information is not always desirable and can hinder decision making and that implementation should be emphasized throughout an environmental assessment.

7.4 CONCLUSIONS

There are two basic approaches to the collection, manipulation, simplification, and display of information for an environmental assessment. One family of methods relies on the quantitative expression of environmental values to allow logical or mathematical manipulation, and display the results in numerical tables. Methods falling into this first group include METLAND, the EES, WRAM, the goals achievement matrix, the surrogate-worth tradeoff method, and decision analysis. Another family of methods makes greater use of qualitative measures and graphic displays. The EQA, KSIM and the Sorenson network fall into this category. The AEA process combines aspects of both types of methods.

Most of the methods reviewed in this chapter rely on experts or a small group of experts and key decision makers to carry out the assessment. Few of the methods address the problems of eliciting and incorporating environmental values from the broad array of groups in affected communities. Since as chapter 3 pointed out, environmental assessment is part of a larger political process, improved methods are needed to accommodate more direct public consultation.

Figure 7-13 summarizes the extent to which these methods meet our seven evaluation criteria. Because some methods do not attempt to serve all of the functions of an environmental assessment, certain criteria are not applicable to particular methods. Readers should be wary of claiming that one method is superior to another because it satisfies a larger number of criteria. The relative importance of any one criterion depends on the purpose and context of a particular environmental assessment. Some important contextual factors include whether the assessment is carried out in the early or final stages of project formulation and design, the seriousness of the potential impacts, and the available resources.

CRITERIA	McHARG'S OVERLAY (McHARG 1969)	METLAND (FABOS, GREENE & JOYNER 1978)	GOALS ACHIEVEMENT MATRIX (HILL 1968)	SURROGATE WORTH TRADEOFF (HAIMES, HALL & FREEDMAN 1975)	DECISION ANALYSIS (KEENEY & RAIFFA 1976)	LEOPOLD MATRIX (LEOPOLD ET AL. 1971)	EES (DEE ET AL. 1972)	EQA (DUKE ET AL. 1977)	WRAM (SOLOMON ET AL. 1977)	WES (GALLOWAY 1978)	NETWORK ANALYSIS (SORENSON 1971)	AEA (HOLLING ed. 1978)	HEP (U.S. FISH & WILDLIFE SERVICE 1976)	KSIM (KANE, VERTINSKY & THOMPSON 1973)
1. Explicitly treats the probabilistic nature of environmental effects	N	N	P	N	S	N	N	N	N	S	N	S	P	N
2. Examines indirect and feedback effects	P	P	O	O	O	N	N	N	N	P	S	S	P	P
3. Considers the dynamic nature of environmental systems	N	N	O	O	O	N	N	N	N	P	P	S	P	S
4. Uses a multiple-objectives approach	N	N	S	S	S	N	P	N	S	N	P	P	N	O
5. Makes a clear distinction between facts and values	N	P	S	P	S	N	N	S	P	N	N	P	N	O
6. Encourages participation by public and decision makers	N	P	S	P	N	N	N	P	N	S	N	P	N	P
7. Parsimonious in requirements of time and money	P	N	N	N	N	S	P	P	N	P	P	N	S	—

KEY: S SATISFIES CRITERION
P PARTIALLY SATISFIES CRITERION
N DOES NOT SATISFY
O NOT APPLICABLE

Figure 7-13 Summary evaluation of fourteen environmental assessment methods

In less developed countries, certain of the criteria
are likely to be of overriding importance due to the (1)
dominance of unfulfilled, basic human needs, (2) scarcity
of trained personnel, (3) lack of baseline data, (4) low
degree of public participation, and (5) high cultural
diversity (Sammy and Canter 1982). In these countries, it
is especially important to choose a multiple-objective
approach with relatively low requirements for trained
personnel and data. Public participation may be less easy
to achieve, but even more important in ensuring the
successful implementation of projects in less developed
countries. Some of the same considerations apply for local
governments undertaking small projects in developed
countries.

Nevertheless, some judgments can be made about the
overall utility of the methods discussed in developed and
less developed countries. For example, the AEA process has
several advantages over checklist approaches because it can
reflect a greater richness of scientific detail, the
dynamic structure of natural systems, and risk and
uncertainty. The disadvantage of the AEA process is that
it relies on the interaction between experts and decision
makers to incorporate social values, so it only partially
satisfies the need to distinguish facts and values.

The goals-achievement matrix also ranks high on many
of the criteria, but it is incomplete as an environmental
assessment method since it does not provide any guidance on
the prediction of environmental effects or on their
aggregation into an environmental quality account.
Decision analysis resembles the goals-achievement matrix in
this regard, but it gives more explicit treatment to
uncertainty. The surrogate-worth tradeoff method is easier
to use than decision analysis in eliciting value weights.
However, the surrogate-worth tradeoff method does not
address uncertainty and also tends to limit participation
to a few key decision makers.

The other methods reviewed here are more limited or
special purpose in character. Although these methods may
satisfy only a few of the criteria, some of them make
important contributions that can be incorporated in the
development of improved methods for environmental
assessment. For example, WRAM contains a useful technique
for representing value judgments in scaling the relative
importance of a large number of different environmental
effects. Computerized maps of the sort produced by METLAND
can be useful in a land-suitability analysis. Similarly, a
Leopold matrix can help in screening potential impacts that
should be considered in a more detailed assessment.
Chapter 8 synthesizes some of the best features of existing
methods and introduces considerations drawn from theories
discusses in previous chapters to develop a new method for
environmental assessment--SAGE.

8

SAGE: A New Participant-Value Method for Environmental Assessment

The review of environmental assessment methods in Chapter 7 shows that substantial advances have occurred over the last decade in identifying the physical, chemical, and biological effects of development as well as in eliciting and displaying expert judgments about the relative importance of these effects. However, most of these methods rely on the values of experts, either alone or with a small group of decision makers. Few methods are concerned with valid ways of representing the values of a broad array of groups for more democratic decision making. In response to this deficiency, the authors have synthesized a new method called SAGE, which builds on the best characteristics of several previous methods. SAGE stands for Social judgment capturing -- Adaptive -- Goals-achievement -- Environmental assessment. This chapter presents the procedures of SAGE and reports the results of a trial application of the method to a watershed management problem in a growing urban area.

Among the methods reviewed in Chapter 7 are two notable advances in the extension of benefit-cost analysis to cover multiple objectives (Haimes and Hall 1974; Keeney and Raiffa 1976). These methods have two key characteristics that distinguish them from other efforts. First, they are careful to group the effects of alternative projects into several accounts representing separate objectives in such a way that the effects within accounts are commensurable, but the effects across accounts are not forced into the same measurement units. Second, they provide a formal means for experts and decision makers to assign relative value weights to each account. The weights are assigned by constructing proxy utility functions to rank the alternatives directly.

225

Instead, SAGE follows the opposite strategy, which is
suggested by social judgment theory (see section 5.2.2).
This strategy is based on deducing the value weights
indirectly by analyzing the decisions that people make. To
do so, the participants are given identical factual
descriptions of the effects of various alternatives on each
objective. The participants are asked to rank the
alternatives in order of their preferences. The analyst can
infer the relative value weights on the objectives from
these rankings. This strategy is likely to produce more
valid weights because it is less demanding of participants
since they do have to make explicit tradeoffs that they are
not used to making among different objectives. It is also
less time consuming. Thus, SAGE makes it possible to elicit
values across a broader range of societal groups. In
addition, the analysis measures the internal consistency of
each participant's assignment of the weights.

SAGE is adaptive because it recognizes the principles
set forth by Holling (1978) for effective fact-finding: the
interdependence between the search for data and the setting
of objectives, and the need for a preliminary analysis to
define the bounds of the problem and the scope of the
information required. Checklists such as those developed by
Leopold *et al.* (1971) or Burchell and Listokin (1975) can
be useful in deciding what information to obtain, but their
relevance is mainly limited to the initial steps in the
process.

Several other methods deal with scaling similar kinds
of effects within accounts and weighting objectives. For
example, the environmental evaluation system (Dee *et al.*
1972) is based on predetermined scaling functions and
weights. WRAM (Solomon *et al.* 1977) also relies on
previously established scaling functions, but it allows the
substitution of expert judgments produced through a
pairwise ranking procedure (Dean and Nishry 1965). By
contrast, SAGE avoids predetermined scales and weights
because each situation is different. SAGE also recognizes
that although scaling factors are a matter of scientific
opinion, value determinations should not be reserved for
experts alone.

One of the most common pitfalls of previous methods is
the blurring of facts and values. SAGE avoids this pitfall
by tabulating the values held by various groups, rather
than aggregating the results into a single index of
societal values. In this way, it presents a wider spectrum
of information to decision makers to help them understand
the sources of agreement and conflict and hence the
political implications of building a consensus or mediating
disputes. A variant of the goals-achievement matrix (Hill
1973) is used in SAGE to cross-tabulate values and
multidimensional effects.

As chapters 3 to 6 noted, there are many valid
approaches to the problem of eliciting societal values.
Political theories suggest either deriving the values from
legislative, executive, and judicial decisions; or

restructuring mechanisms for public choice to increase the direct participation of citizens in decision making. Economic theory offers a menu of approaches that emphasize the use of preferences revealed in actual markets; or, in their absence, values expressed directly through survey techniques. Theories from psychology deal with how environments are perceived and values are formed and can provide some generalizable insights and guidance on techniques for eliciting preferences. Energy analysis highlights the physical and ecological constraints that bound feasible alternatives. Although each of the above approaches has some shortcomings, they can be useful in environmental assessment separately or in conjunction with the SAGE method. Decision makers should not rely exclusively on the values of any one technique rooted solely in political, economic, psychological, or ecological theories. SAGE offers a multiple-objective framework for incorporating diverse values.

8.2   DESCRIPTION OF THE SAGE METHOD

SAGE consists of four tasks: (1) predicting the physical, chemical and biological attributes of alternative actions; (2) scaling the attributes into accounts of beneficial and adverse effects on objectives; (3) eliciting relative value weights that individuals or groups attach to each objective; and (4) presenting the findings in a form useful to decision makers (figure 8-1).

8.2.1   The Prediction of Effects

The first task, the prediction of effects, is primarily scientific and must be adapted to specific problem settings. For a relatively simple project such as a single-purpose, public water supply system, there may be a relatively small number of measurable indicators for the attributes (sub-objectives). Examples of broad categories of attributes include the safe yield of water, water quality, minimum downstream releases, area of terrestrial habitats destroyed, effects on fish populations, and cultural, historic, and scenic impacts. The behaviorial responses to these effects may include changes in land use, rates of water consumption, and recreational use of the reservoir.

8.2.2   Scaling the Attributes Into Accounts

The second task, the grouping of related effects into a few accounts, involves data reduction. Whenever possible, effects on environmental amenities and the productivity of natural resources are reflected under the economic objective using the techniques discussed in chapter 4. This

228

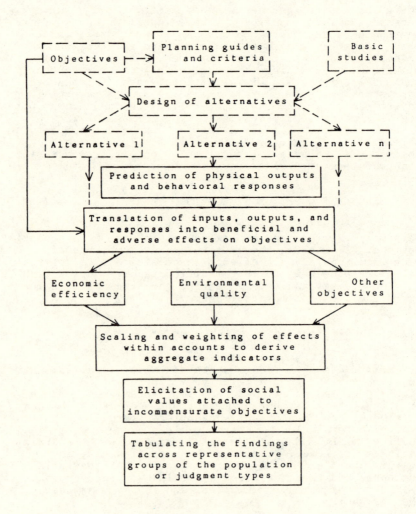

Figure 8-1 Analytical tasks comprising the Sage
method (Adapted from Hyman, Moreau and Stiftel
1984b, p. 214). Reprinted by permission.

allows diverse effects expressed in monetary terms to be added up and compared.

Classifying noneconomic effects into like categories and scaling them to summarize the net change in the account for an objective requires the use of less well-developed measures and procedures. It often is difficult to define measurable indicators for such attributes as aesthetic quality or the maintenance of biological diversity. It also is more complex to make tradeoffs among attributes with the noneconomic accounts. For example, what is the net change in environmental quality when bottomland wildlife habitat is lost while downstream aquatic life is enhanced? Where effects cannot be quantifed in monetary terms, the attributes may be scaled from 0 to 1 and weighted by their relative importance so that they can be combined into accounts.

The relative importance coefficients (RICs) are calculated through a technique involving pairwise rankings of all combinations of attributes such that the sum of all combinations of the RICs within each account equals unity (Dean and Nishry 1965). For each pair, the attribute judged more (less) important is assigned a value of one (zero). Then, a total for each attribute is determined by summing the ones and zeros over all pairs in which that attribute appears. The RIC for attribute k under objective j is calculated by dividing the total points for attribute k by the grand total for all attributes grouped under objective j. To avoid assigning a RIC of zero to a real attribute, a dummy attribute that is less important than all other attributes can be included.

An aggregate index of the account score for an objective may be obtained by taking a linear combination of the scaled effects of the attributes weighted by their respective RICs. This step can be summarized mathematically:

$$x_{ij} = \sum_k (RIC_{jk})(G_{ijk})$$

where $RIC(j)(k)$ is the relative importance coefficient for attribute k under objective j; $G(i)(j)(k)$ is the effect of alternative i on attribute k; and $x(i)(j)$ is the scaled score of alternative i on objective j.

The RICs yield a judgment about the relative importance of attributes within accounts, but do not necessarily imply that the effects across accounts are expressed on comparable scales. To ensure that the effects are commensurable, the $G(i)(j)(k)$ scores for nonmonetary effects must be reduced to common scales. One such scale can be obtained by assigning a value of 0.0 to the least desirable outcome for each attribute, 1.0 to the most desirable outcome, and appropriate values within the interval to intermediate outcomes.

This scaling procedure has some limitations. The largest RIC that can be assigned to any attribute is $(2/n)$, where n is the number of attributes. Also, the selection of a particular scale for each factor is arbitrary and relies heavily upon expert judgment. Nonetheless, when accompanied by an explanatory text and a full description of the actual effects, this procedure can be useful for summarizing and comparing effects.

8.2.3 Eliciting the Value Weights for Accounts

The previous scaling step produced a preferential ranking of alternatives within each of the accounts, but it does not indicate how individuals or groups would weight the net effects on the diverse accounts in making tradeoffs. The third task, elicitation of the value weights placed on the accounts, is critical in assessing the social welfare implications of alternative actions. The value weights for the accounts are elicited by a Q-sort technique (Pitt and Zube 1979). With this technique, participants are asked to sort cards according to their preferred outcomes. Each card contains a verbal description of the effects of alternative decisions or actions on each of the objectives, and also the scaled numerical scores for all of the accounts. The rationale for this technique is that respondents find it easier to make and revise such pairwise comparisons by moving cards, rather than by considering a list of items on paper.

Using regression analysis, the analyst can infer the weights that each individual implicitly places on the objectives and can perform an analysis of variance. To do so, it is necessary to hypothesize a model that relates each participant's rankings to the contribution of the alternative to each objective. Given a set of alternatives, data on the contributions of each alternative to the various objectives, and the scores assigned to each alternative by the participants, the value weights attached to each objective can be estimated. A linear model is simplest, but a polynomial model can be used if there is reason to believe that the rankings include nonlinearities or interactions.

A practical difficulty arises when the number of objectives equals or exceeds the number of alternative projects under consideration. A regression analysis can be conducted only when there are at least $(m+2)$ observations to obtain least squares estimates in a linear model containing m independent variables. If the number of objectives exceeds the number of decision variables, then some objectives must be redundant (Cohon 1978). This difficulty is easily overcome by either reducing the number of objectives or generating hypothetical sets of alternative projects for the purpose of estimating the value weights. Adapting additional combinations of accounts from the real alternatives is a convenient way to generate hypothetical alternatives. This exercise may have the indirect benefit of broadening the range of real alternatives under consideration.

8.2.4 Presenting the Information on Facts and Values

The fourth task, highlighting the range of information on value weights, increases the utility of an environmental assessment to decision makers. Value weights may vary systematically by geographic location, socioeconomic status, political philosophy, and personality type. If decision makers know who expresses what values, it can help them evaluate how widespread the values are and how intensely they are held. The value weights also can be aggregated to identify judgment types--groupings of participants who share similar weights on a set of attributes (Hammond *et al.* 1975). Classification of preferences by judgment types may be useful in conflict resolution because it highlights the differences among groups and indicates whether a constituency is likely to form around a potential compromise.

8.3 REPORT ON A PRELIMINARY FIELD TEST OF SAGE

8.3.1 Description of the Study Area

As a preliminary field test of the method, SAGE was tested in a practical problem concerning alternative urban development patterns for the Falls of the Neuse watershed in piedmont North Carolina (figure 8-2). Construction of the Falls of the Neuse reservoir began in 1982. The reservoir has a design capacity of 396,800 acre-feet and will serve the purposes of flood storage, recreation, and dead storage.

This watershed spans 760 square miles upstream of the dam and is envisioned as the long-term water supply for Raleigh and environs. Urbanization poses a potential threat to use of the reservoir for water supply due to possible nonpoint loadings of phosphorous, sediment, lead, and toxic pollutants (TJCOG 1979). The population of the watershed was 122,000 in 1975 and may reach 200,000 by the year 2000 (TJCOG 1980). While population densities averaged over the entire basin probably will remain relatively low, much of the growth is expected to be concentrated in northeast Durham or north of Raleigh. One concern is that recreation and other amenities associated with the reservoir may induce additional growth in adjacent areas, creating a variety of environmental impacts and difficulties for the delivery of urban services.

The Triangle J Council of Governments(TJCOG) established two committees for planning in the watershed: a Policy Advisory Group (PAG) with interests in areawide water quality planning and land use, and a Watershed

232

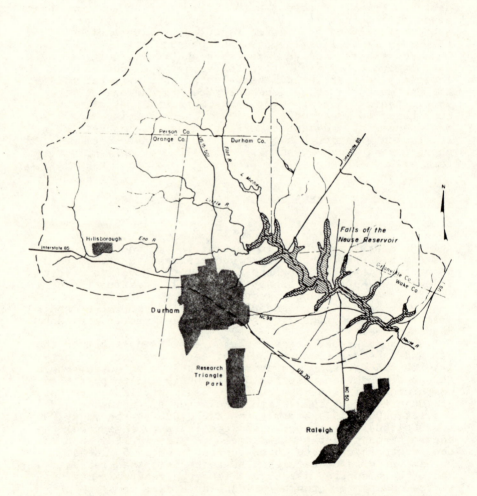

Figure 8-2 Watershed for the Falls of the Neuse Reservoir

Planning Task Force (WPTF) comprising federal, state, and local officials. TJCOG also has its own technical staff. These three groups served as the participants in the preliminary field test of SAGE.

8.3.2   Procedures of the Field Test

The study team began with established statements of objectives for the watershed (TJCOG 1979, 1980; WPTF 1980). We grouped these objectives into five accounts similar to the format of the U.S. Water Resources Council (1973,1980). The accounts considered were (1) national economic development, (2) regional fiscal impacts, (3) environmental quality, (4) public service accessibility, and (5) degree of government intervention. Each account was subdivided into measurable attributes that were expected to differ across development patterns.

In consultation with local planners, the study team developed two alternative growth scenarios for the Falls of the Neuse watershed for the period 1980 to 2000. Since this was a preliminary field test, we did not include a larger number of alternatives. Shuford and Fried (1980) discussed the construction of the scenarios and the growth management strategies needed to bring them about.

The first scenario envisions conventional land use practices with most development occurring as single-family dwellings on relatively large lots scattered widely throughout the southern part of the watershed (figure 8-3). The second scenario assumes advanced land use practices with government policies aimed at reducing the amount of developed land and concentrating the growth more compactly in the watershed (figure 8-4). Under the advanced practices scenario, most new growth would be confined to small lots of multifamily structures within or close to existing urban areas. Industrial or commercial land uses do not occupy a large share of the growth under either scenario.

Estimating the likely effects of the two scenarios on the attributes defined for each account proved to be the most time-consuming aspect of the application. Aggregation of the effects on the attributes within the accounts presented no difficulty for the national economic development and regional fiscal impact accounts because all the attributes in those two accounts are measured on a common, additive scale (money units). However, government intervention was only ranked on an ordinal scale. Since the various attributes of environmental quality and public service accessibility are described in diverse physical units, it was necessary to convert those effects to a common scale.

The first step in calculating the scaled scores for the incommensurable attributes was to determine the relative importance coefficients for each attribute using the technique of pairwise comparison discussed earlier

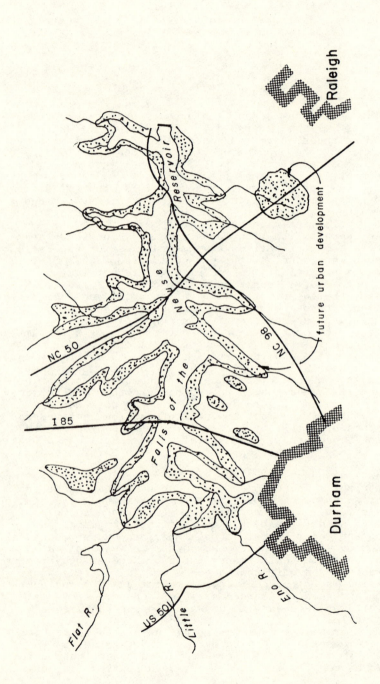

Figure 8-3 Projected land uses under conventional practices.

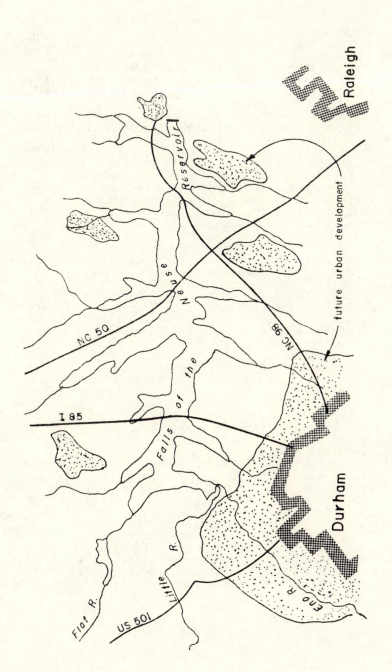

Figure 8-4 Projected land uses under advanced practices.

(table 8-1). For example, farmland losses were ranked as
more important than three other attributes. Dividing three
by fifteen (the sum of the ranks for all attributes under
that objective), yields a scaling factor of 0.20.

The second step in the scaling procedure for each
attribute was to assign one point to the preferred effect
across two scenarios and zero points to the other effect.
For example, since a smaller loss of prime farmland is
preferred, the advanced practices scenario received one
point on this attribute, while the conventional practices
scenario received no points.

The third step was to multiply these point scores by
the relative importance coefficient for the corresponding
attribute; this yields the scaled scores (table 8-2). In
the case of the farmland attribute, the scaled score was
0.2 under the advanced practices scenario and 0.0 under the
conventional practices scenario. The advanced practices
scenario turned out to be superior in four of the five
accounts, but required more government intervention than
the conventional practices scenario.

To estimate the implicit value weights attached to the
accounts, the study team followed the Q-sort technique
discussed earlier. The participants were given identical
decks of cards. Each card contained a description of the
effects of alternative projects on each objective as well
as the verbal scores corresponding to the scaled numerical
scores (figure 8-5). The participants arranged the cards
in order of their preferences and also scored the
alternatives on a scale ranging from 0 to 100.

In this case, weights were estimated for five
accounts, so seven observations were required to estimate
the variance of the error term. Since we had formulated
only two real scenarios, it was necessary to generate at
least five hypothetical scenarios representing variations
in the effects of development. For greater precision in
estimating the weights, we worked with a total of
twenty-five scenarios.

Entries in the hypothetical scenarios were established
by taking combinations of "low," "medium," and "high"
quality levels for the five accounts (table 8-3). For each
account, the low (high) quality level was defined as the
scaled score of the least (most) advantageous of the two
real scenarios. The medium level was defined as the
midpoint between the least and most advantageous scores.
Higher scaled scores represented greater costs for national
economic development and fiscal impacts, but greater
environmental quality and public service benefits. A
higher scaled score indicated more government intervention.

TABLE 8-1
Calculation of scaling factors for the nonmonetary accounts

A. Environmental Quality

| Attributes | Pairwise Comparisons of Attributes | | | | | | Sum of Ranks | Scaling Factors (RIC_{jk}) |
	A	B	C	D	E	F		
A. Forest land losses	–	0	0	0	0	1	1.0	0.07
B. Farmland losses	1	–	0	0	1	1	3.0	0.20
C. Critical habitat losses	1	1	–	0	1	1	4.0	0.27
D. Increases in toxic runoff	1	1	1	–	1	1	5.0	0.33
E. Increases in phosphorus runoff	1	0	0	0	–	1	2.0	0.13
F. Dummy	0	0	0	0	0	–	0.0	0.00
TOTAL							15.0	1.00

B. Public Services

| Attributes | Pairwise Comparisons of Attributes | | | Sum of Ranks | Scaling Factors (RIC_{jk}) |
	G	H	I		
G. Accessibility of transporatation facilities	–	1	1	2.0	0.67
H. Accessibility of recreation facilities	0	–	1	1.0	0.33
I. Dummy	0	0	–	0.0	0.00
TOTAL				3.0	1.00

TABLE 8-2
Effects and scaled account scores under the two scenarios

Accounts and Attributes	Relative Importance Coefficients (RIC_{jk})	Current Practices Scenario		Advanced Practices Scenario	
		Effects (G_{ijk})	Scaled Score (X_{ij})	Effects (G_{ijk})	Scaled Score (X_{ij})
1. Net National Economic Development Costs ($ million/year)	--	58.0	--	37.0	--
a. Space heating costs	--	23.0	--	14.0	--
b. Transportation energy costs	--	61.0	--	48.0	--
c. Lost farm wages	--	0.7	--	0.4	--
d. New construction benefits	--	-26.6	--	-25.0	--
2. Regional Fiscal Impact Costs ($ million/year)	--	41.0	--	29.0	--
a. Road construction	--	37.0	--	26.0	--
b. Water and sewer line construction	--	2.3	--	2.1	--
c. Service transportation	--	1.7	--	1.3	--
3. Environmental Quality			0.0		1.0
a. Forest land lost (acres)	0.07	28,000.0	0.0	4,000.0	0.07
b. Prime farm land lost (acres)	0.20	1,200.0	0.0	360.0	0.20

Accounts and Attributes	Relative Importance Coefficients (RIC_{jk})	Current Practices Scenario Effects (G_{ijk})	Current Practices Scenario Scaled Score (X_{ij})	Advanced Practices Scenario Effects (G_{ijk})	Advanced Practices Scenario Scaled Score (X_{ij})
c. Critical nature areas lost (acres)	0.27	20.0	0.0	0.0	0.27
d. Increase in toxic runoff (%)	0.33	28.0	0.0	15.0	0.33
e. Increase in phosphorus runoff (lbs./year)	0.13	37,000.0	0.0	0.0	0.13
4. Public Service Accessibility			0.0		1.0
a. Population within 1 mile of bus service (%)	0.67	35.0	0.0	46.0	0.67
b. Population within 1 mile of local park (%)	0.33	25.0	0.0	60.0	0.33
5. Degree of Governmental Intervention		[a]	1.0	[b]	0.0

[a] Current Regulations only.
[b] Imposition of new regulations: preferential taxing, capital facilities programming, large lot zoning outside urban areas, public septic tank maintenance.

Source: Hyman, Moreau and Stiftel (1984a, p. 918). Reprinted by permission.

Individual _____

Alternative R   Rank _____   Score _____

The adverse consequences of urban growth on the regional economy are intermediate. There is a **net annual cost of $58 million** to the region resulting from a sizable increase in the costs of space heating and transportation, and a sizable loss in agricultural employment. Increases in home construction employment help to keep total costs from being even greater.

Increases in governmental expenditures to service new development are greatest. **Annually, government budgets increase by $41 million**, $210 for each resident of the watershed.

The **adverse environmental consequences of urban growth are greatest.** Algal blooms are expected to occur frequently in the reservoir during the summer, and will occasionally spread into the lower portions of the lake. Lead loadings increase by 18,000 pounds over present levels and 30,000 acres of forestland is lost to new development.

The effects on **accessibility of social services are least desirable.** Only 35 percent of the population are served by bus transit lines. Only 25 percent of the population live within walking distance of a park or recreation area. One thousand two-hundred acres of prime farm land are lost to farming because they are in urban areas.

The **degree of governmental intervention in development is least restrictive.** Small-lot subdivisions are permitted anywhere provided sewerage is installed or soils meet percolation tests.

National Economic Development Account	Regional Fiscal Impact Account	Environmental Quality Account	Public Service Accessibility Account	Governmental Intervention Account
Medium	Low	Low	Low	High

Figure 8-5 Sample Q-Sort card describing one alternative development pattern. (Source: Hyman, Moreau, and Stiftel 1984a, p. 918). Reprinted by permission.

TABLE 8-3
Scaled account scores corresponding to the three
quality levels for the hypothetical alternatives

Account	Scaled Scores		
	Low	Medium	High
National economic developments[a] ($ million)	58.00	47.00	37.00
Regional fiscal impacts[a] ($ million)	41.00	35.00	29.00
Environmental quality[b] (0.00 to 1.00)	0.0	0.50	1.00
Public service accessibility[b] (0.00 to 1.00)	0.00	0.50	1.00
Degree of government intervention (0.00 to 1.00)[c]	1.00	0.50	0.00

[a] Net costs
[b] Gross benefits
[c] May be considered either a benefit or a cost, depending on value judgments

The study team hypothesized a linear model relating preferences to the scaled account scores:

$$Y_i = b_0 + b_1 X_{1i} + b_2 X_{2i} + b_3 X_{3i} + b_4 X_{4i} + b_5 X_{5i} + e_i,$$

where Y_i is the score assigned to the ith alternative;
b^i coefficients are constants;
X_{ni} variables refer to the contributions of the ith alternative to the nth objective; and
e_i is an error term.

Before we estimated the regression equations for each participant, all of the scaled scores for the twenty-five alternatives were standardized to have zero mean and unit variance by subtracting from each the mean of the scaled scores for each account and then dividing by the standard deviation (table 8-4). That operation also eliminated the constant b_0 from the model. As a result of the

TABLE 8-4
Standardized scaled account scores for the two scenarios[a]

Scenario	National Economic Development Costs	Regional Fiscal Impact Costs	Environmental Quality	Public Service Accessibility	Level of Government Intervention

[a]The standardized scaled scores are positive if the score is above the mean for the hypothetical alternatives and negative if it is below the mean.

Source: Hyman, Moreau and Stiftel (1984a), p. 919. Reprinted by permission.

standardization, a positive (negative) number represented a scaled score above (below) the mean. All other things being equal, we hypothesized negative (positive) value weights for accounts defined in terms of costs (benefits). We hypothesized mixed value weights for degree of government intervention because of differences in individuals' ideologies.

The next step was the identification of judgment types who assigned similar sets of weights to objectives. We employed "hierarchical cluster analysis" in identifying the judgment types. This statistical technique groups the observations that are closest to each other in n-dimensional space without relying on any *a priori* theoretical information.

8.3.3 Findings

Table 8-5 presents the implicit value weights of the three groups of participants. These results imply that for most of these participants, as scaled, the objectives in decreasing order of importance were environmental quality, public service accessibility, national economic development, regional fiscal impacts, and degree of governmental intervention. The rankings for a few individuals showed positive weights on national economic development costs or regional fiscal impact costs. This indicates that these individuals either did not understand the exercise or had additional objectives in mind. In the analysis of judgment types, these counterintuitive weights were converted to zeros so that the weighted and scaled scores would not be misleading to the decision makers. A post-analysis interview with these individuals indicated that their choices were motivated by an additional objective--a preference for which sector, public or private, should bear the costs of development.

Since the sample size was small in this preliminary field test, we accepted as nonzero those mean weights that were significant at the 68 percent level. This level of statistical significance is considered acceptable in market research on people's preferences conducted through focus groups. One possible way of increasing the statistical significance would be to increase sample size. At the 68 percent level, the weights were nonzero on the environmental quality account for all three groups, and on the public service accessibility account for the PAG. When the mean weight for an account was zero, it means that this group was not concerned about marginal changes in the levels of those particular objectives.

A linear model of the relationship between the rankings of the alternatives and the accounts proved quite satisfactory as measured by the coefficients of determination. For the three groups, the model explained between 79 and 87 percent of the variance in rankings. These results indicate a high degree of internal

TABLE 8-5
The value weights the participants implicitly attached to the accounts

Group	National Economic Development	Regional Fiscal Impacts	Environmental Quality	Public Service Levels	Governmental Intervention
Policy Advisory Group					
Mean	-0.08[c]	-0.77[a]	0.77	0.25[b]	0.07[c]
Standard deviation	0.21	0.20	0.24	0.21	0.25
Coefficient of determination = 0.87					
Watershed Planning Task Force					
Mean	0.00[c]	-0.07[c]	0.68[a]	0.10[b]	0.00[c]
Standard deviation	0.27	0.09	0.38	0.18	0.17
Coefficient of determination = 0.79					

Group	National Economic Development	Regional Fiscal Impacts	Environmental Quality	Public Service Levels	Governmental Intervention
TJCOG Staff					
Mean	-0.00[c]	-0.05[c]	0.84[a]	0.08[c]	0.04[c]
Standard deviation	0.27	0.12	0.07	0.17	0.009
	Coefficient of determination = 0.80				
Overall					
Mean	-0.03[c]	-0.076[c]	0.76[a]	0.16[c]	0.04[c]
Standard deviation	0.24	0.15	0.28	0.20	0.20
	Coefficient of determination = 0.83				

[a] Statistically significant at the 90 percent level.
[b] Statistically significant at the 68 percent level.
[c] Not statistically significant at the 68 percent level; converted to 0.0.
[d] Coefficient of determination is the r^2 for the model.

Source: Hyman, Moreau and Stiftel (1984a, p. 919). Reprinted by permission.

consistency on the part of most participants in their use
of the information on impacts in ranking alternatives. We
also estimated a quadratic model, but it added little to
the explanation of the rankings.

The hierarchical cluster analysis classified the
twenty-seven participants into six groups (table 8-6).
Quality-of-life advocates implicitly placed high weights on
both environmental quality and public service
accessibility. Cost-conscious quality-of-life advocates
also showed concern for national economic development costs
and regional fiscal impacts. Environmentalists only
weighted environmental quality heavily. Cost-conscious
environmentalists strongly supported environmental quality,
but exhibited some concern for economic and fiscal costs.
Cost-conscious anti-regulators showed concern for
environmental quality as well as economic and fiscal costs,
but opposed government intervention. Pro-regulators favored
government intervention. One surprising finding was the
relatively low weight most participants attached to the
degree of government intervention.

It is also interesting to examine the composition of
the judgment types by group affiliation. The most common
judgment type for PAG members was cost-conscious
quality-of-life advocates. The WPTF group was well
distributed among all judgment types. TJCOG staff tended to
be environmentalists or cost-conscious environmentalists.
The PAG and WPTF members were chosen to be broadly
representative of the affected areas, but there may have
been some pro-environmental bias in selection of these
advisory committees or in TJCOG staff recruitment.
Additional testing could be conducted to elicit values from
other groups to determine the extent to which these
participants are representative of the regional population.

Table 8-7 summarizes the entire analysis in a
goals-achievement matrix. It shows (1) the standardized
scaled scores for each account under the two scenarios, (2)
the mean weights implicitly placed on each account by the
various judgment types, and (3) the overall evaluations of
the alternative scenarios by the judgment types. The
overall evaluations are derived by multiplying the value
weights for each account by the corresponding, standardized
scaled scores and then summing the results across accounts.
The scores also indicate the relative intensities of the
preferences of each judgment type. In this simple field
test, all of the judgment types preferred the advanced
practices scenario to the conventional practices scenario.

8.4 CONCLUSIONS

This trial application indicates the principal
advantages and disadvantages of the method. With a modest
expenditure of time and resources, SAGE can facilitate
participation by publics and decision makers. It is
applicable to either specific project analyses or regional
planning studies and is consistent with federal guidelines

for environmental assessment in the United States (U.S. Council on Environmental Quality 1978; U.S. Water Resources Council 1983). SAGE clearly separates facts from values in its scaling and weighting procedures. It recognizes the diversity of values held by different groups through its presentation of a cross-tabulated matrix of impacts and value weights. This information can help decision makers understand the sources of agreement and conflict so that a consensus can be built around possible modifications of the proposed project.

SAGE is more useful than ranking methods such as direct polling, which offer little insight into why participants express certain preferences. SAGE relies on a more valid technique for capturing preferences than direct questioning. The high degree of internal consistency in the rankings of alternatives shows that participants are capable of taking an active role in determining values in a realistic setting. Previous applications of techniques to capture social judgment have been in simpler contexts involving fewer variables and decisions (Stewart and Gelberd 1976; Kaplan and Schwartz 1977; Steinmann et al. 1977).

One of the weaknesses of this particular application was the incompleteness of the set of attributes. For example, economic efficiency benefits from people's willingness to pay for large lot, single-family dwellings close to recreational reservoirs were not considered. Additional attributes could be included in future applications. If information is available on the incidence of benefits and costs across groups, the distributional effects could be analyzed explicitly as one of the accounts. Where budget and time permit, value weights could be elicited from a statistically representative sample of the general public. Alternatively, participants who represent identifiable social, economic, or political groups within the affected communities could be selected.

SAGE shares one problem common to nearly all methods for combining facts and values in environmental assessment. While the scaling of attributes is accomplished using ordinal data, the resulting scales are treated as if they were derived from ratio data. Another limitation of this field test was the absence of large differences in the effects of alternatives. As a result, the choices to be made were not very controversial, at least at that time. As land use controls actually begin to limit development or impose higher private sector costs, the issues could become drawn more sharply.

This application did not confront the problems of risk or uncertainty. An interesting follow-up would be to test the ability of participants to handle statements of risk together with multiple objectives. The easiest approach of this type for respondents would be to express the standardized, scaled account scores as ranges rather than single values. More sophisticated approaches could involve probability statements, but it is doubtful that most participants could process such information well. Uncertainty can be handled by postulating different sets of

TABLE 8-6
Classification of participants into judgment types

	National Economic Development	Regional Fiscal Impacts	Environmental Quality	Public Service Levels	Government Intervention
QUALITY-OF-LIFE ADVOCATES (6 participants)					
Mean weights	0.00***	0.00***	0.80*	0.43*	0.00***
Standard deviation	0.00	0.00	0.19	0.15	9.00
COST-CONSCIOUS QUALITY-OF-LIFE ADVOCATES (6 participants)					
Mean weights	-0.10**	-0.15**	0.90*	0.29*	-0.02***
Standard deviation	0.08	0.12	0.05	0.08	0.03
ENVIRONMENTALISTS (7 participants)					
Mean weights	0.00***	-0.02***	0.89*	-0.01***	0.04***
Standard deviation	0.00	0.03	0.08	0.02	0.07
COST-CONSCIOUS ENVIRONMENTALISTS (3 participants)					
Meal weights	-0.32*	-0.15**	0.90*	0.00***	0.08***
Standard deviation	0.08	0.12	0.04	0.00	0.11

	National Economic Development	Regional Fiscal Impacts	Environmental Quality	Public Service Levels	Government Intervention
COST-CONSCIOUS ANTI-REGULATORS (3 participants)					
Meal weights	-0.31**	-0.22**	0.33**	0.00***	-0.16***
Standard deviation	0.29	0.16	0.25	0.00	0.14
PRO-REGULATORS (2 participants)					
Meal weights	-0.30*	0.00***	0.15***	0.00***	0.59***
Standard deviation	0.30	0.00	0.15	0.00	0.30

*Indicates statistical significance at the 90 percent level.
**Indicates statistical significance at the 68 percent level.
***Indicates not statistically significant at the 68 percent level; converted to 0.0.

Source: Hyman, Moreau and Stiftel (1984a, p. 920). Reprinted by permission.

250

TABLE 8-7
A goals-achievement matrix for the two alternative scenarios

Standardized Scaled Scores[a]

Scenario	National Economic Development Costs	Regional Fiscal Impact Costs	Environmental Quality	Public Service Accessibility	Government Intervention
Conventional Practices	1.42	1.59	-1.04	-1.25	-1.33
Advanced Practices	-1.06	-0.98	0.03	1.07	1.33

Mean Weights[b]

Judgment Types	National Economic Development	Regional Fiscal Impacts	Environmental Quality	Public Service Levels	Government Intervention
Quality of life advocates	0.00	0.00	0.80	0.43	0.00
Cost-conscious quality of life advocates	-0.10	-0.15	0.90	0.29	0.00
Environmentalists	0.00	0.00	0.89	0.00	0.00
Cost-conscious environmentalists	-0.32	-0.15	0.90	0.00	0.00

Judgment Types	National Economic Development	Regional Fiscal Impacts	Environmental Quality	Public Service Levels	Government Intervention
Cost-conscious					
Anti-regulators	-0.31	-0.22	0.33	0.00	-0.16
Proregulators	0.00	0.00	0.00	0.00	0.59

Weighted and Standardized Scaled Scores

Judgment Types	Conventional Practices	Advanced Practices
Quality of life advocates	-1.37	0.48
Cost-conscious quality of life advocates	-1.68	0.59
Environmentalists	-0.93	0.03
Cost-conscious environmentalist	-1.63	0.51
Cost-conscious Antiregulators	-0.92	0.34
Proregulators	-0.78	0.78

[a] The standardized, scaled scores are positive if the score is above the mean and negative if below the mean.

[b] Mean weights that were not significantly different from 0.00 at the 68 percent level have been converted to 0.00. Weights should be negative where high standardized scaled scores are undesirable and positive where high standardized scaled scores are desirable.

assumptions about future states of nature and the
socioeconomic context, and testing for the effects of
varying these assumptions.

Aside from these limitations, SAGE holds promise as a
cost-effective means of eliciting societal values in
environmental assessment. It offers a multiple-objective
structure for combining scientific data and value
judgments. Most important, the way in which the findings
are presented can provide substantial insights for decision
makers.

References

Chapter One

Andrews, Richard. 1976. Environmental Policy and Ad-
    ministrative Change: Implementation of the National
    Environmental Policy Act. Lexington, Mass.:
    Lexington Books.
Banfield, Edward. 1955. "Note on a Conceptual Scheme."
    In Politics, Planning, and the Public Interest, by
    Martin Meyerson and Edward Banfield. New York: Free
    Press.
Basta, Daniel and Blair Bower, eds. 1982. Analyzing
    Natural Systems: Analysis for Regional Residuals--
    Environmental Quality Management. Washington, D.C.:
    Resources for the Future.
Beanlands, Gordon and Peter Duinker. 1983. An Ecological
    Framework for Environmental Impact Assessment in
    Canada. Halifax, Nova Scotia: Dalhousie University,
    Institute for Resource and Environmental Studies.
    Prepared for Canadian Federal Environmental Assessment
    Review Office.
Bissett, Ronald. 1981. Problems and Issues in the
    Implementation of Post-Development Audits. Aberdeen,
    Scotland: University of Aberdeen, Department of
    Geography.
Biswas, Asit. 1976. Systems Approach to Water Management.
    New York: McGraw-Hill.
Burchell, Robert and David Listokin. 1975. The
    Environmental Impact Handbook. New Brunswick, N.J.:
    Rutgers University, Center for Urban Policy Research.
California Forest and Range Experiment Station. 1958.
    Soil Vegetation Surveys in California. Sacramento,
    Calif.: California Department of Natural Resources.
Cameron, D. 1981. "Problems of Forest Land Classification
    in Tropical and Subtropical Australia." In Assessing
    Tropical Forest Lands: Their Suitability for
    Sustainable Uses, edited by Richard Carpenter.
    Dublin, Ireland: Tycooly Press.
Canter, Lawrence. 1977. Environmental Impact Assessment.
    New York: McGraw - Hill.
Carpenter, Richard. 1980. "Using Ecological Knowledge for
    Development Planning." Environmental Management 4:13-
    20.
_____, ed. 1983. Natural Systems for Development: What
    Planners Need to Know. New York: Macmillan.
Christian, C. and C. Stewart. 1968. "Methodology of
    Integrated Surveys." In Proceedings, Toulouse
    Conference on Aerial Surveys and Integrated Studies.
    Paris: UNESCO.

253

254

References

Cohon, Jared. 1978. _Multi-objective Programming and Planning_. New York: Academic Press.

Dee, Norbert _et al._ 1972. _An Environmental Evaluation System for Water Resources Planning_. Springfield, Va.: National Technical Information Service. Report PB-208822.

Duke, K.M. _et al._ 1977. _Environmental Quality Assessment in Multi-Objective Planning_. Springfield, Va.: National Technical Information Service. Prepared for the U.S. Bureau of Reclamation.

EIA Worldletter. 1983. 1, No. 1:1-2.

Fabos, Julius, C. Greene and S. Joyner, Jr. 1978. _The METLAND Landscape Assessment, Alternative Plan Formulation and Plan Evaluation: Part 3 of the Metropolitan Landscape Planning Model_. Amherst, Mass.: University of Massachusetts Agricultural Experiment Station, Research Bulletin 653.

Frohock, Fred. 1979. _Public Policy: Scope and Logic_. Englewood Cliffs, N.J.: Prentice-Hall.

Galloway, Gerald. 1978. _Assessing Man's Impact on Wetlands_. Raleigh, N.C.: University of North Carolina, Water Resources Research Institute, Report 78-136.

Gianessi, Leonard, Henry Peskin and G. Young. 1981. "Analysis of National Water Pollution Control Policies: 1. A National Network Model." _Water Resources Research_ 17:796-801.

Haimes, Yacov, Warren Hall and H. Freedman. 1975. _Multiobjective Optimization in Water Resources Systems: The Surrogate Worth Tradeoff Method_. New York: Elsevier.

Hall, Charles and J. Day. 1977. _Ecosystem Modeling in Theory and Practice_. New York: Wiley-Interscience.

Hamilton, Lawrence. 1982. _Land-Use Planning Technologies to Sustain Tropical Forest and Woodlands_. Honolulu, Hawaii: East-West Center Environment and Policy Institute, Prepared for U.S. Congress Office of Technology Assessment.

Hammond, Kenneth. 1978. "Toward Increasing Competence of Thought in Public Policy Formation." In _Judgment and Decisions in Public Policy Formation_, edited by Kenneth Hammond, Boulder, Colo.: Westview Press.

Hart, Stuart, Gordon Enk and William Hornick, eds. 1984. _Improving Impact Assessment: Increasing the Relevance and Utilization of Scientific and Technical Information_. Boulder, Colo.: Westview Press.

Henderson, Jim. 1982. _Handbook of Environmental Quality Measurement and Assessment Methods and Techniques_. Vicksburg, Miss.: U.S. Army Engineer Waterways Experiment Station, Instruction Report E-82-2.

Henderson, Marilyn. 1985. (U.S. Environmental Protection Agency, Office of Federal Activities). Personal communication.

Chapter One

Hill, Morris. 1968. "A Goals-Achievement Matrix for Evaluating Alternative Plans." Journal of the American Institute of Planners 34:19-28.

Hill, William. 1973. "A Review of Selected Materials Relevant to Environmental Impact Assessment." In Analyzing the Environmental Impacts of Water Projects, edited by Leonard Ortolano. Palo Alto, Calif.: Stanford University, Department of Civil Engineering.

_____. 1977. The National Environmental Policy Act and Federal Water Resources Planning: Effects and Effectiveness in the Corps and SCS. Stanford, Calif.: Stanford University, Department of Civil Engineering, Report IPM-4.

Hills, G. Angus. 1961. The Ecological Basis for Land Use Planning. Toronto: Ontario Department of Land Forests, Research Report 46.

Holdridge, Leslie. 1967. Life Zone Ecology. San Jose, Costa Rica: Tropical Science Center.

Holling, C.S., ed. 1978. Adaptive Environmental Assessment and Management. New York: Wiley-Interscience.

Hopkins, Lewis. 1977. "Methods for Generating Land Suitability Maps: A Comparative Evaluation." Journal of the American Institute of Planners 43:368-400.

Horberry, John. 1983. Environmental Guidelines Survey: An Analysis of Environmental Procedures and Guidelines Governing Development Aid. Washington, D.C.: International Institute for Environment and Development.

Hufschmidt, Maynard. 1974. Environmental Statements and Water Resource Planning in North Carolina. Raleigh, N.C.: University of North Carolina, Water Resources Research Institute, Report 94.

_____. 1985. "Adding an Environmental Dimension to Comprehensive Water Resource Management in Developing Countries." In Water Resources for Rural Areas and Their Communities, vol. 2. Brussels: International Water Resources Association.

Hyman, Eric. 1984. "Land Use Planning to Help Sustain Tropical Forest Resources." World Development 12:837-847.

Hyman, Eric, David Moreau and Bruce Stiftel. 1984. "Toward a Participant-Value Method for Presentation of Environmental Impact Data." In Improving Impact Assessment: Increasing the Relevance and Utilization of Scientific and Technical Information, edited by Stuart Hart, Gordon Enk and William Hornick. Boulder, Colo.: Westview Press.

International Planning Associates. 1978. Site Evaluation and Site Selection. Lagos, Nigeria: Federal Capital Development Authority.

Janis, Irving and Leon Mann. 1977. Decision-Making: A Psychological Analysis of Conflict, Choice, and Commitments. New York: Free Press.

Kane, Julius, W. Thompson and I. Vertinsky. 1973. "KSIM, A Methodology for Interactive Resource Simulation." Water Resources Research 9:65-80.

Keeney, Ralph and Howard Raiffa. 1976. Decision Analysis with Multiple Conflicting Objectives: Preferences and Value Tradeoffs. New York: John Wiley and Sons.

Klingbiel, A. and P. Montgomery. 1961. Land Capability Classification. Washington, D.C. U.S. Soil Conservation Service, Agricultural Handbook 210.

Krajina, V. 1973. "Biogeoclimatic Zonation as a Basis for Regional Ecosystems." In Symposium on Planning Utilization of Lowland Tropical Forest. Bogor, Indonesia: Cipayung.

Lacate, Douglas. 1981. "Discussion of Biophysical Land Classification in Canada." In Assessing Tropical Forest Lands: Their Suitability for Sustainable Uses, edited by Richard Carpenter. Dublin, Ireland: Tycooly Press.

Lapping, Mark. 1975. "Environmental Impact Assessment Methodologies: A Critique." Environmental Affairs 4:123-134.

Lee, Peng. 1981. "Forest Land Classification in Malaysia." In Assessing Tropical Forest Lands: Their Suitability for Sustainable Uses, edited by Richard Carpenter. Dublin, Ireland: Tycooly Press.

Leopold, Luna et al. 1971. A Procedure for Evaluating Environmental Impact. Washington, D.C.: U.S. Geological Survey, Circular 645.

Lewis, Phillip. 1963. Landscape Analysis: Lake Superior South Shore Area. Madison, Wis.: Wisconsin Department of Resource Development.

Lichfield, Nathaniel. 1960. "Cost-Benefit Analysis in City Planning." Journal of the American Institute of Planners 26:273-279.

Lim, Gill. 1984. Implementation of Environmental Impact Assessment in Developing Countries. Princeton, N.J.: Princeton University, Research Program in Development Studies, Discussion Paper 115.

Lindblom, Charles. 1959. "The Science of 'Muddling Through'." Public Administration Review 19:79-88.

Maass, Arthur et al. 1962. Design of Water Resource Systems. Cambridge, Mass.: Harvard University Press.

McHarg, Ian. 1969. Design With Nature. New York: Natural History Press.

McClure, J., N. Cost and H. Knight. 1979. Multiresource Inventories -- A New Concept for Forestry Survey. Asheville, N.C.: U.S. Forest Service Southeastern Forest Experiment Station, Paper SE-191.

Chapter One

Mekong Secretariat. 1982. Environmental Impact Assessment
     Guidelines for Application to Tropical River Basin
     Development. Bangkok: Interim Committee for
     Coordination of Investigations of the Lower Mekong
     Basin.
Mishan, Ezra. 1969. Technology and Growth: The Price We
     Pay. New York: Praeger.
Mueller-Dombois, Dieter. 1981. "The Ecological Series
     Approach to Forest Land Classification." In Assessing
     Tropical Forest Lands: Their Suitability for
     Sustainable Uses, edited by Richard Carpenter.
     Dublin, Ireland: Tycooly Press.
Mueller-Dombois, Dieter and H. Ellenberg. 1974. Aims and
     Methods of Vegetation Ecology. New York: John Wiley
     and Sons.
Organization of American States. 1978. Environmental
     Quality and River Basin Development: A Model for
     Integrated Analyses and Planning. Washington, D.C.:
     OAS.
Ott, Wayne. 1978. Environmental Indices: Theory and
     Practice. Ann Arbor, Mich.: Ann Arbor Science Press.
     _____, ed. 1976. Environmental Modeling and Simulation.
     Springfield, Va.: National Technical Information
     Service, Report EPA-60019-76-016.
Patten, B. 1976. Systems Analysis and Simulation in
     Ecology. New York: Academic Press.
Planning Environment International. 1975. Interim Guide
     for Environmental Assessment. Washington, D.C.: U.S.
     Government Printing Office. Prepared for the U.S.
     Department of Housing and Urban Development.
President of the United States. 1981. "Executive Order
     12291, Federal Regulation." Federal Register
     46:13193-13198.
Quade, E. 1975. Analysis for Public Decisions. New York:
     Elsevier-North Holland.
Rau, John and David Wooten, eds. 1980. Environmental
     Impact Analysis Handbook. New York: McGraw-Hill.
Russell, Clifford, ed. 1975. Ecological Modeling in a
     Resources Management Framework. Washington, D.C.:
     Resources for the Future, Working Paper QE-1.
Simon, Herbert. 1975. Administrative Behavior. New York:
     Free Press.
Solomon, R. Charles et al. 1977. Water Resources
     Assessment Methodology (WRAM)-Impact Assessment and
     Alternative Evaluation. Vicksburg, Miss.: U.S. Army
     Engineer Waterways Experiment Station. Technical
     Report Y-77-1.
Sorenson, Jens. 1971. A Framework for Identification and
     Control of Resource Degradation and Conflict in the
     Multiple Use of the Coastal Zone. Berkeley, Calif.:
     University of California, Department of Landscape
     Architecture.
Steiner, Frederick. 1983. "Resource Suitability: Methods
     for Analyses." Environmental Management 7:401-420.

Thom, Gary and Wayne Ott. 1975. Air Pollution Indices: A Compendium of Assessment of Indices Used in the U.S. and Canada. Washington, D.C.: U.S. Council on Environmental Quality.

Thor, E. *et al.* 1978. "Forest Environmental Impact Analysis--A New Approach." Journal of Forestry 76:723-725.

Thor, E., Richard Smardon and R. Adams. 1979. IMPACT in California and Colorado. Berkeley, Calif.: U.S. Forest Service Pacific Southwest Forest and Range Experiment Station. Research Note PSW-336.

Tippetts-Abbett-McCarthy-Stratton. 1980. Environmental Assessment: Accelerated Mahaweli Development Program. New York: TAMS.

Traveler's Research Corporation. 1969. Development of a Procedure and Knowledge Requirements for Marine Resources Planning. Hartford, Conn.: Traveler's Research Corporation.

U.S. Council on Environmental Quality. 1978. "Preparation of Environmental Policy Act: Implementation of Procedural Revisions: Final Regulation." Federal Register 43 (November 29):55977-56007.

U.S. Federal Interagency River Basin Committee. 1950 Proposed Practices for Economic Analysis of River Basin Projects. Washington, D.C.: Government Printing Office.

U.S. Fish and Wildlife Service. 1980. Habitat Evaluation Procedures. Washington, D.C.: Government Printing Office, Documents ESM 101 to 104.

U.S. General Accounting Office. 1984. Report to the Congress: Cost-Benefit Analysis Can Be Useful in Assessing Environmental Regulations Despite Limitations, Washington, D.C.: Government Printing Office.

U.S. Water Resources Council. 1973. "Water and Related-Land Resources: Establishment of Principles and Standards for Planning." Federal Register 38 (September 10):24778-24869.

_____. 1983. Economic and Environmental Principles and Guidelines for Water and Related-Land Resources Implementation Studies." Federal Register 48, No. 48 (March 10): 10259.

Walker, B. and G. Norton. 1982 "Applied Ecology: Towards a Positive Approach. II. Applied Ecological Analysis." Journal of Environmental Management 14:325-342.

Warner, Maurice and E. Preston. 1974. A Review of Environmental Impact Assessment Methodologies. Springfield, Va.: National Technical Information Service, Report PB-236-609. Prepared for the U.S. Environmental Protection Agency.

Chapter Two

Webb, L. *et al.* 1977. "Structural Classification is a
     Method to Predict Site Potential in the Development
     and Conservation of Tropical Humid Forest Lands." In
     Transactions International MAB-IUFRO Workshop on
     Tropical Rain Forest Ecosystems Research, edited by E.
     Brunig. Hamburg: University of Hamburg.

Chapter Two

Andrews, Richard and Mary Jo Waits. 1978. Environmental
     Values in Public Decisions. Ann Arbor, Mich.:
     University of Michigan, School of Natural Resources.
Caldwell, Lyndon. 1970. Environment: A Challenge to
     Modern Society. New York: Natural History Press.
Comar, C. and L. Sagan. 1976. "Health Effects of Energy
     Production and Conversion." Annual Review of Energy
     1:581-600.
Conn, W. David and Nickolaus Feimer. 1985. "Communicating
     With the Public on Environmental Risk: Integrating
     Research and Policy." The Environmental Professional
     7:39-47.
Dee, Norbert *et al.* 1972. An Environmental Evaluation
     System for Water Resource Planning. Springfield, Va.:
     National Technical Information Service, Report
     PB-208822.
Dossani, N., W. Watson and W. Weygart. 1979. "Solar
     Energy: Its Economic and Environmental Consequences."
     Houston, Tex.: Presented at the Annual Meeting of the
     American Institute of Chemical Engineers.
Feagans, Thomas and William Biller. 1981. "Risk
     Assessment: Describing the Protection Provided by
     Ambient Air Quality Standards." The Environmental
     Professional 3:249-264.
Feinberg, Joel. 1974. "The Rights of Animals and Unborn
     Generations." In Philosophy and the Environmental
     Crisis, edited by William Blackstone, Athens, Ga.:
     University of Georgia Press.
Fischoff, Baruch, Paul Slovic and Sara Lichtenstein. 1978.
     "How Safe is Safe Enough? A Psychometric Study of
     Attitudes Toward Technological Risks and Benefits."
     Policy Science 9:127-152.
Fischoff, Baruch *et al.* 1981. "Lay Foibles and Expert
     Fables in Judgments About Risk." In Progress in
     Resource Management and Environmental Planning, vol.
     3, edited by Timothy O'Riordan and R. Turner.
     Chichester, England: Wiley-Interscience.
Goodpaster, Kenneth. 1978. "On Being Morally
     Considerable." Journal of Philosophy 75:308.
Gray, Elizabeth. 1979. Why the Green Nigger? Remything
     Genesis. Wellesley, Mass.: Roundtable Press.
Hobbs, Benjamin. 1980a. "A Comparison of Weighting
     Methods in Power Plant Siting." Decision Sciences
     11:725-737.

_____. 1980b. "Multi-Objective Power Plant Siting Methods." _Journal of the Energy Division, American Society of Civil Engineers_ 106, No. EY2 (October):187-200.

Holdren, John. 1978. _Environmental Impacts of Alternative Energy Technologies for California_. Berkeley, Calif.: Lawrence Berkeley Laboratory.

Holling, C.S., ed. 1978. _Adaptive Environmental Assessment and Management_. New York: Wiley-Interscience.

Hunt, W. Murray. 1980. "Are 'Mere Things' Morally Considerable." _Environmental Ethics_ 2:59.

Hurwicz, L. 1951. _Optimality Criteria for Decision Making Under Ignorance_. Cowles Commission, Discussion Paper 350.

Inhaber, Herbert. 1976. _Environmental Indices_. New York: Wiley-Interscience.

Inhaber, Herbert. 1979. "Risks With Energy From Conventional and Nonconventional Sources." _Science_ 203, No. 4382 (February 23):718-723.

James, A. and L. Evison, eds. 1979. _Biological Indicators of Water Quality_. New York: John Wiley and Sons.

Kates, Robert. 1978. _Risk Assessment of Environmental Hazards--SCOPE_ 8. Chichester, England: Wiley-Interscience.

Keeney, Ralph and Howard Raiffa. 1976. _Decisions With Multiple Objectives: Preferences and Value Tradeoffs_. New York: John Wiley and Sons.

Krutilla, John and Anthony Fisher. 1975. _The Economics of Natural Environments_. Baltimore, Md.: Johns Hopkins University Press.

Landwehr, Jurate. 1974. _Water Quality Indices--Construction and Analysis_. Ann Arbor, Mich.: University of Michigan, Ph.D. dissertation.

Leape, James. 1980. "Quantitative Risk Assessment in Regulation of Environmental Carcinogens." _Harvard Environment Law Review_ 4:86-116.

Leopold, Aldo. 1949. _A Sand County Almanac and Sketches Here and There_. New York: Oxford University Press.

Leopold, Luna, _et al._ 1971. _A Procedure for Evaluating Environmental Impact_. Washington, D.C.: U.S. Geological Survey.

Lowrance, William. 1976. _Of Acceptable Risk_. Los Angeles, Calif.: William Kaufman.

Luce, R. and Howard Raiffa. 1957. _Games and Decisions_. New York: John Wiley and Sons.

Marietta, Don, Jr. 1982. "Knowledge and Obligation in Environmental Ethics: A Phenomenological Analysis." _Environmental Ethics_ 4:155.

McHarg, Ian. 1969. _Design With Nature_. New York: Natural History Press.

Merkhofer, Miley. 1981. "Risk Assessment: Quantifying Uncertainty in Health Effects." _The Environmental Professional_ 3:249-264.

Chapter Two

Moreau, David. 1980. Quantitative Assessments of Health
    Risks by Selected Federal Agencies. Research Triangle
    Park, N.C.: U.S. Enviromental Protection Agency,
    Office of Air Quality Planning and Standards.
Morgan, M. et al. 1978a. "A Probabilistic Methodology for
    Estimating Air Pollution Health Effects from
    Coal-Fired Power Plants." Energy Systems and Policy
    2:287-310.
    . 1978b. "Sulfur Control in Coal-fired Power Plants:
    A Probabilistic Approach to Policy Analysis." Journal
    of the Air Pollution Control Association 28:993-997.
North, D. and Miley Merkhofer. 1976. "A Methodology for
    Analysing Emission Control Strategies." Computer and
    Operations Research 3:185-207.
Organisation for Economic Cooperation and Development.
    1976. Measuring Social Well-Being. Paris: OECD.
Orlando, Joseph and R. Wrightington. 1976. A Review and
    Evaluation of Water Quality Indices and Similar
    Indicators, vol. 2: Review of Available Indices.
    Cambridge, Mass.: Mathtech. Prepared for the U.S.
    Council on Environmental Quality.
Ott, Wayne. 1978a. Environmental Indices: Theory and
    Practice. Ann Arbor, Mich.: Ann Arbor Science Press.
    . 1978b. Water Quality Indices: A Survey of Indices
    Used in the United States. Springfield, Va.:
    National Technical Information Service. Prepared for
    the U.S. Environmental Protection Agency.
Petulla, Joseph. 1980. American Environmentalism:
    Values, Tactics, Priorities. College Station, Tex.:
    Texas A & M University.
Philipson, L. et al. 1974. Investigation of the
    Feasibility of the Delphi Technique for Estimating
    Risk Analysis Parameters. Washington, D.C.: U.S.
    Department of Transportation. Report DOT-05-2011411.
Raiffa, Howard. 1968. Decision Analysis: Introductory
    Lectures on Choice Order Uncertainty. Reading, Mass.:
    Addision-Wesley.
Rosen, Richard et al. 1976. A Review and Evaluation of
    Water Quality Indices and Similar Indicators: vol. 3,
    Evaluation of Available Indices. Cambridge, Mass.:
    Mathtech. Prepared for the U.S. Council on
    Environmental Quality.
Savage, L. 1951. "The Theory of Statistical Decision."
    American Statistical Association Journal 46:55-67.
Schoemaker, Paul. 1982. "The Expected Utility Model: Its
    Variants, Purposes, Evidence, and Limitations."
    Journal of Economic Literature 20:529-563.
Sinden, John. 1974. "A Utility Approach to the Valuation
    of Recreational and Aesthetic Experiences." Journal
    of Agricultural Economics 56:61-72.
Slovic, Paul, Baruch Fischoff and Sarah Lichtenstein.
    1982. "Why Study Risk Perception?" Risk Analysis
    2:83-93.

Solomon, R. Charles *et al.* 1977. Water Resources
    Assessment Methodology (WRAM)--Impact Assessment and
    Alternative Evaluation. Vicksburg, Miss.: U.S. Army
    Engineer Waterways Experiment Station. Technical
    Report Y-77-1.
Spangler, Milton. 1980. "Syndromes of Risk and
    Environmental Protection: The Conflict of Individual
    and Societal Values." The Environmental Professional
    2:274-291.
_____. 1981. "Risks and Psychic Costs of Alternative
    Energy Sources for Generating Electricity." The
    Energy Journal 2:37-59.
Starr, Chauncey. 1969. "Social Benefit Versus
    Technological Risk." Science 165, No. 3899 (September
    19): 1232-1238.
Tversky, Amos and David Kahneman. 1974. "Judgment Under
    Uncertainty: Heuristics and Biases." Science 185, No.
    4157 (September 27):1124-1131.
U.S. National Academy of Engineering, Committee on Public
    Engineering Policy. 1972. Perspectives on
    Benefit-Risk Decision Making. Washington, D.C.: NAE.
U.S. National Academy of Sciences. 1975. Decision Making
    for Regulating Chemicals in the Environment.
    Washington, D.C.: NAS.
U.S. Nuclear Regulatory Commission. 1975. The Reactor
    Safety Study: An Assessment of Accident Risks in U.S.
    Commercial Nuclear Power Plants. Washington, D.C.:
    Government Printing Office, Report WASH-1400 (NUREG
    75/014).
U.S. Toxic Substances Strategy Committee. 1980. Toxic
    Chemicals and Public Protection: A Report to the
    President. Washington, D.C.: U.S. Government
    Printing Office.
Von Neumann, John and D. Morgenstern. 1947. The Theory of
    Games and Economic Behavior, 2nd ed. Princeton, N.J.:
    Princeton University Press.
Wald, Abraham. 1945. "Statistical Decision Functions
    Which Minimize the Maximum Risk." Annals of
    Mathematics 461:265-280.
Walker, Richard. 1973. "Wetlands Preservation and
    Management on Chesapeake Bay: The Role of Science in
    Natural Resource Policy." Coastal Zone Management
    Journal 1:75-101.
Warnock, G. 1971. The Object of Morality. New York:
    Methuen.
Watson, Richard. 1979. "Self-Consciousness and the Rights
    of Nonhuman Animals and Nature." Environmental Ethics
    1:99.
Wilson, Richard *et al.* 1981. Health Effects of Fossil
    Fuel Burning -- Assessment and Mitigation. Cambridge,
    Mass.: Ballinger Press.
Winkler, Robert and Rakesh Sarin. 1981. "Risk Assessment:
    Consulting the Experts." The Environmental
    Professional 3:265-276.

Chapter Three

Almond, Gabriel and Sidney Verba. 1963. The Civic Culture. Princeton, N.J.: Princeton University Press.

Andrews, Richard. 1976. Environmental Policy and Administrative Change: The National Environmental Policy Act of 1969. Lexington, Mass.: Lexington Books.

Andrews, Richard and Mary Jo Waits. 1978. Environmental Values in Public Decisions: A Research Agenda. Ann Arbor, Mich.: University of Michigan, School of Natural Resources.

Arnstein, Sherry. 1969. "A Ladder of Citizen Participation." Journal of the American Institute of Planners 35:261-224.

Bachrach, Peter and Morton Baratz. 1962. "The Two Faces of Power." American Political Science Review 56:947-952.
_____. 1963. "Decisions and Nondecisions: An Analytical Framework." American Political Science Review 57:632-642.

Batchelor, Peter, ed. 1971. Eleven Views. Raleigh, N.C.: North Carolina State University, School of Design.

Borton, Thomas et al. The Susquehanna Communication-Participation Study. Fort Belvoir, Va.: U.S. Army Engineer Institute for Water Resources, Report No. 70-6.

Bouchard, T. 1971. "Whatever Happened to Brainstorming?" Journal of Creative Behavior. 5:182-189.

Checkoway, Barry. 1981. "The Politics of Public Hearings." Journal of Applied Behavioral Science 17:566-582.

Clark, Peter and Francis Cummings. 1981. "Selecting an Environmental Conflict Management Strategy." In Environmental Conflict Management. edited by Philip Marcus and Wendy Emrich, Charlottesville, Va.: University of Virginia, Institute for Environmental Negotitation.

Cole, Richard. 1975. "Citizen Participation in Municipal Politics." American Journal of Political Science 14: 761-781.

Creighton, James. 1980. Public Involvement Manual. Washington, D.C.: U.S. Department of the Interior, Water and Power Resources Service.

Dahl, Robert. 1956. A Preface to Democratic Theory. Chicago: University of Illinois Press.
_____. 1961. Who Governs? New Haven: Yale Press.
_____. 1963. Modern Political Analysis. Englewood Cliffs, N.J.: Prentice-Hall.

Dalkey, Norman. 1967. Delphi. Santa Monica, Calif.: RAND Corporation.

Davidoff, Paul. 1965. "Advocacy and Pluralism in Planning." Journal of the America Institute of Planners 31:331-338.

Davidoff, Paul and Thomas Reiner. 1962. "A Choice Theory of Planning." Journal of the American Institute of Planners 38:103-115.

Davis, Adam, Jill Anderson and Richard Gough. 1975. _Alternative Information and Interaction Approaches to Public Participation in Water Resources Decision-Making_. Raleigh, N.C.: University of North Carolina, Water Resources Research Institute.

Delbecq, Andre, A. de Ven, and D. Gustafson. 1975. _Group Techniques for Program Planning_. Glenview, Ill.: Scott Foresman and Co.

Delp, Peter _et al._ 1977. _Systems Tools for Project Planning_. Bloomington, Inc.: International Development Institute, Indiana University, prepared for the U.S. Agency for International Development.

Downs, Anthony. 1957. _An Economic Theory of Democracy_. New York: Harper and Row.

_____. 1967. _Inside Bureaucracy_. Boston, Mass.: Little, Brown and Co.

Duke, Richard. 1974. _Gaming: The Future's Language_. New York: Sage Publications.

Etzioni, Amitai. 1964. _Modern Organizations_. Englewood Cliffs, N.J.: Prentice-Hall.

Ferejohn, John. 1974. _Pork Barrel Politics: Rivers and Harbors Legislation, 1947-1968_. Palo Alto, Calif.: Stanford University Press.

Freeman, J. Leiper. 1955. _The Political Process: Executive Bureau - Legislative Committee Relations_. New York: Random House.

Friedrich, Carl, ed. 1966. _The Public Interest_. New York: Atherton Press.

Godschalk, David. 1975. "Public Participation in Areawide Waste Treatment Management." In _Field Level Planning for Areawide Waste Treatment Management_, edited by David Moreau. Chapel Hill, N.C.: University of North Carolina, Department of City and Regional Planning.

Gormley, William. 1983. _The Politics of Public Utility Regulation_. Pittsburgh, Pa.: Pittsburgh Press.

Haefele, Edwin. 1973. _Representative Government and Environmental Management_. Baltimore, Md.: Johns Hopkins University Press.

Hardin, Russell. 1982. _Collective Action_. Baltimore: Johns Hopkins University Press.

Helmer, Olaf. 1967. _Analysis of the Future: The Delphi Method_. Santa Monica, Calif.: RAND Corporation.

_____. 1971. "Patterns of Politics in Water Resources Development." _Natural Resources Journal_. 11:102-118.

Ingram, Helen. 1969. _Patterns of Politics in Water Resources Development_. Albuquerque, New Mexico: University of New Mexico, Division of Government Research.

Ingram, Helen, Nancy Laney, John McCain. 1980. _A Policy Approach to Political Representation: Lessons from the Four Corners States_. Baltimore, Md.: Johns Hopkins University Press.

Jordan, D. _et al._ 1976. _Effective Citizen Participation in Transportation Planning, vols. 1 and 2_. Washington, D.C.: U.S. Department of Transportation.

Chapter Three

Kneese, Allen and William Schulze. 1985. "Ethics and
    Environmental Economics." In Handbook of Natural
    Resource and Energy Economics vol. I, edited by Allen
    Kneese and J. Sweeney. Elsevier Science Publishers.
Lipset, Seymour. 1960. Political Man. Garden City, N.Y.:
    Doubleday.
Lowi, Theodore. 1966. "American Business, Public Policy,
    Case-Studies, and Political Theory." World Politics
    16:677-715.
_____. 1969. The End of Liberalism: Ideology, Policy, and
    the Crisis of Public Authority. New York: W.W. Norton.
_____. 1970. "Decision-Making Versus Policy Making: Toward
    and Antidote for Technocracy." Public Administration
    Review 30:314-325.
MacIntyre, Alasdair. 1981. After Virtue. Notre Dame:
    University of Notre Dame Press.
Mazmanian, Daniel and Jeanne Nienaber. 1979. Can
    Organizations Change: Environmental Protection Citizen
    Participation, and the Corps of Engineers. Washington,
    D.C.: The Brookings Institution.
McAllister, Donald. 1980. Evaluation in Environmental
    Planning: Assessing Environmental, Social, Economic
    and Political Tradeoffs. Cambridge, Mass.: MIT Press.
McConnell, Grant. 1966. Private Power and American
    Democracy. New York: Vintage.
Milbrath, Lester. 1965. Political Participation. Chicago,
    Ill.: Rand McNally.
_____. 1981. "Citizen Surveys as Citizen Participation
    Mechaisms." Journal of Applied Behavioral Science 17:
    478-496.
Moe, Terry. 1980. The Organization of Interests. Chicago,
    Ill.: University of Chicago Press.
Morgan, A. 1971. Dams and Other Disasters: A Century of the
    Army Corps of Engineers in Civil Works. Boston, Mass:
    Porter Sargent.
Olson, Mancur. 1965. The Logic of Collective Action.
    Cambridge, Mass.: Harvard University Press.
Ortolano, Leonard. 1976. "Water Plan Ranking and the Public
    Interest." Journal of the Water Resources Planning and
    Management Division, American Society of Civil
    Engineers:35-48.
Ortolano, Leonard and William Hill. 1978. "NEPA's Effect on
    the Consideration of Alternatives: A Crucial Test."
    Natural Resources Journal 18:285-311.
Ozawa, Connie and Lawrence Susskind. 1985. "Mediating
    Science-Intensive Policy Disputes." Journal of Policy
    Analysis and Management 5:23-39.
Page, Talbot. 1977. Conservation and Economic Efficiency.
    Baltimore, Md.: Johns Hopkins University Press.
Pierce, J. and H. Doerksen, eds. 1976. Water Politics
    Public Involvement. Ann Arbor, Mich.: Ann Arbor
    Science Press.
Pyke, Donald and Harper North. 1969. "Technological
    Forecasting to Aid Research and Development Planning."
    Research Management 12:

References

Ragan, James, Jr. 1975. Public Participation in Water
    Resources Planning: An Evaluation of the Program of
    Fifteen Corps of Engineers' Districts. Springfield,
    Va.: National Technical Information Service, Report
    AD-AD 19966.
Rodgers, Joseph. 1977. Citizen Committees. Cambridge,
    Mass.: Ballinger.
Rosenbaum, Walter. 1977. The Politics of Environmental
    Concern, 2nd ed. New York: Holt, Rinehart, and
    Winston.
Schattschneider, E. 1960. The Semi-Sovereign People: A
    Realist's View of Democracy in America. Hinsdale,
    Ill.: Dryden Press.
Schramm, Gunter and R. Burt, Jr. 1970. An Analysis of
    Federal Water Resource Planning and Evaluation
    Procedures. Ann Arbor, Mich.: University of Michigan,
    School of Natural Resources.
Schumpeter, Joseph. 1950. Capitalism, Socialism and
    Democracy. New York: Harper and Row.
Schunk, Peter. 1977. "Public Interest Groups and the
    Political Process." Public Administration Review 37:
    132-140.
Socolow, Robert. 1976. "Failures of Discourse." In
    Boundaries of Analysis: An Inquiry into the Tocks
    Island Dam Controversy, edited by Harold Feiveson,
    Frank Sinden, and Robert Socolow. Cambridge, Mass.:
    Ballinger.
Susskind, Lawrence and Denise Madigan. 1985. "New
    Approaches to Resolving Disputes in the Public
    Sector." Cambridge, Mass.: Massachusetts Institute of
    Technology, Department of Urban Studies and Planning.
Truman, David. 1951. The Governmental Process. New York:
    Knopf.
Verba, Sidney. 1967. "Democratic Participation." The Annals
    of the American Academy of Political and Social
    Science:53-78.
Walker, Jack. 1966. "A Critique of the Elitist Theory of
    Democracy." American Political Science Review 60:284-
    295.
_____. 1983. "The Origins and Maintenance of Interest
    Groups in America." American Political Science Review
    77: 390-406.
Wandesforde-Smith, Geoffery. 1974. "On Doing the Devil's
    Word in God's Country: Legislators and Environmental
    Policy." In Environmental Politics, edited by Stuart
    Nagel, New York: Praeger.
Warner, Katherine. 1971. A State of the Arts Study of
    Public Participation in the Water Resources Planning
    Process. Ann Arbor, Mich.: University of Michigan,
    School of Natural Resources.
Webb, Kenneth and Harry Hatry. 1973. Obtaining Citizen
    Feedback: The Application of Citizen Surveys to Local
    Government. Washington, D.C.: The Urban Institute.

Chapter Three

Wengert, Norman. 1971. "Public Participation in Water
    Planning: A Critique of Theory, Doctrine, and
    Practice." Water Resources Bulletin 7:26-32.
Widditsch, Ann. 1977. Working Effectively with Advisory
    Committees. Washington, D.C.: U.S. Environmental
    Protection Agency.
Willeke, Gene. 1976. "Identification of Publics in Water
    Resources Planning." In Water Politics and Public
    Involvement, edited by J. Pierce and H. Doerksen. Ann
    Arbor, Mich.: Ann Arbor Science Press.
Wilson, James. 1967. "Planning and Politics: Citizen
    Participation in Urban Renewal." In Urban Renewal:
    People, Politics, and Planning, edited by Jewel
    Bellush and Murray Hausknecht. New York: Doubleday.

Chapter Four

Abelson, Peter. 1979. "Property Prices and the Value of
    Amenities." Journal of Environmental Economics and
    Management 6:11-28.
Adams, Richard, Narongsdakdi Thanavibulchai and Thomas
    Crocker. 1979. A Preliminary Assessment of Air
    Pollution Damages for Selected Crops Within Southern
    California. Washington, D.C.: U.S. Environmental
    Protection Agency, Report EPA-600/5-79-001c.
Anderson, Frederick et al. 1977. Environmental
    Improvement Through Economic Incentives. Baltimore,
    Md.: Johns Hopkins University Press.
Armstrong, F. 1974. "Valuation of Amenity Forests." The
    Consultant 19:13-19.
Arrow, Kenneth. 1966. "Discounting and Public Investment
    Criteria." In Water Research, edited by Allen Kneese
    and Stephen Smith, Baltimore, Md.: Johns Hopkins
    University Press.
Arrow, Kenneth and Anthony Fisher. 1974. "Environmental
    Preservation, Uncertainty, and Irreversibility."
    Quarterly Journal of Economics 8:312-320.
Ayres, Robert and I. Gutmanis. 1972. "Technological
    Change, Pollution and Treatment Cost Coefficients in
    Input-Output Analysis." In Population, Resources, and
    the Environment, vol. 3. U.S. Commission on
    Population Growth and the American Future.
    Washington, D.C.: U.S. Government Printing Office.
Bain, J., R. Caves and J. Margolis. 1966. Northern
    California's Water Industry. Baltimore, Md.: Johns
    Hopkins University Press.
Barrett, L. and T. Waddell. 1973. Costs of Air Pollution
    Damage. Research Triangle Park, N.C.: U.S.
    Environmental Protection Agency.
Baumol, William. 1977. "On the Discount Rate for Public
    Projects." In Public Expenditure and Policy Analysis
    2nd ed., edited by Robert Haveman and Julius Margolis.
    Chicago, Ill.: Rand McNally.

Baumol, William and Wallace Oates. 1975. The Theory of Environmental Policy. Englewood Cliffs, N.J.: Prentice-Hall.

Becker, Gary. 1965. "A Theory of the Allocation of Time." Economic Journal 75:493-517.

Bell, F. and E. Canterbury. 1976. Benefits from Water Pollution Abatement: Coastal Waters vols. 1 and 2. Springfield, Va.: National Technical Information Service.

Ben-David, Shaul et al. n.d. Six Studies of Health Benefits from Air Pollution Control, Vol. 2 of Methods Development for Environmental Control Benefits Assessment. Washington, D.C.: U.S. Environmental Protection Agency, Report EPA-230-07-83-007.

Bentham, Jeremy. 1948. An Introduction to the Principles of Morals and Legislation. Oxford: Blackwell (original 1781).

Binkley, C. and W. Hanemann. 1975. The Recreation Benefits of Water Quality Improvement: Analysis of Day Trips in an Urban Setting. Cambridge, Mass.: Urban Systems Research and Engineering.

Bishop, John and Charles Cicchetti. 1975. "Some Institutional and Conceptual Thoughts on the Measurement of Indirect and Intangible Benefits and Costs." In Cost-Benefit Analysis and Water Pollution Policy, edited by Henry Peskin and Eugene Seskin. Baltimore, Md.: Johns Hopkins University Press.

Bishop, Richard. 1978. "Endangered Species and Uncertainty: The Economics of a Safe Minimum Standard." American Journal of Agricultural Economics 60:10-18.

_____. 1982. "Option Value: An Exposition and Extension." Land Economics 58:1-15.

Bishop, Richard, and Thomas Heberlein. 1979. "Measuring Values of Extramarket Goods: Are Indirect Measures Biased?" American Journal of Agricultural Economics 60:926-930.

Blank, Frederick et al. 1977. Valuation of Aesthetic Preferences: A Case Study of the Economic Value of Visibility. Laramie, Wyo.: Resource and Environmental Economics Laboratory.

Blomquist, Glenn. 1979. "Value of Life-Saving: Implications of Consumption Activity." Journal of Political Economy 87:540-558.

Bockstael, N. and K. McConnell. 1981. "Theory and Estimation of the Household Production Function for Wildlife Recreation." Journal of Environmental Economics and Management 8:199-214.

Bohm, Peter. 1972. "Estimating the Demand for Public Goods: An Experiment." European Economic Review 3:111-130.

Bowen, Howard. 1943. "The Interpretation of Voting in the Allocation of Economic Resources." Quarterly Journal of Economics 58:27-48.

Chapter Four

Bower, Blair and Daniel Basta. 1973.
Residuals-Environmental Quality Management: Applying
the Concept. Baltimore, Md.: Johns Hopkins
University Press.
Brookshire, David, B. Ives and W. Schulze. 1976. "The
Valuation of Aesthetic Preferences." Journal of
Environmental Economics and Management 3:325-346.
Brookshire, David. et al. 1979. Experiments in Valuing
Nonmarket Goods: A Case Study of Alternative Benefit
Measures of Air Pollution Control in the South Coast
Air Basin. Washington, D.C.: U.S. Environmental
Protection Agency, Report EPA-600/5-79-79-001c.
_____, 1982. Experimental Approaches for Valuing
Environmental Commodities. Laramie, Wo.: Department
of Economics, University of Wyominng.
_____, et al. n.d. Six Studies on Nonmarket Valuation
Techniques. Vol. 3 of Methods Development for
Environmental Control Benefits Assessment.
Washington, D.C.: U.S. Environmental Protection
Agency, Report EPA-203-07-83-008.
Brown, W., A. Singh and E. Castle. 1965. "An Economic
Evaluation of the Oregon Salmon and Steelhead Sport
Fishery." Journal of Wildlife Management 29:266-279.
Burt, Oscar and Durward Brewer. 1971. "Estimation of Net
Social Benefits from Outdoor Recreation."
Econometrica 39:813-827.
Burton, Ian, Robert Kates and Gilbert White. 1978. The
Environment As Hazard. New York: Oxford University
Press.
Carpenter, B. et al. 1977. Health Costs of Air Pollution
Damages: A Study of Hospitalization Costs.
Washington, D.C.: U.S. Environmental Protection
Agency.
Cesario, Frank. 1976. "Value of Time in Recreation
Studies." Land Economics 52:32-41.
Cesario, Frank and Jack Knetsch. 1970. "Time Bias in
Recreation Benefit Estimates." Water Resources
Research 6:700-704.
Chowdhary, R. 1977. "Estimation of Demand for Forest
Recreation--A Conceptual Framework." Indian Forester
103:2-22.
Cicchetti, Charles and A. Myrick Freeman, III. 1971.
"Option Demand and Consumer's Surplus: Further
Comment." Quarterly Journal of Economics 85:528-539.
Cicchetti, Charles and V. Kerry Smith. 1976. The Costs of
Congestion. Cambridge, Mass.: Ballinger.
Clawson, Marion. 1959. Methods of Measuring the Demand
and Value of Outdoor Recreation. Washington, D.C.:
Resources for the Future, Reprint 10.
Cohen, Bernard. 1980. "Society's Valuation of Life-Saving
in Radiation Protection and Other Contexts." Health
Physics 38:33-51.
Colm, Gerhard. 1966. "The Public Interest: Essential Key
to Public Policy." The Public Interest, edited by G.
Friedrich. New York: Atherton Press.

Common, Michael. 1973. "A Note on the Use of the Clawson Method for the Evaluation of Recreation Site Benefits." Regional Studies 7:401-406.

Cooper, B. and D. Rice. 1976. "The Economic Cost of Illness Revisited." Social Security Bulletin 39:21.

Coughlin, Robert. 1976. "The Perception and Valuation of Water Quality: A Review of Research Methods and Findings." Perceiving Environmental Quality, edited by Kenneth Craik and Ervin Zube. New York: Plenum Press.

Crocker, Thomas et al. 1979. Experiments With the Economics of Air Pollution Epidemiology. Washington, D.C.: U.S. Environmental Protection Agency, Report EPA-600/5-79-001a.

Crutchfield, J. 1976. "The Perception and Valuation of Water Quality: A Review of Research Methods and Findings." In Perceiving Environmental Quality, edited by Kenneth Craik and Ervin Zube. New York: Plenum Press.

Culyer, A. and R. Akehurst. 1974. "On the Economic Surplus and the Value of Life." Bulletin of Economic Research 26:63-78.

Cumberland, John and R.J. Korbach. 1973. "A Regional Interindustry Environmental Model." Regional Science Association Papers 30:61-75.

Dales, J.H. 1968. Pollution, Property, and Prices. Toronto: University of Toronto Press.

Dardis, R. 1980. "The Value of Life: New Evidence From the Marketplace." American Economic Review 70:1077-1082.

d'Arge, Ralph. 1983. "Comments at a Seminar on Environmental Economics at the U.S. Environmental Protection Agency." Washington D.C.

Dasgupta, Partha. 1982. "Environmental Management Under Uncertainty." In Explorations in Natural Resources Economics, edited by V. Kerry Smith and John Krutilla. Baltimore, Md.: Johns Hopkins University Press.

David, Elizabeth. 1971. "Public Perceptions of Water Quality." Water Resources Research 7:453-457.

Desvousges, William, V. Kerry Smith and M. McGivney. 1983. A Comparison of Alternative Approaches for Estimating Recreation and Related Benefits of Water Quality Improvements. Washington, D.C.: Prepared for U.S. Environmental Protection Agency, Report EPA-230-05-83-001.

Dillingham, Alan. 1979. The Injury Risk Structure of Occupations and Wages. Ithaca, N.Y.: Cornell University, Ph.D thesis.

Dornbusch, D. 1975. The Impact of Water Quality Improvements Residential Property Prices. Springfield, Va.: National Technical Information Service.

Chapter Four

Dupuit, Jules. 1952. "On the Measurement of the Utility
    of Public Works." In International Economic Papers
    No. 2, edited by A. Peacock, et al. London: Macmillan
    (orignial 1844).
Ehrenfeld, David. 1978. The Arrogance of Humanism. New
    York: Oxford University Press.
Everett, R. 1978. "The Monetary Value of the Recreational
    Benefits of Wildlife." Journal of Environmental
    Management 8:203-213.
Ferejohn, John. 1974. Pork Barrel Politics. Stanford,
    Calif.: Stanford University Press.
Fink, F. et al. 1971. Technical-Economic Evaluation of
    Air Pollution Corrosion Costs on Metals in the U.S..
    Columbus, Ohio: Battelle-Memorial Institute.
Fisher, Anthony and John Krutilla. 1975. "Resource
    Conservation, Environmental Preservation, and the Rate
    of Interest." Quarterly Journal of Economics
    89:358-370.
Foster, Harold. 1980. Disaster Planning--The Preservation
    of Life and Property. New York: Springer-Verlag.
Freeman, A. Myrick, III. 1979. The Benefits of
    Environmental Improvement: Theory and Practice.
    Baltimore, Md.: Johns Hopkins University Press.
_____. 1980 The Benefits of Air and Water Pollution
    Control. Springfield, Va.: National Technical
    Information Service. Prepared for the U.S. Council on
    Environmental Quality.
_____. 1982 "The Health Implications of Residuals
    Discharges: A Methodological Overview." In
    Explorations in Natural Resource Economics, edited by
    V. Kerry Smith and John Krutilla. Baltimore, Md.:
    Johns Hopkins University Press.
Gibbs, K. Christopher. 1974. "Evaluation of Outdoor
    Recreation Resources: A Note." Land Economics
    55:309-311.
Gordon, Irene and Jack Knetsch. 1979. "The Consumer's
    Surplus Measures and the Evaluation of Resources."
    Land Economics 55:1-10.
Gosselink, J., Eugene Odum and R. Pope. 1974. The Value
    of the Tidal Marsh. Baton Rouge, La.: Center for
    Wetland Resources, Publication LSU-SG-7403.
Graham, D. 1981. "Cost-Benefit Analysis Under
    Uncertainty." American Economic Review 71715-71725.
Gramlich, Fred. 1977. "The Demand for Clean Water: The
    Case of the Charles River." National Tax Journal
    30:183-194.
Hammack, Judd and Gardner Brown. 1974. Waterfowl and
    Wetlands: Towards Bioeconomic Analysis. Baltimore,
    Md.: Johns Hopkins University Press.
Haspel, Abraham and F. Reed Johnson. 1982. "Multiple
    Destination Trip Bias in Recreation Benefit
    Estimation." Land Economics 58: 364-372.
Haveman, Robert. 1969. "The Opportunity Cost of Displaced
    Private Spending and the Social Discount Rate." Water
    Resources Research 5:947-957.

Haveman, Robert. 1983. "Evaluating Public Expenditures Under Conditions of Unemployment." In Public Expenditure and Policy Analysis, 3rd ed., edited by Robert Haveman and Julius Margolis. Chicago, Ill.: Rand McNally.

Heintz, H., Jr., A. Hershaft and G. Horak. 1976. National Damages of Air Pollution. Rockville, Md.: Enviro Control.

Hicks, J. 1944. "The Four Consumer's Surpluses." Review of Economics Studies 11:31-41.

Hirshliefer, Jack, James DeHaven and Jerome Milliman. 1960. Water Supply: Economics, Technology and Policy. Chicago, Ill.: University of Chicago Press.

Hirshliefer, Jack and David Shapiro. 1983. "The Treatment of Risk and Uncertainty." In Public Expenditure and Policy Analysis 3rd edition, edited by Robert Haveman and Julius Margolis. Chicago, Ill.: Rand McNally.

Hitchens, M. et al. 1978. "The Opportunity Cost Criterion for Land Allocations." Review of Marketing and Agricultural Economics 46:275-293.

Hodge, I. 1976. "Social Costs in Modern Agriculture Practice: Some Possible Approaches to Their Evaluation." Journal of Environmental Management 4:225-240.

Hoinville, Gerald. 1975. Multi-Dimensional Tradeoffs: An Appraisal of the Priority Evaluation Approach. London: Social and Community Planning Research.

Hufschmidt, Maynard et al. 1983. Environment, Natural Systems and Development: An Economic Evaluation Guide. Baltimore, Md.: Johns Hopkins University Press.

Hufschmidt, Maynard and Eric Hyman, eds. 1982. Economic Approaches to Natural Resource and Environmental Quality Analysis. Dublin, Ireland: Tycooly Press.

Hyman, Eric. 1981. "The Valuation of Extramarket Benefits and Costs in Environmental Impact Assessment." Environmental Impact Assessment Review 2:227-258.

_____. 1984. "Natural Resource Economics: Relevance in Planning and Management." Resources Policy 10:163-176.

_____. 1985. "Analyzing the Economics of Groundwater Contamination." The Environmental Professional 7: 199-204.

Hyman, Eric and John Dixon. 1986. "Selected Policy Options for Production and Use of Fuelwood in the Philippines." In Case Studies: Environment, Natural Systems, and Development: An Economic Valuation Guide, edited by John Dixon and Maynard Hufschmidt. Baltimore, Md.: Johns Hopkins University Press.

Isard, Walter. 1972. Ecologic-Economic Analysis for Regional Development. New York: Free Press.

Jarrett, Henry, ed. 1966. Environmental Quality in a Growing Economy. Baltimore, Md.: Johns Hopkins University Press.

Chapter Four

Johnson, Manuel and James Bennett. 1979. "An Input-Output Model of Regional Environmental and Economic Impacts of Nuclear Power Plants." Land Economics 55:236-252.

Jones-Lee, M. 1976. The Value of Life: An Economic Analysis. London: Martin Robertson.

Kapp, William. 1950. The Social Cost of Private Enterprise. Cambridge, Mass.: Harvard University Press.

Kim, S. and John Dixon. 1986. "Economic Valuation of Environmental Quality Aspects of Upland Agricultural Projects in Korea." In Case Studies: Environment, Natural Systems, and Development: An Economic Valuation Guide, edited by John Dixon and Maynard Hufschmidt. Baltimore, Md.: Johns Hopkins University Press.

Kneese, Allen. 1964. The Economics of Regional Water Quality Management. Baltimore, Md.: Johns Hopkins University Press.

Kneese, Allen. 1984. Measuring the Benefits of Clean Air and Water. Washington, D.C.: Resources for the Future.

Kneese, Allen, Robert Ayres and Ralph d'Arge. 1970. Economics and the Environment: A Materials Balance Approach. Washington, D.C.: Resources for the Future.

Kneese, Allen, and Blair Bower. 1968. Managing Water Quality: Economics, Technology, Institutions. Baltimore, Md.: Johns Hopkins University Press.

Kneese Allen and William Schulze. 1985. "Ethics and Environmental Economics." Handbook of Natural Resource and Energy Economics, Vol. 1, edited by Allen Kneese and J. Sweeney, Amsterdam: Elsevier Science Press.

Knetsch, Jack and Robert Davis. 1966. "Comparison of Methods for Recreation Evaluation." In Water Research, edited by Allen Kneese and Stephen Smith. Baltimore, Md.: Johns Hopkins University Press.

Kopp, Raymond, William Vaughan and Michael Hazilla. 1983. Agricultural Benefits Analysis for Ozone: Methods Evaluation and Demonstration Research Triangle Park, N.C.: U.S. Environmental Protection Agency.

Krutilla, John. 1967. "Conservation Reconsidered." American Economic Review 57:777-786.

Krutilla, John and Anthony Fisher. 1975. The Economics of Natural Environments. Baltimore, Md.: Johns Hopkins University Press.

Lancaster, Kevin. 1961. "A New Approach to Consumer Theory." Journal of Political Economy 74:132-157.

Leontief, Wassily. 1970. "Environmental Repercussions and the Economic Structure: An Input-Output Approach." Review of Economics and Statistics 52:262-271.

Lerner, L. 1962. "Quantitative Indices of Recreation
    Values." In Proceedings of a Conference on the
    Economics of Outdoor Recreation Policy. Reno, Nev.:
    Western Agriculture Council, University of Nevada.
    Report 11.
Lind, Robert. 1973. "Spatial Equilibrium, the Theory of
    Rents and the Measurement of Benefits from Public
    Programs." Quarterly Journal of Economics 87:188-207.
Loebl, Eugen. 1976. Humanomics. New York: Random House.
Loehman, Ednam, David Boldt and Kathleen Chaikin. 1980.
    Study Design and Property Value Study, Vol. 1 of
    Measuring the Benefits of Air Quality Improvements in
    the San Francisco Bay Area. Menlo Park, Ca.: SRI
    International, Report EPA-230-07-83-009.
Lowi, Theodore. 1969. The End of Liberalism. New York:
    W.W. Norton.
Lowrance, William. 1976. Of Acceptable Risk. Los Altos,
    Calif.: William Kaufmann.
Maler, Karl-Goran. 1977. "A Note on the Use of Property
    Values in Estimating Marginal Willingness to Pay for
    Environmental Quality." Journal of Environmental
    Economics and Management 4:355-369.
Maler, Karl-Goran and Ronald Wyzga. 1976. The Economic
    Measure of Damages in the Domain of the Environment.
    Paris: Organization for Economic Cooperation and
    Development.
Marglin, Stephen. 1963a. "The Opportunity Costs of Public
    Investment." Quarterly Journal of Economics
    77:274-289.
_____. 1963b. "The Social Rate of Discount and the
    Optimal Rate of Investment." Quarterly Journal of
    Economics 77:95-111.
Margolis, Julius. 1977. "Shadow Prices for Incorrect or
    Nonexistent Market Values." In Public Expenditure and
    Policy Analysis, edited by Robert Haveman and Julius
    Margolis. Chicago, Ill.: Rand McNally.
McConnell, K. 1977. "Congestion and Willingness to Pay:
    A Study of Beach Use." Land Economics 53:185-195.
_____. 1979. "Values of Marine Recreational Fishing:
    Measurement and Impact of Measurement." American
    Journal of Agricultural Economics 61:921-925.
McKinney, Michael and Duncan MacRae, Jr. 1978. Survey
    Assessments of Consensus Demand for Publicly Supplied
    Goods: Recreation Facilities. Chapel Hill, N.C.:
    University of North Carolina, Institute for Research
    in Social Science.
Meyer, John and Robert Leone. 1977. "The Urban Disamenity
    Revisited." In Public Economics and the Quality of
    Life, edited by Lowdon Wingo and Alan Evans.
    Baltimore, Md.: Johns Hopkins University Press.
Meyer, Philip. 1975. Recreation and Preservational Values
    Associated With the Salmon of the Fraser River.
    Vancouver: Environment Canada.
_____. 1976. A Comparison of Direct Questioning Methods
    for Obtaining Dollar Values for Public Recreation and
    Preservation. Vancouver, Canada: Environment Canada.

Chapter Four

_____. 1978. Updated Estimates for Recreation Values Associated with the Salmon and Steelhead of the Fraser River. Vancouver, Canada: Department of Fisheries and Oceans.

_____. 1979. "Publicly Vested Values for Fish and Wildlife: Criteria in Economic Welfare and Interface with the Law." Land Economics 55:223-235.

Michelson, I. and B. Tourin. 1966. "Comparative Methods for Studying the Costs of Air Pollution." Public Health Reports 81:505-511.

Mill, John Stuart. 1962. Utilitarianism. London: Collins (original 1863).

Millar, David and Martin Starr. 1967. The Structure of Human Decisions. Englewood Cliffs, N.J.: Prentice-Hall.

Mishan, Ezra. 1976. Cost-Benefit Analysis, 2nd ed. New York: Praeger.

Mitchell, Robert and Richard Carson. 1985. "Option Value: Empirical Evidence From a Case Study of Recreation and Water Quality: Comment." Quarterly Journal of Economics 100:291-294.

Mooney, Gavin. 1978. The Valuation of Human Life. London: Macmillan Press.

Morgan, J. 1969. Bighorn Sheep Investigation in Idaho. Boise, Idaho: Idaho Game Population Census and Range Study Committee.

Muller, Frederick. 1979. Energy and Environment in Interregional Input-Output Models. Boston, Mass.: Martinus Nijhoff.

National Oceanic and Atmospheric Administration. 1983. Assessing the Social Costs of Oil Spills. Washington, D.C.: U.S. Department of Commerce.

Needleman, L. 1976. "Valuing Other People's Lives." Manchester School of Economic and Social Studies 44:309-342.

Niskanen, William and Stephen Hanke. 1977. "Land Prices Substantially Underestimate the Value of Environmental Quality." Review of Economics and Statistics 59:375-377.

Nozick, Robert. 1974. Anarchy, State, and Utopia. Baltimore, Md.: Johns Hopkins University Press.

Odum, Howard. 1971. Environment, Power, and Society. New York: Wiley-Interscience.

O'Toole, R. and A. Walton. 1982. "Intergenerational Equity As It Relates to Conservation and Coal Extraction Standards." Natural Resources Journal 22:53-69.

Page, Talbot. 1977. Conservation and Economic Efficiency. Baltimore, Md.: Johns Hopkins University Press.

_____. 1982. "Intergenerational Justice as Opportunity." In Energy and the Future, edited by Douglas MacLean and Peter Brown. Totowa, N.J.: Rowman and Littlefield.

Payne, B. and R. DeGraaf. 1975. "Economic Values and
    Recreational Trends Associated with Human Enjoyment of
    Nongame Birds." In Proceedings of the Symposium on
    Management of Forest and Range Habitatis for Nongame
    Birds. Washington, D.C.: U.S. Forest Service,
    General Technical Report WO-1.
Pearce, David. 1976. Environmental Economics. London:
    Longman.
_____, ed. 1978. The Valuation of Social Cost. London:
    Allen and Unwin.
Pearce, David and R. Edwards. 1979. "The Monetary
    Evaluation of Noise Nuisance: Implications for Noise
    Abatement Policy." In Progress in Resource Management
    and Environmental Planning, vol. 1, edited by Timothy
    O'Riordan and Ralph d'Arge. New York: John Wiley and
    Sons.
Pearse, P. 1968. "A New Approach to the Evaluation of
    Non-Priced Recreational Resources." Land Economics
    44:87-99.
Pearse, P. and G. Bowden. 1966. Big Game Hunting in the
    East Kootenay: A Statistical Analysis. Vancouver:
    Price Printing.
Pendse, Dilip and J. Wyckoff. 1974. "Environmental Goods:
    Determination of Preferences and Tradeoff Values."
    Journal of Leisure Research 6:64-76.
_____. 1976. "Measurement of Environmental Trade-offs and
    Public Policy: A Case Study." Water Resources
    Bulletin 12:919-930.
Pigou, A. 1920. The Economics of Welfare. New York:
    MacMillan.
Polinsky, A. and S. Shavell. 1976. "Amenities and
    Property Values in a Model of an Urban Area." Journal
    of Public Economics 5:119-129.
Pollak, R. and M. Wachter. 1975. "The Relevance of the
    Household Production Function and Its Implication for
    the Allocation of Time." Journal of Political Economy
    83:255-277.
Portney, Paul. 1981. "Housing Prices, Health Effects and
    Valuing Reductions in Risk of Death." Journal of
    Environmental Economics and Management 8:72-78.
Portney, Paul and John Mullahy. 1983. Ambient Ozone and
    Human Health. Springfield, Va.: National Technical
    Information Service.
Prewitt, R. 1947. "The Economics of Public Recreation."
    Washington, D.C.: National Park Service (mimeograph).
Ramsey, Frank. 1928. "A Mathematical Theory of Saving."
    Economic Journal 38:543-559.
Randall, Alan, B. Ives and C. Eastman. 1974. "Bidding
    Games for Valuation of Aesthetic Environmental
    Improvements." Journal of Environmental Economies and
    Management 1:132-149.
Randall, Alan, John Hoehn and George Tolley. 1981. "The
    Structure of Contingent Markets: Some Results of a
    Recent Experiment." Paper Presented at the American
    Economic Association Annual Meeting, Washington, D.C.

Chapter Four

Rawls, John. 1971. A Theory of Justice. Cambridge,
    Mass.: Belknap Press.
Reiling, S., K. Gibbs and H. Stoevener. 1973. Economic
    Benefits from an Improvement in Water Quality.
    Washington, D.C.: U.S. Environmental Protection
    Agency. EPA-R5-73-008.
Ridker, Ronald. 1967. Economic Costs of Air Pollution:
    Studies in Measurement. New York: Praeger.
Ridker, Ronald and J. Henning. 1967. "The Determinants of
    Residential Property Values with Special Reference to
    Air Pollution." Review of Economics and Statistics
    49:246-257.
Ridker, Ronald and W. Watson. 1980. To Choose a Future.
    Baltimore, Md.: Johns Hopkins University Press.
Romm, Jeffrey. 1969. The Value of Reservoir Recreation.
    Ithaca, N.Y.: Cornell University, Water Resources and
    Marine Sciences Center, Technical Report 19.
Rowe, Robert, Ralph d'Arge and David Brookshire. 1980.
    "An Experiment on the Economic Value of Visibility."
    Journal of Environmental Economics and Management
    1:1-19.
Russell, Clifford. 1973. Residuals Management in
    Industry: A Case Study of Petroleum Refining.
    Baltimore, Md.: Johns Hopkins University Press.
Russell, Milton and William Vaughan. 1976. Steel
    Production: Processes, Products, and Residuals.
    Baltimore, Md.: Johns Hopkins University Press.
Samuelson, Paul. 1954. "The Pure Theory of Public
    Expenditures." Review of Economics and Statistics
    36:387-389.
_____. 1964. "Principles of Efficiency--Discussion."
    American Economic Review 54 (Papers and Proceedings):
    93-96.
Schelling, Thomas. 1968. "The Life You Save May Be Your
    Own." In Problems in Public Expenditures, edited by
    Samuel Chase, Jr. Washington, D.C.: Brookings
    Institution.
Schmalensee, Richard. 1972. "Option Demand and Consumer's
    Surplus: Valuing Price Changes Under Uncertainty."
    American Economic Review 63:813-824.
Schulze, William et al. 1981. The Benefits of Preserving
    Visibility in the National Parklands of the Southwest.
    Washington, D.C.: U.S. Environmental Protection
    Agency, Report EPA-230-07-83-013.
Schulze, William, David Brookshire and Todd Sandler. 1981.
    "The Social Rate of Discount for Nuclear Waste
    Storage: Economics or Ethics?" Natural Resources
    Journal 21:811-832.
Schuman, H. and M. Johnson. 1976. "Attitudes and
    Behavior." Annual Review of Sociology 2:161-207.
Seckler, David. 1966. "On the Uses and Abuses of Economic
    Science in Evaluating Public Outdoor Recreation."
    Land Economics 42:485-494.

References

Sharefkin, M., M. Schecter and Alan Kneese. 1983. Impacts, Costs and Techniques for Mitigation of Contaminated Groundwater. Washington, D.C.: Resources for the Future.

Shelby, B. 1980. "Crowding Models for Background Recreation." Land Economics 56:43-55.

Shucksmith, D. 1979. "The Demand for Angling at the Derwent Reservoir, 1970 to 1976." Journal of Agriculture Economics 30:25-27.

Sinden, John and Albert Worrell. 1979. Unpriced Values -- Decisions Without Market Prices. New York: Wiley-Interscience.

Smith, V. Kerry. 1981. "Congestion, Travel Cost Recreational Demand Models, and Benefit Estimation." Journal of Environmental Economics and Management 8:92-96.

_____. 1983. "Option Value: A Conceptual Overview." Southern Economic Journal 49:654-668.

Smith, V. Kerry and Raymond Kopp. 1980. The Spatial Limits of the Travel Cost Recreation Model. Washington, D.C.: Resources for the Future, Reprint 178.

Smith, V. Kerry and John Krutilla. 1979. "Endangered Species, Irreversibilities, and Uncertainty: A Comment." American Journal of Agricultural Economics 61:371-375.

Sonnen, Mitchell and L. Davis. 1979. "Wild Rivers--Methods for Evaluation." Water Resources Bulletin 15:404-419.

Spindler, J. 1975. The Accuracy of Consumer Surveys in Describing Markets for Hypothetical Goods. Santa Monica, Calif.: Rand Corporation.

Spofford, Walter, Clifford Russell and R. Kelly. 1975. An Integrated Residuals Management Model of the Lower Delaware Valley: The Region, the Model and Preliminary Results. Washington, D.C.: Resources for the Future.

Stanley, J. and A. Rattray. 1978. "Social Severance." In The Valuation of Social Cost, edited by David Pearce. London: Allen and Unwin.

Starkie, D. and D. Johnson. 1975. The Economic Value of Peace and Quiet. Lexington, Mass.: D.C. Heath.

Thaler, Richard and Sherwin Rosen. 1975. "The Value of Saving a Life: Evidence from the Labor Market." In Household Production and Consumption, edited by Nestor Terleckyj. New York: Columbia University Press.

Thayer, Mark. 1981. "Contingent Valuation Techniques Assessing Environmental Impacts: Further Evidence." Journal of Environmental Economics and Management 1:27-44.

Thayer, Mark and William Schultze. 1977. Valuing Environmental Quality: A Contingent-Substitution and Expenditure Approach. Los Angeles, Calif.: University of Southern California Department of Economics.

Chapter Four

Theil, H. and R. Kosobud. 1968. "How Informative are Consumer Buying Intentions Surveys?" Review of Economics and Statistics 50:50-59.

Tussey, R., Jr. 1967. Analysis of Reservoir Recreation Benefits. Lexington, Ky.: University of Kentucky, Water Resources Institute, Report 2.

U.S. Committee on Environment and Public Works. 1977. Pollution Taxes, Effluent Charges, and Other Alternatives for Pollution Control. Washington, D.C.: Government Printing Office.

U.S. Federal Interagency River Basin Committee, Subcommittee on Benefits and Costs. 1950. Proposed Practices for Economic Analysis of River Basin Projects. Washington, D.C.: Government Printing Office.

U.S. Water Resources Council. 1979. "Procedures for Evaluation of National Economic Development Benefits and Costs in Water Resources Planning (Level C); Final Rule." Federal Register 44 (December 14):72892-72976.
_____. 1980. "Environmental Quality Evaluation Procedures for Level C Water Resources Planning, Final Rule." Federal Register 45, No. 190 (September 29):64402-64446.

Vaughan, William and Clifford Russell. 1982. Freshwater Recreation Fishing: The National Benefits of Water Pollution Control, Washington, D.C.: Resources for the Future.

Victor, Peter. 1972. Pollution, Economy, and Environment. London: Allen and Unwin.

Viscusi, W. Kip. 1979. Employment Hazards: An Investigation of Market Performance. Cambridge, Mass.: Harvard University Press.

Walters, Alan. 1975. Noise and Prices. Oxford: Clarendon Press.

Weisbrod, Burton. 1964. "Collective-Consumption Services of Individual-Consumption Goods." Quarterly Journal of Economics 78:471-477.

Wicksell, K. 1967. "A New Principle of Just Taxation." In Classics in the Theory of Public Finance, edited by Richard Musgrave and A. Peacock. New York: Macmillan (original 1896).

Willig, Robert. 1976. "Consumer's Surplus Without Apology." American Economic Review 66:589-597.

Wilman, Elizabeth. 1980. "The Value of Time in Recreation Benefit Studies." Journal of Environmental Economics and Management 7:272-286.

Yang, Edward, Roger Dower and Mark Menefee. 1984. The Use of Economic Analysis in Valuing Natural Resource Damages. Washington, D.C.: Environmental Law Institute. Prepared for National Oceanic and Atmospheric Administration.

Zeckhauser, Richard. 1975. "Procedures for Valuing Lives." Public Policy 23:419-464.

Chapter Five

Agrafiotis, D. 1978. "Social Perception of Industrial
    Odors." In Environmental Assessment of Socioeconomic
    Systems, edited by Dietrich Burkhardt and William
    Ittleson. New York: Plenum Press.
Althoff, Phillip and W. Grieg. 1974. "Environmental
    Pollution Control Policy Making: An Analysis of Elite
    Perceptions." Environment and Behavior 6:259-288.
American Falls International Board. 1974. Preservation
    and Enhancement of the American Falls at Niagara --
    Appendix F: Public Involvement.
Appleyard, Donald. 1979. "The Environment as a Social
    Symbol Within a Theory of Environmental Action and
    Perception." Journal of the American Planning
    Association 45:143-153.
Appleyard, Donald et al. 1973. The Berkeley Environmental
    Simulation Laboratory: Its Uses in Environmental
    Impact Assessment. Berkeley, Calif.: University of
    California, Institute of Urban and Regional
    Development.
Arbuthnot, J. 1977. "The Roles of Attitudinal and
    Personality Variables in the Prediction of
    Environmental Knowledge and Behavior." Environment
    and Behavior 9:217-232.
Barker, M. 1971. "Beach Pollution in the Toronto Region."
    In Perceptions and Attitudes in Resources Management,
    edited by W. Sewell and Ian Burton. Ottawa:
    Information Canada.
Berry, David. 1975. Landscape Aesthetics and
    Environmental Planning. Philadelphia, Pa.:
    University of Pennsylvania, Regional Science Research
    Institute.
Brown, Perry, ed. 1974. Toward a Technique for
    Quantifying Aesthetic Quality for Water Resources.
    Springfield, Va: National Technical Information
    Service, Report AD-A003269.
Brunswick, Egon. 1952. "The Conceptual Framework of
    Psychology." International Encyclopedia of United
    Science, 1, No. 10. Chicago, Ill.: University of
    Chicago Press.
Brush, Robert and James Palmer. 1979. "Measuring the
    Impact of Urbanization on Scenic Quality: Land Use
    Charges in the Northeast." In Proceedings of Our
    National Landscape: A Conference on Applied
    Techniques for Analysis and Management of the Visual
    Resource, edited by Gary Elsner and Richard Smardon,
    Berkeley, Ca.: U.S. Forest Service Pacific Southwest
    Forest and Experiment Station.
Brush, Robert and Edward Shafer. 1975. "Application of a
    Landscape Preference Model to Land Management." In
    Landscape Assessment: Values, Perceptions, and
    Resources, edited by Ervin Zube, Robert Brush and
    Julius Fabos. Stroudsberg, Pa.: Dowden, Hutchinson,
    and Ross.

Chapter Five

Buerger, Robert. 1983. The Perceptual Differences of
    Beach Users and Management Staff Towards the
    Recreation Attributes of the Beach. Syracuse, N.Y.:
    Ph.D. dissertation, State University of New York-
    Syracuse.
Bugliarello, George et al. 1976. The Impact of Noise
    Pollution: A Sociotechnological Introduction.
    Elmsford, N.Y.: Pergamon Press.
Campbell, Angus, P. Converse and W. Rodgers. 1976. The
    Quality of American Life. New York: Russell Sage
    Foundation.
Clary, Bruce. 1978. "Measuring Public Values in
    Environmental Assessment." Carolina Planning 4:30-37.
Constantini, E. and K. Hanf. 1972. "Environmental Concern
    and Lake Tahoe: A Study of Elite Perceptions,
    Backgrounds and Attitudes." Environment and Behavior
    4:209-241.
Coughlin, Robert and K. Goldstein. 1970. The Extent of
    Agreement Among Observers on Environmental Allocation.
    Philadelphia, Pa.: University of Pennsylvania,
    Regional Science.
Coughlin, Robert et al. 1972. Perception and Use of
    Streams in Suburban Areas: Effects of Water Quality
    and of Distance from Residence to Stream.
    Philadelphia, Pa.: University of Pennsylvania,
    Regional Science Research Institute.
Craik, Kenneth. 1968. "The Comprehension of the Everyday
    Physical Environment." Journal of the American
    Institute of Planners 34:29-36.
_____. 1972. "Analyzing the Objectivity of Landscape
    Dimensions." In Natural Environments, edited by John
    Krutilla. Baltimore, Md.: Johns Hopkins University
    Press.
_____. 1975. "Individual Variations in Landscape
    Assessment." In Landscape Assessment: Values,
    Perceptions, and Resources, edited by Ervin Zube,
    Robert Brush and Julius Fabos. Stroudsberg, Pa.:
    Dowden, Hutchinson and Ross.
Daniel, T. and H. Schroeder. 1979. "Scenic Beauty
    Estimation Model: Predicting Perceived Beauty of
    Forest Landscapes." In Proceedings of Our National
    Landscape: A Conference on Applied Techniques for
    Analysis and Management of the Visual Resource, edited
    by Gary Elsner and Richard Smardon Berkeley, Calif.:
    U.S. Forest Service Pacific Southwest Forest and Range
    Experiment Station.
David, Elizabeth. 1971. "Public Perception of Water
    Quality." Water Resources Research 7:453-457.
Dearinger, John et al. 1973. Measuring the Intangible
    Values of Natural Streams: Part 2, Preference Studies
    and Completion Report. Springfield, Va.: National
    Technical Information Service, Report PV-229 838.
Dornbusch, D. 1975. The Impacts of Water Quality
    Improvements on Residential Property Prices.
    Springfield Va.: National Technical Information
    Service.

Dubos, Rene. 1976. "Symbiosis Between Earth and Humankind." Science 193, No. 4252 (August 6):459-462.

Edelstein, Michael. 1982. The Social and Psychological Impacts of Groundwater Contamination in the Legler Section of Jackson, New Jersey. Mahwah, N.J.: Ramapo College.

Elsner, Gary. 1971. Computing Visible Areas from Proposed Recreation Development: A Case Study. Berkeley, Calif.: U.S. Forest Service Pacific Southwest Forest and Range Experiment Station, Report PSW-246.

Feimer, Nickolaus et al. 1979. "Appraising the Reliability of Visual Assessment Methods." In Proceedings of Our National Landscape: A Conference on Applied Techniques for Analysis and Management of the Visual Resource, edited by Gary Elsner and Richard Smardon. Berkeley, Calif.: U.S. Forest Service Southwest Forest and Range Experiment Station.

Feimer, Nickolaus, Richard Smardon and Kenneth Craik. 1981. "Evaluating the Effectiveness of Observer Based Visual Resource and Impact Assessment Methods." Landscape Research 6:12-16.

Felleman, J. 1982. "Visibility Mapping in New York's Coastal Zone: A Case Study of Alternative Methods." Coastal Zone Management Journal 9:249-270.

Finsterbusch, Kurt. 1982. "Psychological Impact Theory and Social Impacts." Impact Assessment Bulletin 1, No. 4 (Summer):71-89.

Foa, Uriel. 1971. "Interpersonal and Economic Resources," Science 171, No. 4166 (January 29):343-351.

Gleser, C., and B. Green and C. Winget. 1981. Prolonged Psychosocial Effects of Disaster: A Study of Buffalo Creek. New York: Academic Press.

Golant, Stephen and Ian Burton. 1976. "A Semantic Differential Experiment in the Interpretation and Grouping of Environmental Hazards." In Environmental Knowing: Theory, Research and Methods, edited by Gary Moore and R. Golledge. Stroudsberg, Pa.: Dowden, Hutchinson and Ross.

Gollub, J. 1976. Identifying and Evaluating Aesthetic Elements of the Landscape: An Aesthetic Quality Assessment Model Based on an Examination of Research in Psychology, Aesthetics, Life-Span Environmental Behavior and Landscape Assessment. Los Angeles, Calif.: University of Southern California.

Gough, H. and A. Heilbrun, Jr. 1965. The Adjective Checklist Manual. Palo Alto, Calif.: Consulting Psychologists Press.

Gramlich, Fred. 1977. "The Demand for Clean Water: The Case of the Charles River." National Tax Journal 30:183-194.

Chapter Five

Gussow, Alan. 1979. "Conserving the Magnitude of
    Usefulness: A Philosophical Perspective." In
    Proceedings of Our National Landscape: A Conference
    on Applied Techniques for Analysis and Management of
    the Visual Resources, edited by Gary Elsner and
    Richard Smardon. Berkeley, Calif.: U.S. Forest
    Service Pacific Southwest Forest and Range Experiment
    Station.
Hammond, Kenneth, et al. 1975. "Social Judgment Theory."
    In Human Judgment and Decision Processes, edited by
    Martin Kaplan and Steven Schwartz. New York:
    Academic Press.
Hart, William and W. Graham. 1967. "How to Size and Rank
    Landscapes." Landscape Architecture 57:121-123.
Hartsough, Don and Jeffrey Savitsky. 1984. "Three Mile
    Island: Psychology and Environmental Policy at a
    Crossroads." American Psychologist 39:1113-1122.
Hendee, John et al. 1968. Wilderness Users in the Pacific
    Northwest -- Their Characteristics, Values and
    Management Preferences. Seattle, Wash.: U.S. Forest
    Service Northwest Forest and Range Experiment Station,
    Report PNW-61.
Hendee, John and R. Harris. 1970. "Foresters' Perception
    of Wilderness-User Attitudes and Preferences." Journal
    of Forestry 68: 759-762.
Hyman, Eric. 1981. "The Uses, Validity, and Reliability
    of Perceived Environmental Quality Indicators."
    Social Indicators Research 9:85-110.
Insko, Chester and John Schopler. 1972. Experimental
    Social Psychology. New York: Academic Press.
Ittleson, William, ed. 1973. Environment and Cognition.
    New York: Seminar Press.
Jain, Ravinder, L. Urban and G. Stacey. 1977.
    Environmental Impact Analysis: A New Dimension in
    Decision Making. New York: Van Nostrand Reinhold.
Kaplan, Martin and Steven Schwartz. 1977. Human Judgment
    and Decision Processes in Applied Settings. New York:
    Academic Press.
Kaplan, Rachel. 1978. "The Green Experience." In
    Humanscape: Environments for People, edited by
    Stephen and Rachel Kaplan. North Scituate, Mass.:
    Duxbury Press.
    . 1979. "Visual Resources and the Public: An
    Empirical Approach." In Proceedings of Our National
    Landscape: A Conference on Applied Techniques for
    Analysis and Management of the Visual Resource, edited
    by Gary Elsner and Richard Smardon. Berkeley, Calif.:
    U.S. Forest Service Pacific Southwest Forest and Range
    Experiment Station.
Kaplan, Stephen. 1978a. "Attention and Fascination: The
    Search for Cognitive Clarity." In Humanscape:
    Environments for People, edited by Stephen and Rachel
    Kaplan. North Scituate, Mass.: Duxbury Press.

_____. 1978b. "On Knowing the Environment." In
Humanscape: Environments for People, edited by
Stephen and Rachel Kaplan. North Scituate, Mass.:
Duxbury Press.

_____. 1979. "Perception and Landscape: Conceptions and
Misconceptions." In Proceedings of Our National
Landscape: A Conference on Applied Techniques for
Analysis and Management of the Visual Resource, edited
by Gary Elsner and Richard Smardon. Berkeley, Calif.:
U.S. Forest Service, Pacific Southwest Forest and
Range Experiment Station.

Kaplan, Stephen and Rachel Kaplan, eds. Humanscape:
Environments for People, North Scituate, Mass.:
Duxbury Press.

Koenig, Daniel. 1975. "Additional Research on
Environmental Activism." Environment and Behavior
7:472-485.

Laurie, Ian. 1975. "Aesthetic Factors in Visual
Evaluation." In Landscape Assessment: Values,
Perceptions and Resources, edited by Ervin Zube,
Robert Brush, and Julius Fabos, Stroudsberg, Pa.:
Dowden, Hutchinson and Ross.

Leff, Herbert, L. Gordon and J. Ferguson. 1974.
"Cognitive Set and Environmental Awareness."
Environment and Behavior 6:395-447.

Litton, R. Burton, Jr. 1972. "Aesthetic Dimensions of the
Landscape." In Natural Environments, edited by John
Krutilla. Baltimore, Md.: Johns Hopkins University
Press.

_____. 1973. Landscape Control Points: A Procedure for
Predicting and Monitoring Visual Impacts. Berkeley,
Calif.: U.S. Forest Service Pacific Southwest Forest
and Range Experiment Station, Paper PSW-91.

Litton, R. Burton, Jr. et al. 1971. An Aesthetic Overview
of the Role of Water in the Landscape. Springfield,
Va.: National Technical Information Service, Report
PB 207 315.

Luchins, Abraham. 1957. "Primacy-Recency in Impression
Formation." In The Order of Presentation in
Persuasion, edited by C. Hovland. New Haven, Conn.:
Yale University Press.

Lynch, Kevin. 1960. The Image of the City. Cambridge,
Mass.: Massachusetts Institute of Technology Press.

McKennell, Aubrey. 1978. "Cognition and Affect in
Judgments of Subjective Well-Being." Social
Indicators 5:389-426.

McKinney, Michael and Duncan MacRae, Jr. 1978. Survey
Assessment of Consensus Demand for Publicly Supplied
Goods: Recreation Facilities. Chapel Hill, N.C.:
University of North Carolina, Institute for Research
in Social Science.

Michelson, William. 1966. "An Empirical Analysis of Urban
Environmental Preferences." Journal of the American
Institute of Planners 32:355-360.

Chapter Five

Miller, G. 1956. "The Magical Number Seven Plus or Minus
    Two: Some Limitations In Our Capacity to Process
    Information." Psychology Review 63:81-97.
Moeller, G., R. MacLachlan and D. Morrison. 1974.
    Measuring Perceptions of Elements in Outdoor
    Environments. Upper Darby, Pa.: U.S. Forest Service
    Northwest Forest Experiment Station.
Moore, Gary and R. Golledge, eds. 1976. Environmental
    Knowing: Theories, Research and Methods.
    Stroudsberg, Pa.: Dowden, Hutchinson and Ross.
Nardi, Bonnie and J. Harding. 1978. "Determining
    Community Attitudes and Preferences for Progress and
    Service." Carolina Planning 4:38-45.
Osgood, Charles, J. Suri, and P. Tannenbaum. 1957. The
    Measurement of Health. Urbana, Ill.: University of
    Illinois Press.
Palmer, James. 1982. "Assessment of Coastal Wetlands in
    Dennis, Massachusetts." In The Future of Wetlands:
    Assessing Visual-Cultural Values. Totowa, N.J.:
    Allanheld, Osmun.
_____. 1983. "Visual Quality and Visual Impact
    Assessment." In Social Impact Assessment Methods,
    edited by Kurt Finsterbusch, Lynn Llewellyn, and
    Charles Wolf, Beverly Hills, Calif.: Sage
    Publications.
Panel on Aesthetic Attributes, U.S. National Research
    Council. 1982. Assessing Aesthetic Attributes in
    Planning Water Resources Projects. Washington, D.C.:
    National Academy of Sciences.
Peterson, George and E. Neumann. 1969. "Modeling and
    Predicting Human Response to the Visual Recreation
    Environment." Journal of Leisure Research 1:219-237.
Pirsig, Robert. 1974. Zen and the Art of Motorcycle
    Maintenance. New York: Morrow.
Pitt, David and T. Anderson. 1975. "Perception and
    Prediction of Scenic Resource Values of the
    Northwest." In Landscape Assessment: Values,
    Perceptions, and Resources, edited by Ervin Zube,
    Robert Brush and Julius Fabos. Stroudsberg, Pa.:
    Dowden, Hutchinson and Ross.
Pitt, David and Ervin Zube. 1979. "The Q-Sort Method:
    Use in Landscape Assessment Research and Landscape
    Planning." In Proceedings of Our National Landscape:
    A Conference on Applied Techniques for Analysis and
    Management of the Visual Resource, edited by Gary
    Elsner and Richard Smardon. Berkeley, Calif.: U.S.
    Forest Service Pacific Southwest Forest Range and
    Experiment Station.
Posner, Michael. 1973. Cognition: An Introduction.
    Glenview, Ill.: Scott, Foresman.

References

Propst, Dennis. 1979. "Policy Capturing as a Method of Quantifying the Determinants of Landscape Preference." In Proceedings of Our National Landscape: A Conference on Applied Techniques for Analysis and Management of the Visual Resource, edited by Gary Elsner and Richard Smardon. Berkeley, Calif.: U.S. Forest Service Pacific Southwest Forest Range and Experiment Station.

Proshansky, H., William Ittleson and L. Rivlin, eds. 1976. Environmental Psychology: People and Their Physical Settings, 2nd ed. New York: Holt, Rinehart and Winston.

Rappaport, Leon and D. Summers. 1973. Human Judgment and Social Interaction. New York: Holt, Rinehart and Winston.

Rau, John and David Wooten, eds. 1980. Environmental Impact Analysis Handbook. New York: McGraw-Hill.

Rosenberg, J. 1960. "An Analysis of Affective-Cognitive Consistency." In Attitude Organization and Change, edited by C. Hovland and M. Rosenberg. New Haven, Conn.: Yale University Press.

Scherer, Ursula and Robert Coughlin. 1971. The Influence of Water Quality in the Evaluation of Stream Sites. Philadelphia, Pa.: University of Pennsylvania, Regional Science Research Institute.

Shafer, Elwood, Jr. and H. Burke. 1965. "Preferences for Outdoor Recreation Facilities in Four State Parks." Journal of Forestry 63:512-518.

Shafer, Elwood, Jr., J. Hamilton, Jr. and E. Schmidt. 1969. "Natural Landscape Preferences: A Predictive Model." Journal of Leisure Research 1:1-19.

Shafer, Elwood, Jr. and J. Mietz. 1970. It Seems Possible to Quantify Scenic Beauty in Photographs. Upper Darby, Pa.: U.S. Forest Service Northeast Forest Experiment Station, Paper NE-162.

Shafer Elwood, Jr. and M. Tooby. 1973. "Landscape Preferences: An International Replication," Journal of Leisure Research 5:60-65.

Simon, Herbert. 1957. Models of Man. New York: Wiley.

Smardon, Richard et al. 1983. "Assessing the Reliability, Validity and Generalizability of Observer-Based Visual Impact Assessment Methods for the Western United States." In Managing Air Quality and Scenic Resources at National Parks and Wilderness Areas, edited by Robert Rowe and Lauraine Chestnut, Boulder, Co.: Westview Press.

Smardon, Richard. 1984. Visual Impact Assessment Procedure for U.S. Army Corps of Engineers. Syracuse, N.Y.: College of Environmental Sciences and Forestry, State University of New York.

Shuttlesworth, S. 1980. "The Evaluation of Landscape Quality." Landscape Research 5:14-20.

Chapter Five

Sonnenfeld, Joseph. 1966. "Variable Values in Space Landscape: An Inquiry into the Nature of Environmental Necessity." Journal of Social Issues 5:71-82.

Spindler, J. Andrew. 1975. The Accuracy of Consumer Surveys in Describing Markets for Hypothetical Goods. Springfield, Va.: National Technical Information Service, Report AD-AO22 218.

Sproule-Jones, Mark. 1978. "The Social Appropriateness of Water Quality Management for the Lower Fraser River." Canadian Public Administration 21:176-194.

Stankey, G. 1972. "The Use of Content Analysis in Resource Decision Making." Journal of Forestry 10:148-151.

Stewart, Thomas and Linda Gelberd. 1976. "Analysis of Judgment Policy: A New Approach for Citizen Participation in Planning." Journal of the American Institute of Planners 42:33-41.

Strumpel, Burkhard. 1974. "Economic Well-Being as an Object of Social Measurement." In Subjective Elements of Well-Being. Paris: Organization of Economic Cooperation and Development.

Tognacci, L. et al. 1972. "Environmental Quality: How Universal Is Public Concern?" Environment and Behavior 4:73-86.

U.S. Bureau of Land Management. 1978. Upland Visual Resource Inventory and Evaluation. Washington, D.C.: BLM Manual Sections 8411 and 8431.

U.S. Bureau of Land Management. 1980a. Visual Resource Management Program. Washington, D.C.: Government Printing Office.

U.S. Bureau of Land Management. 1980b. Visual Simulation Techniques. Washington, D.C.: Government Printing Office.

U.S. Forest Service. 1974. National Forest Landscape Management: The Visual Management System, Washington, D.C.: Government Printing Office, Agricultural Handbook 462, vol. 2.

Ward, Barbara. 1976. The Home of Man. New York: W. W. Norton.

Wellman, J., G. Buhyoff. 1980. "Effects of Regional Familiarity on Landscape Preferences." Journal of Environmental Management 11:105-110.

Wellman, J. and M. Dawson and J. Roggenbuck. 1982. "Park Manager's Prediction of the Motivations of Visitors to Two National Park Service Areas."

Wenger, W., Jr. and R. Videbeck. 1969. "Eye Pulillary Measurement of Aesthetic Response to Forest Scenes." Journal of Leisure Research 1:149-161.

Zube, Ervin. 1974. "Cross-Disciplinary and Inter-Mode Agreement on the Description and Evaluation of Landscape Resources." Environment and Behavior 6:68-69.

Chapter Six

Alessio, Frank. 1981. "Energy Analysis and the Energy
 Theory of Value." Energy Journal 2:61-74.
American Physical Society. 1975. Efficient Use of Energy:
 A Physics Perspective. New York: American Institute
 of Physics.
Berndt, Ernst. 1978. "Aggregate Energy Efficiency, and
 Productivity Measurement." In Annual Review of
 Energy, edited by Jack Hollander. Palo Alto, Calif.:
 Annual Reviews.
Berry, R. and M. Fels. 1973. "The Energy Cost of
 Automobiles." Science and Public Affairs 29, No.
 10(December):11-17.
Berry, R. and Hiro Makino. 1974. "Energy Thrift in
 Packaging and Marketing." Technology Review 76, No.
 8(February):32-43.
Bullard, Clark, P. Penner and David Pilati. 1976. Energy
 Analysis Handbook. Urbana, Ill.: University of
 Illinois, Center for Advanced Computation. Report CAC
 214.
Chapman, Peter. 1977. "Energy Costs: A Review of
 Methods." In Energy Analysis, edited by John Thomas.
 Boulder, Colo.: Westview Press.
Chapman, Peter, Gerald Leach and Malcolm Slesser. 1977.
 "The Energy Costs of Fuels." In Energy Analysis,
 edited by John Thomas. Boulder, Colo.: Westview
 Press.
Chapman, Peter and W. Mortimer. 1974. "Energy Inputs and
 Outputs for Nuclear Power Stations." In Energy
 Accounting as a Policy Analysis Tool, edited by David
 Gushee, Congressional Research Service. Washington,
 D.C.: U.S. Government Printing Office.
Development Sciences, Inc. 1976. A Study to Develop
 Energy Estimates of Merit for Selected Fuel
 Technologies. East Sandwich, Mass.: Development
 Sciences, Inc.
_____. 1977. Application of Net Energy Analysis to
 Consumer Technologies. Washington, D.C.: Energy
 Research and Development Administration, Report 77-14.
Elsner, Henry, Jr. 1967. The Technocrats: Prophets of
 Automation. Syracuse, N.Y.: Syracuse University
 Press.
Georgescu-Roegen, Nicholas. 1976. Energy and Economic
 Myths. New York, N.Y.: Pergamon Press.
_____. 1979. "Comments on the Papers by Daly and
 Stiglitz." In Scarcity and Growth Reconsidered,
 edited by V. Kerry Smith. Baltimore, Md.: Johns
 Hopkins University Press.
Gilliland, Martha. 1975. "Energy Analysis and Public
 Policy." Science 189, No. 4208 (September
 26):1051-1056.
Gilliland, Martha, ed. 1978. Energy Analysis: A New
 Public Policy Tool. Boulder, Colo.: Westview Press,
 AAS Selected Symposium 9.

Chapter Six

Gosselink, J., Eugene Odum and R. Pope. 1974. The Value
    of the Salt Marsh. Baton Rouge, La.: Louisiana State
    University Center for Wetland Resources.
Hannon, Bruce. 1973. "An Energy Standard of Value."
    Annals of the American Academy of Political and Social
    Science 410 (November):139-153.
_____. 1975. "Energy Conservation and the Consumer."
    Science 189, No. 4197 (July 11):95-102.
Herendeen, Robert. 1978. "Energy Analysis of Two
    Technologies: Gasohol and Solar Satellite Power
    Station." Energy Abstracts for Policy Analysis 5,
    No.11:4574.
Herendeen, Robert and Clark Bullard. 1974. Energy Cost of
    Goods and Services. Urbana, Ill.: University of
    Illinois, Center for Advanced Computation.
Holling, C.S., ed. 1978. Adaptive Environmental
    Assessment and Management. New York:
    Wiley-Interscience.
Huettner, David. 1976a. "Net Energy Analysis: An
    Economic Assessment." Science 192, No. 4235 (April
    19):101-104. International Federation of Institutes
    for Advanced Study. 1976a. "Energy Analysis Workshop
    on Methodology and Conventions." In Energy Accounting
    as a Policy Analysis Tool, edited by David Gushee.
    Washington, D.C.: Congressional Research Service.
_____. 1976b. "Workshop on Energy Analysis and
    Economics." In Energy Accounting as a Policy Analysis
    Tool, edited by David Gushee. Washington, D.C.:
    Congressional Research Service.
Lenchek, T. 1976. "Energy Expenditures in a Solar Heating
    System." Alternate Sources of Energy 21:13-18.
Marshall, Alfred. 1922. Principles of Economics. London:
    MacMillan.
Odum, Howard. 1971. Environment, Power, and Society. New
    York: Wiley.
Odum, Howard and Elizabeth Odum. 1976. Energy Basis for
    Man and Nature. New York: McGraw-Hill.
Pilati, David. 1977. "Energy Analysis of Electricity
    Supply and Energy Conservation Options." Energy
    2:1-7.
Pimentel, David et al. 1975. "Energy and Land Constraints
    in Food Protein Production." Science 190, No. 4216
    (November 21):754-761.
Price, John. 1974. "Dynamic Energy Analysis and Nuclear
    Power." In Energy Accounting as a Policy Analysis
    Tool, edited by David Gushee. Washington, D.C.:
    Congressional Research Service.
Ricardo, David. 1911. Principles of Political Economy and
    Taxation. New York: E.P. Dutton (original 1817).
Scott, Howard. 1933. Introduction to Technocracy. New
    York: John Day.
Shabman, Leonard and S. Batie. 1977. Estimating the
    Economic Value of Natural Coastal Wetlands: A
    Cautionary Note. Blacksburg, Va.: Virginia
    Polytechnic Institute.

References

Slesser, Malcolm. 1977. "Letter." Science 196, No. 4287
    (April 15):259-260.
    . 1978. Energy in the Economy. London: Macmillan.
Slesser, Malcolm and Gerald Leach. 1973. Energy
    Equivalents of Network Inputs to Food-Producing
    Process. Glasgow, Scotland: Strathclyde University.
Smith, Adam. 1910. An Inquiry Into the Nature and Causes
    of the Wealth of Nations. New York: E.P. Dutton
    (original 1776).
Smith, V. Kerry, ed. 1979. Scarcity and Growth
    Reconsidered. Baltimore, Md.: Johns Hopkins
    University Press.
Soddy, Frederick. 1933. Wealth, Virtual Wealth, and
    Death. New York: E.P. Dutton.
Williamson, Richard. 1978. "Energy Analysis in Energy R,
    D, and D: Planning and Decision-Making." In Energy
    Analysis: A New Public Policy Tool, edited by Martha
    Gilliland. Boulder, Colo.: Westview Press.

Chapter Seven

Adams, David. 1980. "Wildlife Habitat Models As Aids to
    Impact Evaluation." The Environmental Professional
    2:253-262.
Bisset, Ronald. 1980. "Methods for Environmental Impact
    Analysis: Recent Trends and Future Prospects."
    Journal of Environmental Management 11:27-43.
Bonnicksen, Thomas and Robert Becker. 1983.
    "Environmental Impact Studies: An Interdisciplinary
    Approach for Assigning Priorities." Environmental
    Management 7:109-117.
Boyce, Stephen. 1982. A Decision and Control Tool
    (DYNAST)." The Environmental Professional 4:261-266.
Burchell, Robert and David Listokin. 1975. In The
    Environmental Impact Handbook. New Brunswick, N.J.:
    Rutgers University, Center for Urban Policy Research.
California State Water Resource Control Board. 1972.
    Environmental Impact Statement: Policies and
    Procedures, Grants for the Clean Water Program.
    Sacramento, Calif.: Government of California.
Canter, Lawrence. 1977. Environmental Impact Assessment.
    New York: McGraw-Hill.
Canter, Lawrence and Loren Hill. 1979. Handbook of
    Variables for Environmental Impact Assessment. Ann
    Arbor, Mich.: Ann Arbor Science Press.
Dean, B.V. and M.J. Nishry. 1965. "Scoring and
    Profitability Models for Evaluating and Selecting
    Engineering Projects." Journal of the Operations
    Research Society of America 13:550-569.
Dee, Norbert et al. 1972. An Environmental Evaluation
    System for Water Resource Planning. Springfield, Va.:
    National Technical Information Service. Report PB-
    208822.

Chapter 7

Duke, K.M. *et al.* 1977. Environmental Quality Assessment
in Multiobjective Planning. Springfield, Va.:
National Technical Information Service. Prepared for
the U.S. Bureau of Reclamation.

Ellis, J. *et al.* 1979. "Appraising Four Field Methods of
Terrestrial Habitat Evaluation." Transactions of the
North American Wildlife and Natural Resources
Conference 44:369-379.

Fabos, Julius. 1979. Planning the Total Landscape: A
Guide to Intelligent Land Use. Boulder, Colo.:
Westview Press.

Fabos, Julius and S. Caswell. 1977. Composite Landscape
Assessment. Amherst, Mass.: University of
Massachusetts Agricultural Experiment Station,
Research Bulletin 637.

Fabos, Julius, Christopher Greene and Spencer Joyner, Jr.
1978. The METLAND Landscape Planning Process:
Composite Landscape Assessment, Alternative Plan
Formulation and Plan Evaluation: Part 3 of the
Metropolitan Landscape Planning Model. Amherst,
Mass.: University of Massachusetts Agricultural
Experiment Station, Research Bulletin 653.

Galloway, Gerald. 1978. Assessing Man's Impact on
Wetlands. Raleigh, N.C.: University of North
Carolina, Water Resources Research Institute, Report
78-136.

Guseman, Patricia and K. Dietrich. 1978. Profile and
Measurement of Social Well-Being Indicators for Use in
the Evaluation of Water and Related-Land Management
Planning. Washington, D.C.: U.S. Army Corps of
Engineers, Office of the Chief of Engineers.

Guter, G., J. Westermeier and T. Ryan. 1976. "Computer
Simulation of Long-Term Secondary Impacts of Water and
Wastewater Projects." In Environmental Modeling and
Simulation, edited by Wayne Ott. Washington, D.C.:
U.S. Environmental Protection Agency.

Haimes, Yacov *et al.* 1977. Multiobjective Analysis in the
Maumee River Basin: A Case Study on Level B Planning.
Cleveland, Ohio: Case Western Reserve University.

Haimes, Yacov and Warren Hall. 1974. "Multiobjectives in
Water Resources Systems: The Surrogate Worth Tradeoff
Method." Water Resources Research 10:615-624.

Haimes, Yacov, Warren Hall and H. Freedman. 1975.
Multiobjective Optimization in Water Resource Systems:
The Surrogate Worth Tradeoff Method. New York:
Elsevier.

Hill, Morris. 1968. "A Goals-Achievement Matrix for
Evaluating Alternative Plans." Journal of the
American Institute of Planners 34:19-28.

_____. 1973. Planning for Multiple Objectives: An
Approach to the Evaluation of Transportation Plans.
Philadelphia, Pa.: University of Pennsylvania,
Regional Science Research Institute, Monograph 5.

Hill, Morris, and Rachel Alterman. 1974. "Power Plant
    Site Evaluation: The Case of the Sharon Plant in
    Israel." Journal of Environmental Management
    2:179-196.
Holling, Charles, ed. 1978. Adaptive Environmental
    Assessment and Management. New York:
    Wiley-Interscience.
Kane, Julius, I. Vertinsky and W. Thompson. 1973. "KSIM:
    A Methodology for Interactive Resource Simulation."
    Water Resources Research 9:65-80.
Keeney, Ralph and Howard Raffia. 1976. Decisions with
    Multiple Objectives: Preferences and Value Tradeoffs.
    New York: Wiley.
Keeney, Ralph and G. Robilliard. 1977. "Assessing and
    Evaluating Environmental Impacts at Proposed Nuclear
    Power Plant Sites." Journal of Environmental
    Economics and Management 4:153-166.
Kruzic, Pamela. 1974. Cross-Impact Simulation in Water
    Resource Planning. Fort Belvoir, Va.: U.S. Army
    Engineer Institute for Water Resources.
Leopold, Luna et al. 1971. A Procedure for Evaluating
    Environmental Impact. Washington, D.C.: U.S.
    Geological Survey, Circular 645.
Lichfield, Nathaniel. 1960. "Cost-Benefit Analysis in
    City Planning." Journal of the American Institute of
    Planners 26:273-279.
Maass, Arthur et al. 1962. Design of Water Resources
    Systems. Cambridge, Mass.: Harvard University Press.
McHarg, Ian. 1969. Design With Nature. New York:
    Natural History Press.
Mekong Secretariat. 1981. Nam Pong Environmental
    Management Research Project. Bangkok: Interim
    Committee for Coordination of Investigations of the
    Lower Mekong Basin, Report MKG/R.322/INF.
Miller, Donald. 1980. "Project Location Analysis Using
    the Goals-Achievement Method of Evaluation." Journal
    of the American Planning Association 46:195-205.
Nichols, Robert and Eric Hyman. 1982. "Evaluation of
    Environmental Assessment Methods." Journal of the
    Water Resources Planning and Management Division,
    American Society of Civil Engineers 108, No. WR1:87-
    105.
Odum, Eugene. 1969. "The Strategy of Ecosystem
    Development." Science 164:262-270.
Raiffa, Howard. 1968. Applied Statistical Decision
    Theory. Cambridge, Mass.: Massachusetts Institute of
    Technology Press.
Richardson, Sue et al. 1978. Preliminary Field Test of
    the Water Resources Assessment Methodology (WRAM):
    Tensas River, Louisiana. Vicksburg, Miss.: U.S. Army
    Engineer Waterways Experiment Station, Report
    WES-MP-4-78-1.

Chapter Seven

Sammy, G. and Lawrence Center. 1982. "Environmental
    Impact Assessment in Developing Countries: What are
    the Problems?" Impact Assessment Bulletin 2, No.
    1(Fall):29-43.
Schamberger, Melvin. 1982. "Habitat: A Rational Approach
    to Assessing Impacts of Land Use Changes on Fish and
    Wildlife." The Environmental Professional 4:251-259.
Schamberger, Melvin, A. Farmer and J. Terrell. 1982.
    Habitat Suitability Index Models: Introduction.
    Washington, D.C.: U.S. Fish and Wildlife Service,
    Report FWS/OBS-82-10.
Solomon, R. Charles et al. 1977. Water Resources
    Assessment Methodology (WRAM) -- Impact Assessment and
    Alternative Evaluation. Vicksburg, Miss.: U.S. Army
    Engineer Waterways Experiment Station. Technical
    report Y-77-1.
Sorenson, Jens. 1971. A Framework for Identification and
    Control of Resource Degradation and Conflict in the
    Multiple Use of the Coastal Zone. Berkeley, Calif.:
    University of California, Department of Landscape
    Architecture.
Travelers Research Corporation. 1969. Development of a
    Procedure and Knowledge Requirements for Marine
    Resource Planning. Hartford, Conn.: Travelers
    Research Corporation.
U.S. Federal Aviation Administration. 1973. Procedures
    for Environmental Impact Statement Preparation.
    Washington, D.C.: FAA, Order 1050.1A.
U.S. Fish and Wildlife Service. 1980. Habitat Evaluation
    Procedures, Revised ed. Washington, D.C.: Government
    Printing Office, Documents ESM 101 to 104.
U.S. Water Resources Council. 1973. "Water and
    Related-Land Resources: Establishment of Principles
    and Standards for Planning." Federal Register 38
    (September 10):24778-24869.
_____. 1979. "Procedures for Evaluation of National
    Economic Development Benefits and Costs in Water
    Resources Planning (Level C); Final Rule." Federal
    Register 44 (December 14):72892-72976.
_____. 1980. "Final Rule: Principles and Standards For
    Water and Related-Land Resources Planning." Federal
    Register 43 (November 29):55977-56007.
Wallace-McHarg Associates. 1964. Plan for the Valley.
    Philadelphia, Pa.: Wallace-McHarg Associates.

Chapter Eight

Brunswick, Egon. 1952. "The Conceptual Framework of
    Psychology." International Encyclopedia of Unified
    Science 1, No. 10. Chicago, Ill.: University of
    Chicago Press.

Burchell, Robert and David Listokin. 1975. The Environmental Impact Handbook. New Brunswick, N.J.: Rutgers University, Center for Urban Policy Research.

Cohon, Jared. 1978. Multiobjective Programming and Planning. New York: Academic Press.

Dean, B. and M. Nishry. 1965. "Scoring and Profitability Models for Evaluating and Selecting Engineering Projects." Journal of the Operations Research Society of America 13:550-569.

Dee, Norbert et al. 1972. An Environmental Evaluation System for Water Resource Planning. Springfield, Va.: National Technical Information Service. Report PB-208822.

Haimes, Yacov and Warren Hall. 1974. "Multiobjectives in Water Resources Systems: The Surrogate Worth Tradeoff Method." Water Resources Research. 10:615-624.

Hammond, Kenneth et al. 1975. "Social Judgment Theory." In Human Judgment and Decision Processes, edited by Martin Kaplan and Steven Schwartz. New York: Academic Press.

Hill, Morris. 1968. "A Goals-Achievement Matrix for Evaluating Alternative Plans." Journal of the American Institute of Planners 34:19-28.

Holling, C.S., ed. 1978. Adaptive Environmental Assessment and Management. New York: Wiley-Interscience.

Hyman, Eric, David Moreau and Bruce Stiftel. 1984a. "SAGE: A New Participant-Value Method for Environmental Assessment." Water Resources Bulletin 20:915-922.

_____. 1984b. "Toward a Participant-Value Method for the Presentation of Environmental Impact Data." In Improving Impact Assessment: Increasing the Relevance and Utilization of Scientific and Technical Information, edited by Stuart Hart, Gordon Enk and William Hornick. Boulder, Colo.: Westview Press.

Johnson, Stephen. 1967. "Hierarchical Clustering Schemes." Psychometrika 32:241-254.

Kaplan, Martin and Steven Schwartz. 1977. Human Judgment and Decision Processes in Applied Settings. New York: Academic Press.

Keeney, Ralph and Howard Raiffa. 1976. Decisions with Multiple Objectives. New York: John Wiley and Sons.

Leopold, Luna et al. 1971. A Procedure for Evaluating Environmental Impact. Springfield, Va.: National Technical Information Service. Report N71-36757.

Pitt, David and Ervin Zube. 1979. "The Q-Sort Method: Use in Landscape Assessment Research and Landscape Planning." In Proceedings of Our National Landscape: A Conference on Applied Techniques for Analysis and Management of the Visual Resource, edited by Gary Elsner and Richard Smardon. Berkeley, Calif.: U.S. Forest Service Pacific Southwest Forest and Range Experiment Station.

Chapter 8

Shuford, Scott and Sarah Fried, eds. 1980. Examination of Alternative Development Patterns for the Falls of the Neuse Watershed. Chapel Hill, N.C.: University of North Carolina, Department of City and Regional Planning.

Solomon, R.C. *et al.* 1977. Water Resources Assessment Methodology (WRAM): Impact Assessment and Alternative Evaluation. Vicksburg, Miss.: U.S. Army Engineer Waterways Experiment Station. Technical report 77-1.

Steinmann, Derick *et al.* 1977. "Application of Social Judgment Theory in Policy Formulation: An Example." Journal of the American Institute of Planners 42:33-41.

Stewart, Thomas and Linda Gelberd. 1976. "Analysis of Judgment Policy: A New Approach for Citizen Participation in Planning." Journal of the American Institute of Planners 42:33-41.

Triangle J Council of Governments. 1979. Proposed Work Program: Comprehensive Planning for Watersheds. Research Triangle Park, N.C.: TJCOG.

———. 1980. A General Inventory of the Falls of the Neuse Reservoir Watershed. Research Triangle Park, N.C.: TJCOG.

U.S. Council on Environmental Quality. 1978. "National Environmental Policy Act: Implementation of Procedural Revisions; Final Regulation." Federal Register 43 (November 29):55977-56007.

U.S. Water Resources Council. 1983. "Economic and Environmental Principles and Guidelines for Water and Related Land Resources Implementation Studies." Federal Register 48, No. 48 (March 10):10259.

Watershed Planning Task Force. 1980. Statement of Problems and Goals. Research Triangle Park, N.C.: Triangle J Council of Governments.

About the Authors

Eric L. Hyman is currently Evaluation Economist with Appropriate Technology International. His prior affiliations include the U.S. Congress' Office of Technology Assessment, the U.N. Food and Agriculture Organization, and the East-West Center Environment and Policy Institute. He has written in the areas of environmental impact assessment, small-scale technologies for rural development in the Third World, renewable energy, tropical forestry, and the monitoring and evaluation of development projects. He holds a Ph.D. in City and Regional Planning from the University of North Carolina at Chapel Hill.

Bruce Stiftel is Assistant Professor of Urban and Regional Planning at Florida State University where he teaches environmental planning, planning theory, and dispute resolution. His prior affiliations include the Center for Urban and Regional Studies of the University of North Carolina, and the U.S. Environmental Protection Agency. His work focuses on environmental impact assessment, planning theory, natural hazards management, and environmental policy and mediation. He holds a Ph.D. in City and Regional Planning from the University of North Carolina at Chapel Hill.

David H. Moreau is Professor of City and Regional Planning at the University of North Carolina and Director of the Water Resources Research Institute of the University of North Carolina. His most recent books concern flood plain land use management, water supply protection, and planning for urban water and sewer systems. He holds a Ph.D. in water resources from Harvard University.

Robert C. Nichols is an Environmental Policy Specialist at the Research Triangle Institute in North Carolina where he studies the implementation of national water quality standards. His prior affiliations include the Center for Urban and Regional Studies and the Institute for Environmental Studies of the University of North Carolina, and the U.S. Environmental Protection Agency. He holds a M.R.P. in environmental planning form the University of North Carolina at Chapel Hill.

Index

Adaptive environmental
assessment (AEA) 16,
156, 218-223, 226
Advisory committees 41, 50,
51, 246
Advocacy 17, 24, 46
Aesthetic quality 24, 53,
115-118, 125, 130, 134,
159, 229
Affect 112
Air quality (air pollution)
15, 35-38, 64, 66, 79,
98, 99, 100
Alternative cost approach
86-87, 89, 106-107
See also Revealed
preference measures
Antagonistic effects 20, 29
Attitudes 22
Australian Land System 11
See also Land
classification
Benefit-cost analysis 8, 9,
13, 55, 60, 63, 65, 67,
68, 108, 109, 225
Bequest value 66-67, 74
See also Option value
Bias 26-28, 50, 72-74, 78,
80-83, 105-107, 127,
132-135, 157, 246
Bidding games 70-75, 79-82,
96, 100, 105-107
Brainstorming 49
See also Group process
techniques
Bureau of Land Management
landscape rating system
122-124

California Soil Vegetation
Survey 12
See also Land
classification
Canadian Biophysical System
11
See also Land
classification
Cassandra method 78
See also Tradeoff
analysis
Certainty 29-30, 33, 38,
80
Chance node 35, 37
Charette 52
Checklists 9, 15, 86, 105,
121-122, 155, 170,
172, 180, 183, 193,
212, 223, 226
Coefficients of optimism
33-35
See also Game theory
strategies
Cognition 112
Collective action 43
Collective goods 64, 66
See also Pure public
goods
Complementary goods 87
Conflict resolution 42, 51,
52, 114, 231
Consumer's surplus 55-59,
65, 67, 73, 85, 90,
92, 98, 108
Cost-effectiveness analysis
65, 68
Costless choice method 78
See also Tradeoff
analysis

299

304